NEWSPAPER EXTRACTS FROM "THE HOOSIER STATE"

Newport
Vermillion County
Indiana

January 4, 1882 to December 27, 1882
January 3, 1883 to April 4, 1883
April 11, 1883 to April 1, 1885 Unavailable
April 8, 1885 to December 30, 1885

Abstracted by
Carolyn Schwab

HERITAGE BOOKS
2007

HERITAGE BOOKS
AN IMPRINT OF HERITAGE BOOKS, INC.

Books, CDs, and more—Worldwide

For our listing of thousands of titles see our website
at
www.HeritageBooks.com

Published 2007 by
HERITAGE BOOKS, INC.
Publishing Division
65 East Main Street
Westminster, Maryland 21157-5026

Other Heritage Books by Carolyn Schwab and the Marin County Genealogical Society:

Newspaper Extracts from Sausalito News, *Sausalito, Marin County, California, February 12, 1885 to December 26, 1890*

Newspaper Extracts from The Marin Journal, *San Rafael, Marin County, California, January 6, 1881 to December 25, 1884*

Newspaper Extracts from The Marin Journal, *San Rafael, Marin County, California, January 1, 1885 to December 27, 1888*

Newspaper Extracts from The Marin Journal, Marin County Tocsin
San Rafael, Marin County, California, January 3, 1889 to December 27, 1890

Newspaper Extracts from The Marin Journal, Marin County Tocsin
San Rafael, Marin County, California, January 1, 1891 to December 31,1892

Newspaper Extracts from The Marin Journal, Marin County Tocsin
San Rafael, Marin County, California, January 5, 1893 to December 27, 1894

Other Heritage Books by Carolyn Schwab:

The Hoosier State Newspapers, 1880-1881

Newspaper Extracts from "The Hoosier State", Newport, Vermillion County, Indiana, January 2, 1868 to December 25, 1873

Newspaper Extracts from "The Hoosier State", Newport, Vermillion County, Indiana, January 1, 1874 to December 30, 1875

Newspaper Extracts from "The Hoosier State", Newport, Vermillion County, Indiana, January 6, 1876 to December 27, 1877

Newspaper Extracts from "The Hoosier State", Newport, Vermillion County, Indiana, January 3, 1878 to December 31, 1879

Newspaper Extracts from "The Hoosier State", Newport, Vermillion County, Indiana, January 7, 1880 to December 28, 1881

Newspaper Extracts from "The Hoosier State", Newport, Vermillion County, Indiana, January 4, 1882 to December 27, 1882; January 3, 1883 to April 4, 1883; April 11, 1883 to April 1, 1885 Unavailable; April 8, 1885 to December 30, 1885

Newspaper Extracts from "The Hoosier State", Newport, Vermillion County, Indiana, January 6, 1886 to December 28, 1887

International Standard Book Number: 978-0-7884-4205-8

Table of Contents

INTRODUCTION

Early newspapers contain information that is very useful to the genealogist. Sometimes you can find early births and deaths that were never recorded. It was not required by law to report these until after 1882. They were not too complete or very reliable. Other information is also found here. I hope what I have found is very useful to you in writing a story about your family.

NEWPORT HOOSIER STATE 1882

Wednesday, January 4, 1882

Summit Grove
A large and merry crowd of over 50 young folks assembled at Mr. JOE JAMES' last Saturday, being in honor of his son CHARLES JAMES' wedding dinner. All enjoyed themselves, especially at dinner, which was elegant. May happiness and good cheer attend the young couple through life.

A Sad Accident
Mr. BIRELY, of this place, received a telegram from Baltimore, MD, week before last, that his old father, aged 76 years, had met with an accident and was not expected to live. Mr. BIRELY took the first train after getting the word, and when he arrived there, his father was dead. He was hurt by a threshing machine, which was at work in his barn. It was one of those old style tumbling shaft rod machines. His coat caught in one of the knuckles of the rod, and in trying to extricate himself his hand was caught, winding his arm around the shaft and crushing every bone in it up to the elbow. His arm had to be amputated, which caused his death in two days afterwards.

Scandal Mongers
A few weeks ago, scandal mongers circulated the report that Miss MARY H. MAST, a daughter of Rev. JOHN A. MAST of Bono, Helt township, had been unfortunate in love affairs, and was in a delicate situation. When approached on the subject, she positively denied the charge, although outer indications made it appear that there was something the matter with her. She had dropsical affections for several years, but not bad until within the last two or three months. She was examined about three weeks ago by Dr. SWAFFORD, of Terre Haute, and he pronounced her disease dropsy or ovarian tumor. Since then she gradually grew worse until Monday of last week, when Dr. G.W. McCUNE and Dr. E.B. CANNON of Montezuma were sent for, her attending physician, Dr. TWEEDY of Jonestown, and H.C. EATON of Bono, being present. On Tuesday morning, the day following, Dr. CANNON tapped her, taking from her, two wooden buckets of water. We hope scandal mongers will now give the poor girl a rest, and be more cautious in the future about assailing the character of respectable young girls.

Highland
The wife of WILLIAM FRENCHA, living west of town, is lying dangerously ill with typhoid fever.

HENRY and BILLY JOHNSON, of Douglas County, IL, are visiting relatives at this place.

DUTCH BALMER and wife, of IL, were visiting LAFE LEATHERMAN during the holidays.

WILLIAM HOUCHIN, is at present, not expected to live. Disease – typhoid fever.

Old Mr. SWINDELL, aged 78 years, and BETSEY CLARK, aged about 60 years, were married at the residence of the bride in Montezuma, December 22, 1881. May success crown their efforts, and their anticipations be fully realized.

Clinton and Vicinity
JIM CRANE is on the sick list. He suffers from a bilious attack.

MORRY EDWARDS has flown to Texas. This climate was becoming uncongenial to his enfeebled constitution.

S.H. VANSANT, recently of this place, now of Greencastle, was over last week, looking after his accounts.

WILLIS HEDGES, JAMES BAILEY, MORT KNOWLES, and MAY WHITCOMB returned to the I.A.U. at Greencastle today.

Montezuma
Mrs. INDIA OSBORN, of Decatur, IL, came on Friday to visit her friends, Mr. and Mrs. GUS BAILEY.

In Memoriam

Unity Lodge No. 344, F. & A.M.
In memory of Brother LEWIS FRAZEE, deceased

J.C. McKIBBEN, Chairman
J.F. COMPTON
D.B. JOHNSON
J.M. HOWARD

Home News
BEN BLANCHARD, excursion agent, and HENRY DILLOW returned home yesterday morning from Kansas. HENRY is not favorably impressed with Kansas, and will remain in Newport a while longer.

BILLY MOORE, of Danville, IL, was down here last week putting the finishing touches on the monument erected last fall in the Zener Cemetery in memory of the late Mrs. JANE BIRELY. The monument is a handsome piece of workmanship, and speaks in high terms of praise for the skilled artists who made it. Mr. MOORE does honest work and always guarantees satisfaction.

Matrimony
On last Sunday afternoon, Rev. F.E. PENNY, of the U.B. Church, united in wedlock ALFRED H. ALLISON and Miss CHARLOTTE E. FOX, of Gessie. We wish the young couple a long and pleasant life.

United in Wedlock
Clerk ROBERTS issued the following marriage licenses since our last report:

WILLIAM L. MORRIS to MARIA SHEWARD
ALFRED H. ALLISON to CHARLOTTE E. FOX
BENJAMIN F. FOLTZ to NANCY A. BUMGARDNER

Through the influence of Congressman PIERCE, Captain R.B. SEARS has secured a clerkship in the pension department at Washington, which pays a salary of $1500 a year. The Captain's many friends will be glad to hear of his good luck. He will not leave for Washington until about the first of March.

Personal
Attorney J.C. SAWYERS was over in Hendricks County last week visiting his mother.

J.J. PADRICK, a teacher in the primary department at Eugene, was in town on Saturday last.

W.E. LINDSEY, of Sidney, IL, spent last Sunday and Monday in town. His wife arrived here last week on a visit, and will remain several days yet.

JOE E. ALDRIDGE, of Helt township, is going out near Long, IL, on the new Narrow Gauge railroad, to open out a grocery and confectionary store. We wish him success.

Married
On the 22nd instant, at the residence of the bride's parents, in Annapolis, by Rev. R.G. ATCHESON, WATSON C. BLACK to Miss JENNIE PASSMORE.

D.R. GRAY now plays the cornet in the M.E. Church Choir.

Wednesday, January 11, 1882

Nearly a Fatal Case of Vaccination
In the forepart of last week, Dr. M.L. HALL vaccinated FRANK LAMB of this place, a young man aged about 16, who is very chicken hearted and cannot stand the sight of blood. After the operation was performed, he stepped out the door to start for home, when he fainted and fell on the flag pavement, striking his head on the stone, and fracturing his skull. He was insensible for several days, and it is thought he could not recover, but at present he is mending, and the opinion is expressed that he is going to get well.

Elopement Extraordinary
The Danville, Il, Daily Commercial of Saturday last, says Mrs. MARIA LEATHERMAN, aged 41 years, the educated and accomplished wife of EDWARD D. LEATHERMAN, one of the richest farmers in Iroquois County, eloped on Thursday with DAVE GERMAN, aged 26, a poor, uneducated, ugly looking tenant on a neighboring farm. The young man leaves a wife and 2 children in want, while the rich lady leaves a husband frantic with rage and 4 children, 2 of whom are nearly grown. Mrs. LEATHERMAN had been married 22 years, but had become tired of the humdrum life of the farm, and desired to visit other scenes. The ill mated but loving couple departed on the train unobserved, and were seen subsequently at Danville, but quickly disappeared. LEATHERMAN offers a large reward for the apprehension of GERMAN. It seems that Mrs. LEATHERMAN carried off 3 trunks filled with silverware and valuables, and $12,000 in money. GERMAN is described as a young Frenchman, with a frightful scar in his cheek and neck, resulting from a burn.

Highland
Mrs. VAL CONLEY, of Broad Land, IL, is visiting her father, JOHN RUSSELL.

JOHN PEALER, ANDREW JACKSON's son-in-law, has bought the SIMPSON saloon property in Dana and expects to engage in the liquor traffic.

JESS JOHNSON, a silver miner and prospector of New Mexico, is in this vicinity visiting his brother, JOHN JOHNSON.

MORGAN LINDSEY of New Goshen, will move to this place the coming week.

SAM AIKMAN and JOHN BROWN, after spending a week's vacation at home, returned to Dayton last Monday week, where they are preparing for the ministry.

CHARLES LOWE, our blacksmith, talks of moving to St. Bernice. CHARLES is the best blacksmith in this part of the country.

Mr. BUSKIRK, our schoo teacher, and Mr. HUSTON, our former teacher, deserve much credit as the school has been more successful during their management than ever before.

Clinton and Vicinity
JOE WHITE went to Greencastle last Thursday where he intends to attend school.

JAMES ROBERTS of Newport, has bought an interest in A.L. WHITCOMB & Co.'s dry goods store at this place.

Montezuma
Mrs. MARY BAILEY started on Saturday last to visit her daughter, Mrs. INDIA OSBORN, living at Decatur, IL.

ALF McDONALD has rented his property lately occupied by DAVIS & AKINS to AARON HISE and BEN LAMB, of Lodi, who are fitting it up as a first class saloon.

Dr. KEMP, of our town, who is attending WILLIAM HOUCHIN, of Helt township, and who is down with typhoid fever, thinks there is a good show for his recovery.

The infant child of S.A. RICHEY died on Thursday last of heart disease, and was buried on Friday.

Home News
On last Friday, Prof. JOHN COLLETT, State Geologist, celebrated his 54th birthday.

Grandmother HALL, of this place, who makes her home with Mrs. HIRAM HASTY, celebrated her 83rd birthday yesterday. She is in excellent health for one of her years.

Fire in Eugene Township
The residence of WORTH PORTER, near Walnut Grove, in Eugene township, caught fire on last Sunday night and burned down, destroying all the household contents. The family was at church. It is supposed to have caught from the fireplace. The loss will reach about $500. There was no insurance.

Stricken With Paralysis
One day last week, Aunt PATSY DICKEN, an old lady of this place, about 76 years, was suddenly stricken down with paralysis, and is now in a dying condition. She cannot possibly live many days. She is not able to speak or move a muscle. Mrs. DICKEN, although she bears the name of Mrs. B.K. DICKEN, who was stricken down a few weeks ago, is no relation, but is similarly affected. She lives on the same street.

List of Real Estate Transfers for Month of December 1881

RUFUS P. SPAULDING etal to MARTIN G. RHOADS
136 acres in Eugene township - $2,158.80

RUFUS P. SPAULDING etal to JAMES A. ARRASMITH
100 acres in Vermillion township - $1,700

RUFUS P. SPAULDING etal to JOHN MANGES
80 acres in Vermillion township - $808

JOHN H. BOGART to D.W. GARDNER
Lots 4 & 5, block 2, in Clinton - $225

HERBERT W. MOREHOUSE and wife to JACOB WIMSETT
3 acres in Vermillion township - $100

HAMILTON BETSON and wife to ALFRED R. NEWLIN
40 acres in Vermillion township - $1,820

SAMUEL J. TAYLOR and wife to SAMUEL J. BOEN
30 acres in Eugene township - $575

ARAMANTA CARRICO to HENRY F. TAYLOR and wife
½ acre in Vermillion township - $9.50

BEN BLANCHARD and wife to JACKSON A. SEARS
Lot 1 in Sexton's addition to Newport - $650

JACKSON H. SEARS and wife to BEN BLANCHARD
20 acres in Vermillion township - $600

NORMAN SKINNER etal to HIRAM CHENOWETH
Outlot No. 9 adjoining Perrysville - $218

NORMAN SKINNER etal to MILO J. RUDY
Lot No. 3 in Steven's addition to Perrysville - $185

JOHN M. GIVENS etal to JOHN HAINS etal
W ½ lots 73 & 74, in Perrysville - $385

REBECCA McLAUGHLIN to CLAUDE MATTHEWS
2 ½ acres in Clinton township - $12

ANNIE SLATER to JOHN WRIGHT
1/3 interest in lots 6, 7, & 10, block 14, in Clinton - $50

THOMAS EVASTON and wife to ENOCH WHITTED
One acre in Clinton township - $150

NEWTON HUMPHRIES and wife to JAMES KING
1/3 of 24 acres in Clinton township - $120

JAMES A. ROLL and wife to HELEN A. McKNIGHT
Lots 17 & 18, in Newport - $300

P.C. BULLINGTON and wife to CHARLES HAYS and wife
Lot 26, block 4, in Jonestown - $25

MARY RUMSPIRT etal to HENRY VOLKEL
20? Acres in Highland township - $900

DANIEL C. DICKEN etal to JOSEPH A. MOREHEAD
31 ½ acres in Vermillion township - $300

JOHN W. PARRETT etal to PHOEBE M. HASTY
Part lot 28 in Newport - $100

JOHN W. PARRETT etal to ABEL SEXTON
Lot 63 in Newport - $500

ABEL SEXTON and wife to JOHN W. PARRETT etal
Outlot adjoining Newport - $100

RUHAMA E. UNDERWOOD etal to JOHN BRINDLEY
80 acres in Vermillion township - $2,400

EDWARD O. WATTEN and wife to THOMAS McFALL
57.36 acres in Vermillion township - $3,857.40

JOHN BRINDLEY and wife to CHARLES P. POTTS
80 acres in Vermillion township - $2,440

PHILIP M. HARRIER and wife to FRED HIBERLY
89.18 acres in Vermillion township - $1,800

MARTIN G. RHOADS and wife to ENOCH WHITE
157.76 acres in Eugene township - $1,800

LOUISA DALLAS to SAMUEL MOREHEAD
Undivided ½ of lots 9 & 10, in L. and A.'s addition to Newport - $225

NANCY J. FENNIMORE and husband to JOHN RUNYAN
11 and 2/3 acres in Clinton township - $225

NANCY KIRKPATRICK and husband to JAMES C. STUTLER
Lots 3 & 4 in Gessie - $100

JAMES C. STUTLER and wife to SILAS HUGHES
Lots 3 & 4 in Gessie - $150

PLATT Z. ANDERSON and wife to JOHN H. BOGART
Undivided ¼ of part lot 1, block 12, in Clinton - $1,000

CRAWFORD FAIRBANKS and wife to WILLIAM H. SALTSGAVER
Lots 7 & 10, in C's addition to Gessie - $25

WILLIAM FULWIDER and wife to LEGLAND J. PLACE
Undivided ½ of out lot adjoining Newport - $75

SAMUEL E. PATTON to SAMUEL N. TAYLOR
20 acres in Clinton township - $400

HANNAH T. LOWE etal to JONATHAN CARITHERS
Part of 61.20 acres in Highland township - $1,050

JOHN H. BOGART and wife to JOHN KING
Lots 2 & 3, block 1, in M's addition to Clinton - $150

CECILIA ROBERTS to PAUL WILSON
Outlot adjoining Clinton - $600

PAUL WILSON and wife to DANIEL W. GARDNER
Part outlot 13, adjoining Clinton - $175

EMELINE BRADSHAW and husband to JOHN H. BOGART
Part outlot 6, adjoining Clinton - $500

JAMES E. KNOWLES etal to DANIEL W. GARDNER
One acre adjoining Clinton - $150

JOSEPH W. MOREY and wife to MARTIN J. FRADER
S ½ lot 3, block 19, in Clinton - $200

CLAUDE MATTHEWS and wife to STEPHEN FRADER
Lot 4, block 19, in Clinton - $10

ELIZABETH S. CRANOR and husband to JAMES CHIPPS
Lot 65 and outlot adjoining Newport - $300

GEORGE BRADSHAW to EMELINE BRADSHAW
Lot 1, block 7, in Clinton - $500

SAMUEL W. MALONE etal to WESLEY MALONE
3 acres in Eugene township - $100

JOHN L. WHITE and wife to ELIZABETH J. McKANNON
20 acres in Vermillion township for $300

BENJAMIN R. FUQUA and wife to SHUBB Y. TAYLOR
26 ¾ acres in Clinton township - $1,075

PLATT Z. ANDERSON and wife to NELSON C. ANDERSON
Part outlot 6 adjoining Clinton - $250

HENRY C. SMITH and wife to MILO J. RUDY
Outlot adjoining Perrysville - $575

SEYMOUR NEBEKER and wife to THIRZA ANDERSON
Outlot adjoining Clinton - $300

THOMAS MARRS and wife to JAMES L. BREWER
40 acres in Clinton township - $1,050

TYLER HALSTEAD to JOHN F. DUGGER
40 acres in Clinton township - $6,000

BENJAMIN F. PEER to TAYLOR SIMPSON
Lot 1, in B's addition to Dana - $1,200

TAYLOR SIMPSON to ANDREW JACKSON
Lot 1, B's addition to Dana - $1,200

Personal
E.H. BURNS of Montezuma, left on Monday last for Ann Arbor, MI, to attend college.

JAKE HALL, of Fairmount, IL, and his good looking daughter, ALICE HALL, are in town visiting, the guests of Mrs. HASTY and family.

F.M. MALONE of Pana, IL, as in town yesterday. We met him in the post office, but failed to recognize him on account of his silvery locks.

F.M. BISHOP returned home on last Saturday night. He was favorably impressed with Kansas, and talks of moving to that State sometime in the spring. He also visited JAMES ZENER and his daughter HATTIE ZENER. He found them well and in prosperous circumstances. He says HATTIE is as fat as she can roll.

Wednesday, January 18, 1882

Eugene Items
JOE McCORMICK, who has been in Mexico for more than a year, running a construction train on a railroad, returned to Eugene Saturday. JOE says only lots of money would induce him to go back. He says that none of the Americans like the country, and only those who are making money stay.

Mrs. ELIZABETH LUNGER, wife of OMER LUNGER, died suddenly at her home one and a half miles W of town Sunday morning. We did not learn the cause.

JAMES B. PERRIN talks of going to Hutchinson, KS, in the spring to teach school.

Montezuma
WILLIAM McKEY, of Rockville, passed through our town on Saturday evening from Paris, IL, on his way home.

CHARLEY SOLOMON and family, who moved from our town a few months since to Camargo, IL, will return here this week to again live out of mud.

Mrs. JOHN COOK returned home from Scotland, IL, whither she had been called to the bedside of a dying brother.

LAFE NEWELL's wife of Highland, has the typhoid fever.

No school in the grammar department; the teacher, Mr. LINDLEY, having resigned.

Clinton and Vicinity
BOB WISHARD was under the weather the first of this week from the effects of vaccination.

Miss EVA ANDERSON, the prettiest girl in town, returned home last week after a pleasant visit to relatives and friends in Kokomo, this State.

Home News
Mrs. ELIJAH KNIGHT, of Helt township, is lying very low with typhoid fever, and is not expected to live.

HAM BETSON has just purchased a nice little farm of 112 ½ acres of WILSON TERRY, lying half a mile W of the State line. He paid $1,500.

E.D. WHEELER still has to go upon crutches, and don't seem to be improving much. It is doubtful where he ever will regain the full use of his leg.

Two of JESSE HOUCHIN's sons, both young men, have died of typhoid fever within the last three or four weeks. Mr. HOUCHIN has the sympathy of all his acquaintances in his affliction.

Closing Out at Cost
JOE ERLANGER, of 513 Main St., Terre Haute, is closing out his immense stock of ready made clothing at cost, preparatory to engaging strictly in the merchant tailoring business.

Personal
C.W. SHAW, of Helt township, is lying dangerously low.

Mrs. PATSY DICKEN still lingers, but cannot possibly survive many days.

Mrs. N. DORA, of Kansas, is in town visiting, the guest of her half sister, Mrs. POLLY CRAIG.

Mrs. JAMES F. WELLER, of Ridgefarm, IL, is here visiting her daughter, Mrs. NORTH CRAIG, and numerous old friends.

JOHN HASTY and wife have returned from Streator, IL, where they went a few weeks since to attend the bedside of their sick son, who died shortly after their arrival.

E.F. DAVIS went up to Delphi, this State, last week, to visit relatives and old friends. Delphi is his native home.

Obituary
WILLIAM EWING HOUCHIN departed this life January 7, 1882, at the age of 21 years, 8 months, and 16 days. He was the third son of JESSE HOUCHIN. The funeral rites were conducted by Rev. WILLIAM McMASTERS, of the Baptist Church, at Spring Hill Church, Monday, January 9, 1882. He leaves his father, mother, 2 brothers, and 4 sisters, to mourn his early death. He was not a member of church, though dying in full faith of a blessed immortality, and a happy life beyond the grave. His remains were interred in the Pisgah Cemetery by kind friends beside his brother DANIEL V. HOUCHIN, who preceeded him to the grave only 22 days before. They are both buried together on the same section where they were born, lived, and died. Their lives were spent together in play, work, and at school, scarcely being apart any length of time.

Highland
WILLIAM HOUCHIN, of this township, departed this life on Saturday, January 7, 1882. He was a brother of DANIEL HOUCHIN, who died a few weeks ago.

MARIA RUSSELL, wife of WILLIAM RUSSELL, died on last Thursday morning of consumption. She was a daughter of the widow HARTMAN, of Sidney, IL.

Another Pioneer Gone
Died of dropsy on Saturday morning, January 7, 1882, at half past 2 o'clock, JOSEPH WIMSETT of Edgar County, IL, aged 72 years and 7 months. The deceased was born in Delaware County, OH, and emigrated to Indiana with his parents at the age of 12 years, and was married to CYNTHIA POWERS at the age of 25 years, and was a resident of Vermillion County, IN, up to the year 1849, at which time he emigrated with his family to Edgar County, IL, where he resided until the time of his death. The funeral services were conducted by the Rev. J.W. NYE on Sunday the 8th, at Wesley Chapel, after which his remains were followed by a large concourse of weeping relatives and kind neighbors and deposited in the cemetery near the Chapel. The deceased has been a member of the U.B. Church for about 50 years, all of which time he has tried to live a devoted and exemplary Christian life. A large portion of that time he was a licensed exhorter in the church. He leaves a wife and 7 children to mourn his loss, but they need not mourn, as those who have no hope, for we firmly believe that Uncle JOE, as he was familiarly called, has gone from labor to reward.

Notice of Final Settlement of Estate
Estate of NORMAN SKINNER, deceased
January 9, 1882
JAMES ROBERTS, Clerk

Notice of Final Settlement of Estate
Estate of WILLIAM L. MALONE, deceased
January 10, 1882
JAMES ROBERTS, Clerk

Wednesday, January 25, 1882

Montezuma
Born to G.M. ABBOTT and wife, Friday last, a daughter.

C.F. DAVIS and wife were made happy by the appearance of a fine daughter.

AARON HISE and wife rejoice over a daughter born on Thursday last.

Toronto
MOLLIE MAST is getting so she is able to sit up some now.

Miss BELLE FORD is teaching an excellent school here this winter.

HATTIE ELDER is still visiting with her grandmother in Kansas.

Prof. ADAMS, of Chicago, commences a singing class here this week.

Clinton and Vicinity
FRANK MARLEY has resigned his position as teacher of the school south of town.

PETER LAMB returned home last week from Lafayette, where he had been visiting in the hope of recuperating his health.

Highland
ANDREW WILSON, living 3 ½ miles NW of here, is now father in the truest meaning of the term. Although it came too late for a holiday gift, it is a fine, large boy and weighs 9 pounds.

FRANK JOHNSON has sold his interest in the store, and in the spring thinks he will go West to engage in stock raising.

ABE STEPP, living south of here, has moved to Yankee Point, IL, where he expects to engage in farming.

GEORGE HAMMOND, who was arrested in this township last winter and taken to Chicago for trial on the charge of robbing or being implicated in a U.S. mail robbery near that city, returned home a few days ago. After having repeated trials before the U.S. court, was finally acquitted week before last, the charge not being sustained. His brother JERRY HAMMOND, of Iowa, well known in this township, being one of Vermillion County's old school teachers, was his attorney, and it was no doubt through his indefatigable efforts that brought about his brother's acquittal.

Home News
F.M. BISHOP has been confined to his bed for the last week with rheumatism.

Mrs. MARIA NIXON, who is afflicted with rheumatism, is talking of going to the Arkansas Hot Springs in a few weeks.

M.G. RHOADS is certainly the happiest and best pleased man in Newport. It is of the piano thumping gender, and made its appearance on last Monday evening.

Mrs. ELIZABETH B. CLARK, an old lady of this township, aged 77 years, has returned from a three months visit to relatives and friends in Bartholomew County, this State.

An Indian Hunter
FRED AMMERMAN, a 14 year old boy living near Clinton locks, ran away from home on Thursday, taking with him a shotgun and a valise. His relatives are considerably worried.

United in Wedlock
An Old Farmer of Helt's Prairie Marries a Terre Haute Prostitute
Justice WHARRY yesterday united in the holy bonds, JOHN STRAIN and LIZZIE BINGHAM. The former is 60 years old, and said to be the owner of a large farm in Vermillion County, and the latter is an inmate of GABE St. CLAIR's bagnio. The couple has been arrested several times for associating.

Fourty-Sixth Anniversary

Last Thursday was the 46th anniversary of Mr. and Mrs. ROBERT DAVIS. The children thought they deserved a party. All the children, except ROBERT, who is in California, and most of their nieces, nephews, and grandchildren, were present, making about 40 in all. It was a complete surprise to them.

ROBERT DAVIS and MELVINA TAYLOR were both born in Virginia, and were united in marriage on January 19, 1836. In the second year of their marriage, they emigrated to this State in a one horse wagon, stopping first in Parke County, where they resided several years, and afterwards at Helt's Prairie, Vermillion County, where they now reside. They endured the toils, the hardships, and privations which were incident to early settlers, and did their part in removing the brush and preparing the way for the wholesome rays of civilization. ROBERT was a mason by trade, and when he visited Virginia, one year ago last fall, he found houses still standing that had been built by him 50 years before. After coming to this State, he undertook the business of farming, though while he remained in Parke County, he still worked at his trade when not engaged in work on the farm. When he removed to this county, he bought the tract of land which he now occupies and which by his own labor, with the help of his sons, he has greatly improved. There are perhaps few men in this county who have uprooted more stumps, burnt more logs, or cleared more ground than father DAVIS. Neither has MELVINA failed in bearing her share of the burden. In household affairs, she has always been found at the post of duty. Thus the aged couple has walked hand in hand, and by industry, frugality, and economy, have obtained competence of this world's goods. Father's head is whitened by the frosts of 72 winters, and the elastic step and vigor of his youth have become the victims of relentless time. He has come to his second eye-sight, and can see to read the finest print without glasses. Mother, who is 8 years younger, has not yet a great many gray hairs, and on her brow old time has not so visibly set his seal. Both are in the enjoyment of good health, and have a fair prospect for many years.

Smallpox in the County

We have a genuine case of smallpox in this county. JOHN RANDOLPH, residing 3 ½ miles N of here, near the Porter School house, is down with this terrible disease. It is probable several others will be down sick with the same disease in less than a week from this time. Mr. RANDOLPH caught the disease while in Chicago with a carload of hogs. It was several days after he was taken down with the disease, before they knew what ailed him, and a number of neighbors had called to see him.

Wednesday, February 1, 1882

Eugene Items

The old Good Templar Lodge which was first organized here January 24, 1873, and went down two years ago, was reorganized last Thursday night. The following officers were elected:

W.H. HOOD – W.C.T.
Mrs. ELLA MEEKS – W.V.T.
H. STURM – W.S.
H.H. HOSFORD – W.F.S.
MARY LANE – W.T.
ROBERT HOLD – W.M.
MARY HOLTZ – W.C.
MINNIE MORRIS – W.I.G.
JOHN BISHOP – W.O.G.

Montezuma

Born – on Wednesday, January 28, 1882, to Mr. and Mrs. PETERS, a 9 pound son.

Mr. and Mrs. JAMES PECK are happy over a fine daughter, born on Wednesday, January 28, 1882.

Mr. SAMUEL KALER was called very suddenly to Ohio. A telegram announced his father is dying.

Old Grandma LEMONS, who was taken to the poor farm last fall, died at that place on Thursday, and was buried in our Cemetery on Friday.

Highland
A.C. LOVE is teaching a writing class at the Redman Schoolhouse.

Old Mr. LONG, living N of here, is in a very bad situation, being sick himself and unable to work, and his wife not in a condition to attend to household duties. He has sons and daughters living in this county who could partly relieve his suffering if they felt a disposition to do so, and also relieve the neighbors who night after night have sat up with him and carried provisions to his family. It is sad that the children for whom he had spent days that they might not go unclothed and unfed, that they now will not cast one ray of sunlight to administer his wants and bidding their old father a kind farewell.

Home News
D.R. GRAY united with the M.E. Church on Sunday last.

Capt. R.B. SEARS and WILLIAM L. TRIPLETT united with the M.E. Church on last Monday afternoon.

W.B. FOLAND is now traveling for a Cincinnati buggy firm. He gets $100 a month and expenses.

WILLIAM H. HASKELL, who is teaching school at Libertyville, Vigo County, was in our city on Saturday last.

LEN WHEELER has ordered a cargo of catnip. It is a gal and made its first appearance at about 4 o'clock on last Thursday evening.

J.C. JACKSON is a candidate for Road Superintendent of Helt township. Mr. JACKSON having lost his health by sickness, is not able to do hard manual labor anymore, and if the people would give him the office, it would afford him a means of making a living.

JAMES ASBURY, of this township, is going to sell all his personal property and household effects, at public sale, on February 21st.

Dr. O.M KEYES, of Dana, is a candidate for renomination to the office of Trustee of Helt Township, subject to the will of the Republican nominating convention. The doctor has made a good officer, and we see no reason why the people should not re-elect him. He always employs the best teachers to be found, and carefully watches the interests of the schools under his charge.

Personal
Hon. WILLIAM EGGLESTON and lady, of Terre Haute, were in town several days last week visiting relatives and friends.

Dana
JOE FILLINGER has gone to Pittsburg with cattle for HENRY JORDAN.

We have heard the name of REUBEN CLEARWATERS favorably spoken of as a candidate for Road Superintendent. He is fully competent and would undoubtedly make a good officer.

Wednesday, February 8, 1882

Real Estate Transfers for Month of January 1882

ADDISON L. WHITCOMB to SARAH J. HISE
Lot 2, block 19, in Clinton - $25.00

PLATT Z. ANDERSON and wife to ALMEDA HAGENBAUGH
Lot 10, block 4, in Clinton - $1,000

ELVIRA ODELL and husband to JOHN B. BROWN
Lots 7 & 8, Parrett's addition to Newport - $1,700

WASHINGTON KING and wife to NANCY J. FENNIMORE
Part lots 3, 6, & 7, block 2, Morey's addition to Clinton - $300

JAMES S. ROGERS to TAYLOR ADAMS
20 acres in Vermillion township - $200

SAMUEL AIKMAN etal to JOHN O. ROGERS
Lots 5 & 6, block 9, in Dana - $100

JOSEPH HOWARD and wife to PETER CORSEY
35 acres in Highland township - $700

BEN HARRISON and wife to JOSEPH A. HARRISON
------- acres in Clinton - $340

JAMES M. MOORE and wife to JOSEPH W. MOREY
Lots 2, 3, 6, 7, & 10, block 19, in Clinton - $450

JOHN TATE and wife to THOMAS J. MITCHELL Jr.
Outlot adjoining Perrysville - $100

REZIN METZGER and wife to THOMAS J. MITCHELL Sr.
Lots 15 & 16, in G. and C.'s addition to Perrysville - $325

THOMAS J. WILLIAMSON and wife to WILLIAM J. LAKE
Lots 32 & 33, in Alta - $125

JESSE HOUCHIN and wife to WILLIAM J. LAKE
Lots 22 & 31, in Alta - $25

SERENA J. WASHBURN to CLAUDE MATTHEWS
Outlot 1 & 2, adjoining Clinton - $1,000

JAMES ASBURY to URE A. JOHNSON
141.10 acres in Vermillion Township - $6,000

ABRAHAM SOEY and wife to HENRY STAHL
10 acres in Vermillion Township - $125

HEZEKIAH CASEBEER and wife to SAMUEL HAMERSLEY
40 acres in Helt township - $1,200

JOHN FORD and wife to JACOB A. SOUDERS etal
17 ½ acres in Helt township - $350

ANDREW R. REED to SARAH A. BURGESS
120 acres in Clinton township - $2,400

GOTTLIEB D. HEIDBREDER and wife to CHRISTIAN GLINDMEIR
Lot 29, and outlot adjoining Eugene - $640.34

ANNA M. RANDELS etal to BARBARA A. McCALLA
100 ¾ acres near Highland - $3,475

Indiana & Illinois Central Railway Co. to L.T. DICKASON etal
231 acres in Vermillion township - $5,000

BEN BLANCHARD and wife to JOHN B. BROWN
Lot 50, in Newport - $1,500

JOHN B. BROWN and wife to BEN BLANCHARD
Lots 7 & 8, in Parrett's addition to Newport - $1,700

ELIZA J. DARRINGTON to MARY J. LOVE
Lot 4, square 4, in Highland - $200

MARY J. LOVE and husband to DAVID N. DOUGLAS
Lot 4, in Highland - $200

HENRY NEBEKER etal to SEYMOUR NEBEKER
30 acres adjoining Clinton - $4,000

SEYMOUR NEBEKER etal to LAURA WASHBURN
Lot 10, block 34, in Clinton - $100

WILLIAM C. WALKER and wife to LAURA N. WASHBURN
Lot 7, block 34, in Clinton - $125

JAMES M. REEDER to FRANK L. REEDER
20 acres in Clinton township - $4,000

ROBERT J. GESSIE and wife to WILLIAM CAYWOOD
Lot 15, in Riley's addition to Perrysville - $500

OBADIAH UNDERWOOD to EDGAR VANSICKLE etal
Lot 2, in Hillsdale - $500

WILLIAM L. HAYS and wife to ANDREW CARMACK
Lots 3 & 4, block 11, in Dana - $100

PLATT Z. ANDERSON and wife to HENRY NEBEKER
9 feet, side lot 7, block 4, in Clinton - $90

LEWIS MORGAN and wife to ELIAS E. ANDREWS
40 acres in Clinton township - $950

OLIVE TAYLOR etal to JOEL G. CARSON
3 acres in Vermillion township - $100

SAMUEL AIKMAN etal to MARGARET A. McGEE
Lots 9 & 10, block 8, in Dana - $100

MARY H. CAMPBELL to EDMOND EDMONDS
144 acres in Eugene township - $7,200

Perrysville
JAMES HEMPHILL, a former resident of this place, is here visiting relatives and friends, and will return to his home in a day or two near Champaign, IL.

Mrs. MARIAH LONG, wife of JACOB LONG of this place, was buried on last Tuesday in the graveyard on the Mound Prairie.

ROBERT DICKENSON has purchased the groceries in HAIN'S saloon building which formerly belonged to DICK MORRIS, and has restocked it, and is now doing a fair business.

MILT STEVENS has opened a grocery in the building formerly occupied by J. GIVENS as a boot and shoe store.

PETER COSSEY, one of our most prominent farmers, living 3 ½ miles NW of this place, who has been suffering with heart disease for some time past, we understand is able to be about again.

Montezuma
Mr. JAMES ROAR and Mrs. NICHOLS were married here last week. May happiness attend them.

Mrs. EVA PECK died at the residence of her father, L.R. YOUNG, Thursday evening. She leaves an infant daughter about 10 days old and a husband. Funeral services were conducted by Rev. MERIDITH on Sunday afternoon.

Highland
Mrs. RANDALL is suffering from a severe attack of bone erysipelas.

HENRY DINSMORE is lying very low with lung disease.

Application for Liquor License
ISAAC BISHOP – Clinton township
JEREMIAH CONELY – Dana township
LEONIDAS H. BELLUS – Clinton township
JOHN F. PEELER – Dana township

Home News
JAMES A. PRATHER, of Gessie, is a candidate for Road Superintendent of Highland township.

WILLIAM GIBSON has united with the M.E. Church.

RICHARD HAWKINS and lady, Miss FRANK TROTTER, and Miss ELLA PRITCHARD, united with the M.E. Church last Sunday.

L.A. MORGAN of Perrysville, is announced as an Independent candidate for Trustee of Highland township.

On last Monday evening in the Courthouse, RICHARD SEARCY and JENNIE DONEY, both of Eugene, were united in the holy bonds of matrimony by Judge DAVIDSON. The couple has our best wishes.

MILES H. COOK has been appointed administrator of the Estate of ISAAC COOK, deceased.

Personal
WALTER PLACE will take charge of the Newport Hotel after the first of March.

WILLIAM F. THORNTON, a compositor in this office, has a new baby boy at his house. The little fellow arrived here about 9 o'clock on last Friday morning.

NATHAN KILGORE, aged 16, was sentenced to the House of Correction until he is 21, by Judge DAVIDSON on last Tuesday.

Agents for the Hoosier State

J.J. RABB	Perrysville
W.H. SALTSGAVER	Gessie
HOSFORD & BELL	Eugene
Postmaster	Hillsdale
J.E. BILSLAND	Dana
F.N. AUSTIN	Toronto
J.R. FINNELL	St. Bernice
THOMAS C. DAVIS	Summit Grove
JOHN F. LEITON	Clinton
Mrs. H.M. WOOSTER	Montezuma

List of Lands and Lots Delinquent for non-payment of Taxes for the Year 1880
Vermillion Township

NAME	SEC	TWP	RANGE	ACRES	TAX
COLLUM, JOHN	30	17	10	2	
COLLUM, JOHN	30	17	10	1	6.35
PENCE, MARSA A.	29	17	10	80	25.28

Clinton Township

NAME	SEC	TWP	RANGE	ACRES	TAX
HUFF, JOHN H.	27	14	10	40	
HUFF, JOHN H.	27	14	10	40	
HUFF, JOHN H.	27	14	10	40	44.18
McLAUGHLIN, JAMES, heirs	9	14	9	2 ½	2.95
NICHOLS, JOHN F.	33	14	10	5	
NICHOLS, JOHN F.	33	14	10	9	7.98
SHEPARD, JAMES N.	33	14	9	40	19.75

Town Lots in Gessie

NAME	LOTS	TAX
KIRKPATRICK, NANCY C. & JOHN S.	Lease, Railroad addition, Inlot 1	
KIRKPATRICK, NANCY C. & JOHN S.	Lease, Railroad addition, Inlot 3 & 4	37.87

Town Lots in Perrysville

NAME	LOTS	TAX
KIRKPATRICK, NANCY C. & JOHN S.	Lease, Railroad addition, Inlot 6 & 7	
KIRKPATRICK, NANCY C. & JOHN S.	Lease, Railroad addition, Outlot 45	2.27
BAKER, SOLOMON	Smith & Parish addition, Inlot 14 & 15	14.37
HUNTER, JANE, heirs	East half, outlot 3	5.29

PERRIN, AMOS, heirs	Gessie & Cushman's addition, inlot 23	8.01
SEAL, HENRY I., heirs	Gessie & Cushman's addition, inlot 26	2.73

Town Lots in Hillsdale

NAME	LOTS	TAX
GARRETT, CAROLINE	Inlot 20 & 21	4.21
HERD, CYNTHA A.	South fourth, block 1	5.26

Town Lots in Clinton

NAME	LOTS	TAX
DAILY, SOLOMON, estate	SW corner outlot Knowles addition, block 4	9.45
PATTEN, RACHEL J.	Inlot 2 & 3, block 31	108.37
SPRAGUE, ELONZO	W ½, inlot 10, block 5	14.67

Wednesday, February 15, 1882

Committed Suicide

On last Saturday, CHARLES W. SHAW, who resided 3 miles SW of Dana, committed suicide at Chrisman, IL, by shooting himself in the temple with a revolver. He had been in feeble health for about 2 months, and had been worrying over the death of his daughter who died recently, and a sum of money, something over $2,000, which he had to pay twice on account of the rascally C.E. HOSFORD. Those two troubles weighed upon his mind so heavily, and being in poor health, he finally became slightly deranged. Last week he went out to Paris, IL, accompanied by his niece, a young lady aged about 20, and from there to Danville and back down to Chrisman on Saturday morning. While waiting at this place for the train to take them home, his niece went into a store to do some shopping. Mr. SHAW, although a temperate man, took advantage of her absence, and went to a saloon, and purchased a half pint of whiskey. He went into the coal house of the M.E. Church, drank the half pint of whiskey, and then shot himself. A woman who saw him go in there, gave the alarm when she heard the shot, but it was too late. The deceased was born in Virginia in 1823, and had been a resident of this county since 1864. He was a wealthy farmer, being worth between $50,000 and $75,000. He leaves 4 children, all grown, and many friends to mourn his sad death. His wife died a number of years ago.

Highland

A Mr. OLIVER of Greenfield, this State, is stopping with his brother-in-law, SMITH JONES.

Montezuma

Born – Wednesday, February 8, 1882, to JAMES & MARY BLUR, a daughter.

FRANK SMITH and wife of St. Louis, came here on Thursday morning to bury a lovely babe, aged one year, which death had taken from them. FRANK is still railroading there, and they returned home on Monday.

JOSIAH CAMPBELL, the teacher of Hillsdale School, reports getting along well with his school.

Executor's Sale of Land

Tuesday, March 21, 1882

At residence of FIELDING RABOURN, deceased

W 1/4 of SW ¼ of Sec 4, T 19, N R 10

Lies S of Danville & Covington Road – 47 acres

Also adjoining parcel – 10 acres

Also adjoining parcel – 10 acres

The first 2 tracts are good prairie farmland, the last tract is timber.

WILLIAM L. RABOURN, Executor of Will

Birthday Anniversary
On Wednesday, February 8, 1882, at the residence of Mrs. S.H. HARRINGTON, 2 miles W of Summit Grove, her children and grandchildren arrived to celebrate her 66th birthday. Because of the weather, not all attended. Her eldest child, Mrs. JOHN McDOWELL, who was born on her 19th birthday, was not present. Mrs. HARRINGTON was born February 8, 1816, in Harden County, KY, near or at Elizabethtown and emigrated to Vermillion County with her parents in her 13th year. Mrs. HARRINGTON's maiden name was PEARMAN. In this family there were 7 boys and 7 girls, 7 born in KY, and 7 born in IN. Seven had black hair, and 7 had red hair. Mrs. HARRINGTON has 9 grandchildren and 30 grandchildren.

Home News
A son was born to GEORGE & EMMA CHUNN, of Helt township, on February 3, 1882.

JOSEPH C. LYNN has been appointed the administrator of Dr. WAKEFIELD TWEEDY, deceased.

Clerk ROBERTS issued marriage license to HENRY B. JAMES and CAROLINE DINSMORE on Monday last.

J.F. LANGSTON, C.C. AIKMAN, and PETE AIKMAN are announced as candidates for Road Superintendent of Helt township.

W.T. FERGUSON of Perrysville, and B.K. DICKEN of this place, have been elected Directors of the Fountain and Vermillion Agricultural Society.

Sheriff MYERS took Mrs. ELIZABETH GRIFFIN over to the Insane Asylum on last Monday night. She had become deranged again from trouble and religious excitement.

Dying
J.Y. DURHAM started for Topeka, KS, last Saturday, on receipt of a message that his brother, JERRE B. DURHAM, was not expected to live but a few days at most. J.B. DURHAM is an old acquaintance of ours, who formerly resided on a farm near Waveland, Montgomery County. He is a Christian gentleman, and a man who is very highly esteemed by all of his acquaintances. We hope to hear of his recovery. He is between 75 and 80 years of age, and has always been blessed with good health.

E. WHITE JAMES is announced as a candidate for Trustee of Helt township.

Court Report

HENRY S.S. FORD etal vs. CLARA A. FORD
Partition – continued

Trustees Springhill M.E. Church vs. W.L. LITTLE, Trustee of Funds
Petition for order – dismissed

SAMUEL REED etal vs. ACHA REED etal
Partition – continued

RUHAMA E. UNDERWOOD etal vs. ROBERT B. STOKES etal
Partition to quiet title – report of full payment and Commissioner discharged

SAMUEL MOREHEAD vs. JOHN S. BUSH
Trial by jury, judgment for plaintiff for $40

CHARLES W. WARD vs. ROBERT BURNETT etal
Partition – report of receipts and expenditures approved and Commissioner discharged

FRANK WELLS, admr. vs. ANNA EADS etal
Partition – continued

Frankfort & State Line RR Co. vs. JOHN GRONENDYKE etal
Right of way – continued

Frankfort & State Line RR Co. vs. SAMUEL GRONENDYKE etal
Right of way – continued

LUCINDA BROWN vs. HUGH M. KILGORE
Note & account – dismissed at plaintiff cost

WILLIAM ALEXANDER vs. MARY ALEXANDER
Divorce – dismissed at plaintiff cost

JOHN G. SPIESS vs. HENRIETTA SPIESS
Divorce – decree for plaintiff at his costs

CLAUDE MATTHEWS vs. ADDISON L. WHITCOMB
Injunction – decree for plaintiff

GEORGE W. ANDREWS etal vs. L.H. BELLUS etal
Note & mortgage – decree of foreclosure, judgment for $283.21

GAAR, SCOOT & Co. vs. ISAAC VANNEST etal
Note – judgment for $266

THOMAS BASINGER vs. JEROME B. THOMAS
To recover personal property and damages – dismissed by plaintiff

JOSEPHUS COLLETT vs. WILLIAM ANDERSON
Note – judgment for $150

HOMER LUSADDER vs. JULIA A. LUSADDER
Divorce – Decree for defendant, order that maiden name be restored
Judgment for $500 alimony

WILLIAM F. BARNETT vs. THOMAS J. STARK
Note – judgment for $489.67

EDWARD W. JOHNSON etal vs. L.H. BELLUS etal
Attachment – default – judgment for $233.31

ISAAC VANNEST vs. CHARLES CHEEKS
Appeal – dismissed by agreement

SOLOMON HINES vs. PETER F. STUTLER
Note – dismissed

Aetna Life Insurance Co. vs. MILTON SHOWALTERS etal
Note & mortgage – decree of foreclosure, judgment for $1,095

JAMES QUINLAN vs. WILLIAM WOOSTER
Change of venue – license granted

JAMES RARIDAN ex parte
Application for liquor license – granted

JOHN VANDUYN vs. WILLIAM P. HELT
Seduction – dismissed

WILLIAM HAGENBAUGH vs. ABEL HOOVER etal
Appeal – dismissed

JAMES McMEEN vs. THOMAS J. STARK
Not & account – default, judgment for $186

LUCINDA BROWN vs. THOMAS W. STEPHENS
Note & account – default, judgment for $139.80

MARY A. STANLEY vs. JESSE L. STANLEY
Divorce – continued

HENRY SHANNON vs. LAURA SHANNON
Divorce – dismissed

NELSON C. ANDERSON vs. CEPHUS MACK
Note – default, judgment for $322

ROBERT H. NIXON vs. SAMUEL G. MALONE etal
Note & mortgage – default, foreclosure, judgment for $1,023.31

ISAAC B. HEDGES vs. EDMOND D. JAMES etal
Note & mortgage – continued

MARY J. LOVE vs. ARTHUR C. LOVE
Petition for change of order – continued

Cleveland Burial Lease Co. vs. ROBERT B. BAILEY etal
Account – default, judgment for $119.65

PHILLIP C. PERKINS etal vs. ALBERT F. FULTZ
Note – default, judgment for $45.78

OLIVER P. BUSH vs. JAMES MAXWELL etal
Note – default, judgment for $56.45

Trustees Insurance Co. vs. CHARLES E. HOSFORD etal
Note & mortgage – JAMES CHIPPS appointed receiver
To take rent and profits until foreclosure

ELAM S. McBROOM vs. I.R. & W.R.R. Co.
Change of venue – continued

JOSEPH C. LYNN, guardian vs. JOHN H. FINNELL, DAVID E. FINNELL
Ex parte partition – report of commissioner approved

Personal
Mrs. E. HITE has returned home, and is now prepared to contract for carpet weaving.

A.M. CARPENTER, of Veedersburg, a former citizen of this place, was in town visiting this week.

Mrs. LOU WOODMAN, of Rio, Knox County, IL, is visiting her cousin, JESSE HOUCHIN, of Helt township.

Miss DOLLIE HAYS, only daughter of Mr. and Mrs. J.M. HAYS, of Clinton, died last week, aged about 15 years.

Mrs. S.A. HOUCHIN, wife of D.V. HOUCHIN, who died December 16, 1881, gave birth to a bright girl baby on January 29, 1882.

Mrs. J.L. HOFFMAN, of Indianapolis, spent several days in town last week, the guest of her sister, Mrs. IVY A. SEARS.

Notice of Non-Residence

EDWARD W. JOHNSON, ROBERT FLYNN
Vs.
LEONIDAS H. BELLUS, JAMES WILLS
Complaint 2153
P.Z. ANDERSON, JUMP & WARD attorneys
JAMES WILLS is not a resident of Indiana
Must appear before fourth Monday of April 1882
Date February 10, 1882

JAMES ROBERTS, Clerk

Wednesday, February 22, 1882

W.F. HENDERSON & Co., prominent grain dealers of Danville, IL, has failed. It is thought their assets will be sufficient to pay liabilities.

Montezuma
Our county has lost another good citizen in JONATHAN DeMOTTE on Wednesday, February 15, 1882, who died after an illness of several weeks, from lung fever, aged about 50 years. He was a kind husband and father and leaves a widow and 4 children to mourn their loss.

Hon. O.P. BROWN has bought the PERLEY TENBROOK farm of 60 acres lying one mile W of Rockville, for which he paid the round sum of $8,000, or over $133 per acre.

THOMAS LETNER, one of our barbers, throws up the sponge and will remove to Putnam County. TOM and his family are good people and we are sorry to part with them.

WILLIAM WOOSTER has been confined to the house by sickness for nearly a week. Some form of liver complaint is what is the matter.

ED WICKENS, a former resident of our town, died at his home near Hillsdale on last Saturday morning from pneumonia. He had been in town but a few days since, and but few heard of his illness until after his death. He leaves a wife and 2 children.

Highland
The following persons are on the sick list: A.J. PITTS, ANDREW JACKSON, and MARY MITCHELL.

JOHN TAYLOR, of Dana, paid his sister, Mrs. EMMA HOPKINS, a visit last week.

ANDREW JACKSON had a fine monument erected at his wife's grave in Pisgah Cemetery, a few days ago.

JOHN OLIVER, a young man who came to this township about 5 years ago from the State of TN, died on last Wednesday. JOHN was a model young man and was beloved by all who knew him. Although he has no relatives in this county, he had many friends who think of him as a brother and all his acquaintances mourn at their loss.

Perrysville
Mrs. P.S. MOUDY has purchased the McNEILL property, opposite the U.B. Church in this place.

JIM HAINS has returned from the Hot Springs, Arkansas, and is looking well.

Died – on the evening of February 17, 1882, Mrs. BARSHEBA JAMES, of this place, aged 79 years, of consumption.

Died – on February 17, 1882, the wife of JOHN BURNETT, living 3 miles E of this place, of consumption (age not known).

The wife of ROBERT DICKERSON, of this place, has gone to some town in Illinois to be operated on for cancer of the breast.

Notice of Administration

Estate of WAKEFIELD TWEEDY, deceased
February 9, 1882

JOSEPH C. LYNN, Admr.

Home News
OSCAR GIBSON is now Deputy County Treasurer. OSCAR is honest and faithful and will make a good officer.

JOHN GIVENS, of Highland township, has leased the Newport Hotel, and will take possession sometime next month.

Sheriff MYERS brought Miss NETTIE SCONCE, of Eugene, home from the Asylum on last Saturday evening. She is pronounced cured.

JOHN W. PARRETT has sold his farm lying N of the Little Vermillion, and containing about 160 acres, to JOSEPH A. MOREHEAD, for $6,000.

WILLIAM B. SIMPSON, who is subject to hemorrhage of the lungs, had a severe attack one day last week, and was confined to his room for several days.

HURON SOUTHARD, of Helt township, is announced as a candidate for Trustee of Helt township.

JOE CARTER and his family, who moved to Kansas a few years ago, returned to Helt township, their old home, on last Friday. They are satisfied to live out the rest of their days in old Vermillion.

United Again
LEWIS L. BISHOP and ANNA McNAIR, his lately divorced wife, were again reunited in wedlock last week. The ceremony took place at Terre Haute. We wish them better luck this time.

Personal
Little KATIE GIBSON is down with scrofula.

R.H. NIXON and lady and Postmaster STEPHENS left yesterday for the Arkansas Hot Springs.

JAMES W. HALL, of Seely, Cowley County, KS, writes back that he has joined church and been converted.

FRANK JONES left for the Arkansas Hot Springs yesterday morning, to see if he could not recuperate his health.

HARRISON MAXIDON, of Moultrie County, IL, is now visiting his uncle, JESSE HOUCHIN, of Helt township. It is probable he will remain here and work for Mr. HOUCHIN this season.

GEORGE SKIDMORE, of Helt's Prairie, was in town on last Friday. He is laboring under considerable trouble and pain at the present time. There is a hard lump on the right side of his neck which has been 15 years forming, and gradually getting a little larger each year. A number of physicians have examined it, and some of them pronounce it a cancer. At times it is very painful, and Mr. SKIDMORE is beginning to get uneasy about it.

JAMES ROBERTS has bought ¼ interest in A.L. WHITCOMB's dry goods store at Clinton, and will probably not be a candidate for re-election to the Clerk's office. NORTH CRAIG, who is familiar with the duties of the office, has been installed as Deputy Clerk. Mr. ROBERTS intends to move to Clinton shortly.

Mrs. ORPHA WIGLEY, an old lady 75 years of age, united with the U.B. Church on last Sunday evening. She was formerly a Cumberland Presbyterian.

Obituary
Mrs. MARTHA DICKEN, widow of SIMEON DICKEN, who was stricken down with paralysis about 7 weeks ago, died at 11 o'clock on last Saturday morning, aged 78 years. The deceased was born in Kentucky in 1804, and emigrated to this county in 1822, two years before it was organized. At that date the county was sparsely settled with white people, but Indian camps were numerous. Mrs. DICKEN did not belong to any church organization, but was a good Christian lady, and tried to live an honorable and upright life. Her funeral took place on last Tuesday, and was conducted by Rev. JONES of the U.B. Church, from the late family residence. Her remains were interred in the Thomas Cemetery.

Sheriff's Sale

Saturday, March 18, 1882
Aetna Life Insurance Co. vs.
MILTON SHOWALTERS, MARY E. SHOWALTERS, LIDA HOSFORD, SIDNEY B. DAVIS, Assignee of CHARLES E. HOSFORD
$1,149.85
Sale to be held at 4 p.m. at Courthouse
NW ¼ of NE ¼
SW ¼ of NE ¼
Also 24 acres in E ½ of NW ¼
Land in Section 22, T 16 N R 9 W
Total of 104 acres
Land in Vermillion County, IN
February 22, 1882
WILLIAM C. MYERS, Sheriff

Wednesday, March 1, 1882

An Old Citizen of Helt Township Murdered In His Hen Roost

Another murder was committed in Helt township. The victim was EVAN THOMAS, an old man aged 69 years, who resided on the bluff, in a little log cabin, 4 miles S of here. On last Sunday night, after Mr. THOMAS and his wife had retired for the night, they heard the chickens making unusual noises. Mr. THOMAS got his shotgun and went to the hen house to check. His wife heard the sound of two shots, one right after another. Upon investigation, Mrs. THOMAS found her husband on the ground, in the throes of death. An inquest was held on his body by Coroner BRINDLEY the next morning, and it was found that over 70 large shot had struck him on the thigh, groin, his privates, and the pit of his stomach. Upon investigation, it was determined that a warrant should be issued for GEORGE WHITTED, JOSEPH HART, and JAMES RIDDLE. They were found and arrested.

JOSEPH HART was raised in Vigo County. At one time he worked for T.J. STARK of this township. About 3 months ago, he came to this county from southern Illinois, where he had been stopping for some time. He is unmarried and claims to be 30 years of age.

JAMES RIDDLE hails from Kentucky and has only been a resident of this county for a short time. He says that he is only 23 years of age, and unmarried.

GEORGE WHITTED was born and raised in this county. His parents are still living and reside in Clinton township and are said to be respectable people. WHITTED is 28 years of age, has a wife and 4 children who reside in Clinton township.

The three, along with 30 or 40 other men, have been engaged for several weeks getting out ties for DICKERSON & ENGLISH, in Danville, IL. Alcohol played a part in the crime.

JOHN H. BOGART, of Clinton, has announced that he is a candidate for County Treasurer. He held the office for two terms, and made one of the best Treasurers ever elected in this county.

S.V. ODEKIRK, of Opedee, is announced as a candidate for County Treasurer. He is a man of business capacity, and in every way fitted and qualified to discharge the duties.

FRANK M. RILEY, of Highland township, is announced as a candidate for County Treasurer. He is a man of good business qualifications.

Montezuma
J.F. STACY died Sunday evening, about 6 o'clock, from intermittent fever. Mr. STACY has been in poor health for sometime. He has been one of our best and most respected citizens, universally loved by all. His funeral took place Tuesday noon.

JOSEPH STILLWELL, formerly of this place, now of Ironton, KS, returned here last week to settle up some unfinished business; also to visit his many friends. Mr. STILLWELL has been studying under Mr. WILSON, a well known occulist. He has been doing a good business since he left. We wish him success.

THOMAS LETNER has moved to Greencastle.

Highland
A man by the name of BENNETT died of lung fever on last Friday.

Dr. HARRISON informs us that JOHN MALONE and wife were made happy by the arrival of a female youngster last Saturday morning.

Old Mr. HOSS, of Greenfield, was visiting his daughter, MARGARET JONES, last week.

Home News
BOB WHITE has become a citizen of Newport.

DICK MITCHELL has moved on his farm, just W of town.

SAMUEL STOVER, of Helt township, has been appointed administrator of the Estate of JOHN H. OLIVER, deceased.

WILLIAM MALONE has closed out his business here and will move his stock of dry goods and groceries up to Eugene today.

Mrs. ISABEL KEYS gives legal notice that she will apply at the next term of circuit court for a divorce from her husband, WILLIAM C. KEYS.

Sheriff MYERS' wife is still confined to her bed of affliction. It was 5 months ago last Monday since she has been out of the house.

Personal
JOHN S. JAMES has moved on to a farm 1 ½ miles E of Danville, IL.

Miss CHARITY THORNTON, of Sadorus, IL, is in town visiting, the guest of W.P. HENSON and family.

MEL JAMES, who has been stopping at Oskaloosa, IA, for the last 4 months, spent last Sunday in town.

W.B. FOLAND, of Troy, OH, a former resident of this place, was in town a few hours last Monday evening. BILL looks hale and hearty, and says he has not touched a drop of liquor for over a year.

Notice of Non-Residence
ISABEL KEYS vs. WILLIAM C. KEYS
Complaint 2188
Divorce
CONLEY & DAVIS attorneys
WILLIAM C. KEYS is not a resident of Indiana
Must appear before fourth Monday of April 1882
February 28, 1882
JAMES ROBERTS, Clerk
By NORTH CRAIG, Deputy Clerk

Administrator's Sale
Estate of JOHN H. OLIVER, deceased
Saturday, March 25, 1882
All personal property
Horses, wagons, sleigh, buggy, harness, saddle, bridle, etc.
SAMUEL STOVER, Admr.
Date February 28, 1882

Notice of Non-Residence
JAMES M. SAVAGE vs. FLORIDA SAVAGE
Complaint 2186
Divorce
J.C. SAWYERS attorney
FLORIDA SAVAGE is not a resident of Indiana
Must appear before fourth Monday in April 1882
February 17, 1882
JAMES ROBERTS, Clerk
By NORTH CRAIG, Deputy Clerk

Notice of Non-Residence

HELEN A. McKNIGHT vs.
Unknown heirs of WILLIAM C. DON CARLOS
Unknown heirs of CUTHBERT H. SPANGLER
Unknown heirs of JOHN W. BUSH
JACOB L. THOMAS, JAMES A. ELDER, & JAMES R. DUNLAP – Commissioners
Complaint 2178
Quiet Title
BEN BLANCHARD attorney
Unknown heirs of WILLIAM C. DON CARLOS, Unknown heirs of CUTHBERT H. SPANGLER, Unknown heirs of JOHN W. BUSH, WILLIAM C. CLOVER, WILLIAM P. DOLE are not residents of State of Indiana
Must appear before fourth Monday in April 1882
February 27, 1882

JAMES ROBERTS, Clerk
By NORTH CRAIG, Deputy Clerk

Miss FLORA JOHNSON, who has been at Cincinnati for several months having her eyes treated by a skilled occulist of that city, has returned and reports that her eyesight has been much improved.

Wednesday, March 8, 1882

Miss MAY GREEN, aged 14, and the daughter of Rev. M.L. GREEN, Parke County, eloped last week with a young man by the name of JOE HUNT, aged 19. They boarded a C. & E.I. train and went to Danville, IL, where they were united in marriage.

Death

JERRE B. DURHAM, formerly of this county, died at his home in Topeka, KS, last Saturday. He was an honored man, and leaves to mourn his death, many friends and kinsman in this county. At the time of his death, he was in his 76th year. He was a prominent and active member of the Methodist Church, and during his long life was a most exemplary Christian.

Crawfordsville Journal

Death

Mrs. MARY CAMPBELL died at Crawfordsville on Tuesday evening, February 28, 1882. She was the widow of JOHN P. CAMPBELL, an old citizen of Crawfordsville, and a sister of Messrs. JOSEPHUS, JOHN, and S.S. COLLETT, Mrs. J.H. TURNER, Mrs. CRAWFORD FAIRBANKS, Mrs. DAVIS, and Mrs. JONES, of Newport. Mrs. CAMPBELL was born in Terre Haute 56 years ago, and was well known to our older citizens. She was a member of the Presbyterian Church. She left 3 children – two sons and a daughter, all grown. Mrs. CAMPBELL was ill a considerable time. The funeral takes place at Crawfordsville this (Thursday) afternoon.

Terre Haute Express

Montezuma

It is rumored that S.P. HANCOCK was united in marriage to a Terre Haute belle on Thursday last.

Mrs. JANE MUSHETT bought at Sheriff's sale the property of JOHN STILLWELL, paying for the same the sum of $200.

Mrs. MARY BALDWIN, aged about 60 years, died at 1 o'clock on Monday last. The funeral took place at Friends Church on Wednesday. She was buried at Coloma. She leaves 3 children, all grown.

Mr. F.S. CUMBERLAND showed great respect to our departed friend J.F. STACY, by decorating the inside of the grave with evergreens. No earth could be seen.

Real Estate Transfers for the Month of February 1882

HENRY A. ANDREWS and wife to WILLIAM D. McFALL
13 1/3 acres in Helt township - $330

AMOS E. WELLS and wife to JOHN T. BOREN
2 acres in Helt township - $100

JAMES CHIPPS and wife to WILLIAM F. THORNTON etal
Lot 65 in Newport - $200

ANDREW R. REED to TILGHMAN FONCANNON
25 acres in Helt township - $300

ELIAS E. ANDREWS and wife to GEORGE WELLMAN
40 acres in Clinton township - $1,000

GEORGE R. HOPKINS to SARAH A. DAVIS
40 acres in Clinton township - $650

LEWIS C. WELLMAN and wife to JOHN N. WELLMAN
40 acres in Helt township - $1,000

ANDREW JACKSON etal to DAVID PEARMAN etal
13 acres in Helt township - $400

PETER AMMERMAN and wife to MARGARET BURNS
1 acre in Helt township - $150

LIDA A. BENTON etal to Charity Lodge No. 32
Part of lot 36 in Perrysville - $1,000

JAMES A. GREENAWELT and wife to WILLIAM M. HAMILTON
Lot 5 in block 1, Morey's addition to Clinton - $100

WILLIAM M. HAMILTON and wife to WASHINGTON KING
Lot 5, block 1, Morey's addition to Clinton - $72.50

JAMES E. KNOWLES etal to MARIA HAMILTON
Lot 1, block 4, Knowles addition to Clinton - $250

JOHN PAYTON to SARAH A. PORTER
Lot 8, block 24, in Clinton - $110

GEORGE SMITH and wife to EDWARD Y. STOKES
60 acres in Vermillion township - $900

CLINTON WATSON to PETER AMMERMAN
11/12 of an acre in Helt township - $25

JOHN W. SLACK to ALFRED R. HOPKINS
40 acres in Vermillion township - $7.85

JACOB W. REED to TILGHMAN FONCANNON
15 acres in Helt township - $500

MARY NEWLIN to AMOS FOREMAN
133 ¼ acres in Vermillion township - $400

SAMUEL AIKMAN etal to WILLIAM E. FULWIDER
Lot 24, block 6, in Dana - $50

E.T.H. & C. RR Co. to SPENCER MACK
Lot 7 in Summit Grove - $25

WILLIAM SPERRY to HENRY HOLLINGSWORTH
Lot 7, Gessie - $3.26

CHARLES B. McDOWELL and wife to JOHN D. McDOWELL
14.3 acres in Helt township - $350

MARY GIBSON to EDGAR VAN SICKLE etal
Lots 3, 4, & 5, Hillsdale - $120

JOHN W. PARRETT and wife to JOSEPH MOREHEAD
155 acres in Vermillion township - $5,900

ROBERT BURNETT etal to RICHARD S. ALDERSON
20 acres in Eugene township - $450

WAKEFIELD TWEEDY and wife to Helt township
Lot near Jonestown - $50

BENJAMIN K. DICKEN to JOHN W. PARRETT
Lot 103, and part lot 102, Newport - $1,000

SAMANTHA A. PLACE and husband to SILAS HOLLINGSWORTH
Lot 6, Newport - $600

HENRY R. INGRAHAM to SARAH J. ROBERTS
Lot 4, Riley's addition to Perrysville - $108

HENRY HOLLINGSWORTH and wife to WILLIAM I. HALL
Lot 7, in Gessie - $20

FERNANDO C. OAKS and wife to GEORGE T. RICHARDSON
88 acres in Indiana and Illinois - $3,000

JOHN MANGES and wife to LIVINGSTON T. RICHARDSON etal
10 acres in Vermillion township - $225

WILLIAM H. RIGGS to NELSON C. ANDERSON
Part lot 7, block 3, in Clinton - $6.03

WILLIAM E. LIVENGOOD to NELSON C. ANDERSON
2 acres in Clinton township - $3.20

JAMES HENRY to NELSON C. ANDERSON
Lots 7 & 10, block 6, in Clinton - $13.86

AUGUST VAN HOUSTON to NELSON C. ANDERSON
6 acres in Clinton township - $4.22

JOHN FLETCHER to WILLIAM GIBSON
5.87 acres in Vermillion township - $2.31

MALISSA NICHOLS to WILLIAM GIBSON
5 acres in Clinton township - $4.20

EMILY BALES etal to JOHN RICHARDS
10 acres in Helt township - $200

ELI BRINDLEY and wife to OLIVER P. DAVIS
38 acres in Vermillion township - $1,520

DANIEL W. FINNEY and wife to SOLON JOHNSON
160 acres in Helt township - $7,600

WILLIAM SWAN and wife to JOHN SALYARDS
40 acres in Clinton township - $400

WILLIAM H. DUGGER and wife to ROSA J. UNDERWOOD
1/15 of 40 acres in Helt township - $75

JOHN W. PARRETT and wife to JOSHUA N. DAVIS
Lot 20, Zener's addition to Newport - $55

Home News
BEN BLANCHARD has bought the mill lot. He paid $1,500.

JAMES ASBURY has bought the old BRICKER farm at Highland. He paid $4,000.

WILLIAM C. BOGART has been appointed administrator of the Estate of C.W. SHAW, deceased.

A little daughter of STEPHEN MILLER, of Opedee, has been lying dangerously ill for several weeks.

SOLON JOHNSON has bought D.W. FINNEY's farm near Dana. Consideration $7,600.

JOE C. DILLOW has a young blacksmith at his house. The little son of Vulcan made his appearance at about 10 o'clock on last Wednesday night.

J.E. WHIPPLE, of Eugene township, announced he is a candidate for Assessor of this township.

JOHN H. BEADLE, editor of the Rockville Tribune, has a new youngster at his house, of the piano thumping gender.

On Monday last, the Board of Commissioners granted retail liquor licenses to JERRE CONLEY, and JOHN PEELER, of Dana. The cases of L.H. BELLUS and ISAAC BISHOP were continued to next Monday.

EBER HOLLINGSWORTH has announced he is a candidate for Road Superintendent of this township. He is familiar with all the roads in this township, and thinks he could put them in a much better condition.

SEYMOUR NEBEKER, of Clinton, was in the city Sunday, visiting his nephew, Dr. WASHBURN. Mrs. LAURA WASHBURN is here visiting her sister, Mrs. General WASHBURN, who is still sick.

Greencastle Banner

Death of a Former Citizen of Newport
V.E. WHITMER, a former resident of Newport, died at Covington, OH, Saturday, February 25, 1882, after a short illness. He was 43 years of age.

Death
Mrs. ETTA ASBURY, wife of JOHN ASBURY and daughter of Dr. GILMORE, died at about 12 o'clock noon on Saturday last, aged 24 or 25 years. The deceased was taken down with typhoid fever 3 months ago, and lingered until death released her from her sufferings. Her funeral took place on Sunday, her remains being interred at the Vermillion Chapel Cemetery.

Wedding
FRANK HASTY of this place, and Miss JOSIE HUMPHRIES, of Perrysville, will be united in wedlock at 11 o'clock today, at the residence of the bride. Miss LAURA McCONNELL, of this place, is going up to witness the ceremony.

Some of the citizens of Eugene township are talking of the lazy fellow by the name of HENRY WOOTAN, who resides 1 ½ miles NW of Eugene, and does not provide better for his family. He lays around and does nothing while he has a little child, without medical attention or anything to eat, except as the neighbors bring it in.

Personal
Mrs. JANE PIERCE's youngest child has been quite sick for several days.

HENRY LONGFELLOW and wife, and JOHN HOLLINGSWORTH, all of this township, left yesterday morning for Superior, NB, where they intend to locate.

Administrator's Sale of Personal Property

Estate of CHARLES W. SHAW, deceased
Sale to be held Friday, March 31, 1882
Public auction of personal property

Household furniture, wagon, buggy, 2 spring wagons, horses, mules, harnesses, cattle, etc.

WILLIAM C. BOGART, Admr.

Notice to Non-Residents

URIAH HADLEY vs. GEORGE W. ROGERS
JUMP & WARD attorneys
Garnishment to collect money on account
GEORGE W. ROGERS is not a resident of Indiana
Must appear before Third day of May, 1882
March 8, 1882

NATHAN M. TUTT, J.P.

Wednesday, March 15, 1882

J.M. HARPER, of Helt's Prairie, is announced as a candidate for Assessor of Helt township.

Perrysville
WARREN VATES has moved to Kansas.

TAYLOR JONES, of Champaign, IL, is here on a visit to friends and relatives.

The little child of JOHN BRILES, of this place, that has been lying at the point of death for some days past, has taken a change for the better and there is now some prospect of it getting well again.

Rumor says that Mr. METZER will run the hotel again after the first of April, and that Mr. SABIN will retire to the bluff again where he has a nice property of his own.

Lost Her Mind
Mrs. MARY E. WALLACE, an old and estimable widow lady of this township, has become insane, and attempted to kill herself by hanging on Wednesday last. She was discovered and cut down just in time to save her life. The necessary papers have been made out and forwarded, asking that she be received at the Insane Asylum for treatment.

Death
WILLIAM NELSON, a saloon keeper of Dana, died on Sunday last, of consumption. The deceased was born in this county in 1836, and had been a resident of it ever since up to the day of his death. He was buried on Sunday last. He was buried on Sunday last, at the Jaggers' Cemetery, in this township. Mr. NELSON, like all the rest of us, he had his faults, but was kind and generous hearted.

Montezuma
Sorry for the report that S.P. HANCOCK was married to a Terre Haute Belle. The report was false.

JOHN OSBORN has been appointed administrator of the Estate of the late JONATHAN DeMOTTE, and will sell the personal property at public auction, April 14th.

Mrs. PHELUN WATT has been quite sick for some time with lung fever.

W.P. STANLEY, of Annapolis, has rented the JESSE HOUCHIN property and will shortly move. Mr. STANLEY will engage in the dry goods and grocery business.

Highland
Mrs. BURNETT, of Rockville, is visiting her son, ANDREW WILSON.

Miss EDMONDS is teaching the Spring Hill School.

JOHN MIDDLEBROOK will leave in a few days for Russellville where he will take charge of a tile factory.

JOSHUA SNIDER has a young dishwasher at home.

MORGAN SINSEY was made happy by the arrival of a boy baby last week.

JOHN CRAFTON, who moved to this place about one year ago from Illinois, died on last Thursday. He walked to the Junction about one mile in the morning, went back home and spoke of feeling better than he had for some time, sat down in a chair and was smoking when his wife noticed his pipe fall and saw that something was wrong. He only lived a few moments. He was about 60 years of age, and leaves a wife and 7 small children in destitute circumstances. The family has the deepest sympathy of all their neighbors.

Home News
E.F. DAVIS has closed out here and will leave for Goodland, Newton County, IN, tomorrow.

J.C. SAWYERS has sworn off and quit chewing tobacco.

A little 4 year old daughter of STEPHEN MILLER, of Opedee, died on Wednesday last.

JOHN BILSLAND, of Helt township, has been making his children feel happy. He has just deeded Mrs. SAM MALONE 108 acres of land, JOHN E. BILSLAND 110 acres, and Mrs. CHARLEY TAYLOR 120 acres.

A.R. HOPKINS is announced as a candidate for County Clerk. He was born and raised in this county and is favorably known by many of our leading and influential citizens.

Obituary
The wife of WESLEY WILTERMOOD, of Eugene township, died at 6 o'clock on last Friday evening, and was buried at the Wimsett Cemetery on Sunday last. The remains were accompanied to their last resting place by quite a number of her friends. The deceased was an exceptional good woman, a kind neighbor, and esteemed and respected by everybody. She leaves a husband and 3 little children to mourn her death.

On Thursday, March 9, 1882, at the residence of JOSEPH MOREHEAD, one half mile N of town, the marriage of his daughter MAGGIE MOREHEAD to WILSON J. HARSHAW of Savana, IL was consummated. The ceremony was performed by Rev. W.H. JONES, of the U.B. Church.

Personal
Mrs. ETTA DAVIS, of Indianapolis, is here visiting her brother, MARTIN SEELY. She will remain with us a couple of weeks.

Public Sale

March 25, 1882
Late residence of WILLIAM L. MALONE, deceased, in Dana
Personal property

Sheep, cattle, one horse and buggy, harness, wagon, farming utensils, household and kitchen furniture

MALINDA MALONE FRASIER

Final Settlement of Estate

Estate of JOHN SLATER, deceased
April 24, 1882
Dated March 8, 1882

JAMES ROBERTS, Clerk

Notice of Non-Resident

J.W. PARRETT, & CLARA C. FAIRBANKS vs. JOHN S. JAMES
Collect money due on account
JOHN S. JAMES is not a resident of Indiana
Must appear before April 8, 1882
March 15, 1882

JOHN W. PARRETT, J.P.

Sheriff's Sale

ROBERT H. NIXON vs. SAMUEL G. MALONE
$1,088.31
Saturday, April 8, 1882
Sale at courthouse between 10 and 4
NE of SE ¼ Sec 36 T 16 R 10 W, containing 73 acres
SAWYER & GIBSON attorneys
March 15, 1882

WILLIAM C. MYERS, Sheriff

Wednesday, March 22, 1882

Sentenced
ALEXANDER KILPATRICK, a former citizen of Perrysville, was tried in the circuit court at Bloomingdale, IL, on Wednesday last, and was tried and convicted of stealing a horse and buggy, and set of harnesses. He was sentenced to 13 years in the Joliet Penitentiary. This makes his second trip to Joliet. He was sent up for 3 years from Danville, IL, for killing a man. He is now over 50 years of age.

Clinton township
The Republicans met and nominated the following candidates:

Trustee	GEORGE W. STULTZ
Assessor	JAMES M. HAYS
Road Superintendent	J.O. WRIGHT
Justice of the Peace	Rev. D.H. BIRT
Constables	FRANK VANDUYN, SAMUEL DAVIDSON, HORACE PERRIN

Helt township
The Republicans met and nominated the following candidates:

Trustee	O.J. KEYES
Road Superintendent	PETER AIKMAN
Assessor	I.V. JORDAN
Justice of the Peace	G.W. SAXTON, ALEX MURPHY
Constables	ALEX DUGGER, HENRY ANDREWS, W.F. EATON

D.C. SMITH, of Perrysville, was in the city Wednesday and Thursday of the present week. He will become a citizen of Frankfort in the near future.
Frankfort Banner

Highland
Old WILLIAM RUSSELL, of this place, is lying at the point of death.

Clinton
Mrs. ANNA PITMAN, nee KNOWLES, of Evansville, is visiting her parents here this week.

Montezuma
WILLIAM PHILLIPS Sr., died of old age on Tuesday last, aged 84 years. He had been married over 60 years, his aged companion still living. The old man was much respected and leaves many friends to mourn.

THOMAS J. WATKINS' health continues very precarious. He has not been able to leave his room for several weeks.

DAVIS & AKINS have sold out to STANLEY & WEAVER, of Annapolis, who in addition to the grocery will also open out a dry goods store here. Mr. AKINS will have charge of the grocery house.

Mr. WEAVER, of Indianapolis, has rented the property lately bought by JESSE HOUCHIN, and now occupies it with his family.

OL AKINS is now RR agent at Newman, IL, and is getting along first rate.

Home News
Mrs. JOHN GIBBENS is ailing.

JESSE SMITH, of Eugene township, is lying seriously ill.

JOE GARRETT has a nine pound boy baby at his house. The little fellow arrived last Friday.

A lady by the name of IDA ROBINSON is publishing a very neat little local paper in Fairmount, IL.

J.A. WILTERMOOD, teacher in the intermediate department, is under the weather, and not able to teach.

C.S. DAVIS is announced as a candidate for Recorder.

JOE CHUNN has left the poor farm and gone to live with friends in Clinton township. He and the Superintendent had a falling out.

R.H. NIXON has bought the HARRIET C. DALLAS farm, located 6 miles SW of here. The farm contains 320 acres, for which Mr. NIXON paid $35 per acre, amounting to $11,200.

FRANK SHELATOE, of Eugene township, is announced as a candidate for Road Superintendent.

WILLIAM C. MYERS is announced as a candidate for Sheriff, the office which he has so efficiently and satisfactorily filled during the past 2 years. He has made a good officer and should be given another term.

Commissioner's Court
Allowances

JOHN O. ROGERS, road viewers fees	1.75
JAMES KAUFMAN, road viewers fees	1.50
ISAAC WALTERS, road viewers fees	1.50
WILLIAM STARKEY, criminal	2.50
MAURICE HEGARTY, County offices	3.40
JOSEPH CONRAD, county Poor Asylum	630.03
RICHARD E. NICHOLS, keeping poor	15.00
S.B. DAVIS, printing	230.55
J.A. & J.W. THOMAS, on account, NW gravel road	23.45
H.H. CONLEY, County School Superintendent	211.80
JOHN S. BUSH, tilling on Poor Farm	94.50
W.B. BURFORD, books and stationary	221.95
J.C. SAWYERS, poor, Vermillion township	205.57
J.C. SAWYERS, bridges, Vermillion township	54.19
M.L. HALL, Clerk County Board of Health	78.79
H.C. SMITH, poor Highland township	237.75
H.C. SMITH, services as overseer poor	15.00
M.C. HOSFORD, poor Eugene township	176.61
M.C. HOSFORD, services as overseer poor	15.00
WILLIAM L. PORTER, poor Clinton township	246.25
WILLIAM L. PORTER, services overseer poor	15.00
H.O. PETERS, 3 mo. Salary, County Treasurer	200.00
CASEY & BISHOP, printing	76.50
R.E. STEPHENS, school books for pauper children	6.10
THOMAS BRINDLEY, janitor service	66.67
H.O. PETERS, interest coupons, NW & Eugene road	36.50
H.O. PETERS, interest coupons, Hazel Bluff road	35.35
H.O. PETERS, interest coupons, Clinton & Paris road	455.00
C.M. KEYES, poor Helt township	154.80

O.M. KEYES, services overseer poor	15.00
JAMES A. BARNES, township physician	25.00
H.H. JAMES, township physician	21.25
JAMES WALLACE, township physician	48.75
THOMAS CUSHMAN, account N & Quaker road	5.60
DANIEL SEARS, keeping poor	30.00
ELIAS PRITCHARD, account Hazel Bluff road extension	5.00
ELIAS PRITCHARD, account NW & Eugene gravel road	40.00
ELIAS PRITCHARD, account Clinton & Paris road	50.00
ELIAS PRITCHARD, account Hazel Bluff road	40.00
ELIAS PRITCHARD, fees and salary	305.06
J.C. SAWYERS, services overseer poor	15.00
JACOB L. THOMAS, account bridges	32.24
JACOB L. THOMAS, NW & Eugene road	10.09
JACOB L. THOMAS, commissioners fees	17.50
WILLIAM C. MYERS, criminals	100.80
JAMES ELDER, commissioners fees	17.50
JAMES R. DUNLAP, commissioners fees	18..00

License Granted to sell intoxicating liquors

JEREMIAH CONLEY – Dana
JOHN F. PEELER – Dana
ISAAC BISHOP – Clinton

Superintendent for Poor Asylum

JOSEPH CONRAD employed for one more year from April 1, 1882.

E.F. DAVIS and family left for their new home in Goodland, Newton County, IN, on Saturday last. Mrs. DAVIS was a good citizen. He is a live and energetic merchant and will make friends wherever he goes. We wish him success.

Nuptials

On Thursday last, at the residence of the bride, DANIEL MILLER and Miss JOHANNA SHAW, daughter of the late CHARLES W. SHAW, were united in wedlock, Rev. C.H. FELTS, of the Protestant Methodist Church officiating. Both are residents of Helt township, and we predict for them a happy and prosperous future.

Perrysville

DUNCAN McCULLUM is going to Clay County to bore for coal.

JACK MITCHELL, a farmer and a candidate for Road Superintendent, living 3 ½ miles N of Perrysville, while working on a ditch near his home, was stricken with paralysis on the right side, caused by the rupturing of a blood vessel. He has been lying in a critical condition since last Friday.

WILLIAM SINKS, a carpenter of this place, is lying at the Sabin House in a very critical condition, with consumption.

Report says that ALBERT CHEZEM and BELL BOLEY, were married at Danville, IL, one day last week.

Mr. D.C. JOHNSON has announced he is a candidate for County Clerk. He was principal of the Clinton Schools for 2 years, has a good business education, and is very well qualified for the position. He is a good citizen of temperate habits and would make an excellent officer. He enlisted in the army at the age of 18, and spent 3 years in fighting for the flag of his country.

Wednesday, March 29, 1882

Republicans of Eugene township has announced its candidates:

Trustee	JAKE WHITLOCK
Road Superintendent	W.F. SHELATOE
Assessor	J.E. WHIPPLE
Justices of Peace	Rev. R.B. VAN ALLEN, J.J. PADRICK
Constables	J.F. RANDOLPH, J.W. CRAIG, W.W. PORTER

WILLIAM Y. RICE is announced as a candidate for Road Superintendent of this township. He is an old farmer, and thoroughly understands road work.

Highland
MIRT CLARK, a 13 year old boy of this place, weighing 175 pounds, is the champion swag puller in our city.

CHARLES LOWE, our blacksmith, moved out to Liberty corner last week. A good smith could do well here for it is a good point for that business.

SMITH JONES is going to sprout some sweet potatoes this spring.

Miss JENNIE STOKESBERRY is teaching the school at No. 17, N of here.

Miss MATTIE FILLINGER is visiting her niece, LAURA AIKMAN, this week.

Montezuma
WILL HILL, who has been clerking for Col. BENSON for several years, has made an engagement to clerk for a Terre Haute firm, his place being taken by JOE ARN.

HENRY OSBORN, an old Vermillion county boy, is no longer a bachelor, but is now enjoying his honeymoon at Buena Vista, CO, where he has chosen to make his home. His spouse was formerly a Mrs. COLEMAN, of Seneca, KS. His mining property is proving quite productive and his many friends here hope to hear of his becoming a millionaire.

Home News
FRANK BURRIS has a new boy baby at his house. He made his appearance on last Sunday.

J.A. WILTERMOOD, teacher in the primary department of our public schools, has had a severe attack of the lung fever, but is now slowly on the mend.

Little SCOTT HARRISON of this place, was seriously hurt on last Monday evening. WALTIE PLACE was jumping and using heavy rocks as weights, which he would throw in jumping. One of them struck SCOTT on the temple, knocking him insensible, and fracturing the skull, it is feared.

Sheriff MYERS took Miss JENNIE CHURCH, of Helt township, over to the Insane Asylum on Monday last. She was sent to the Asylum once before, but was returned home after being there awhile on account of her delicate health. She is now robust and healthy, but crazy as a loon. It is now thought the physicians will succeed in effecting a cure.

Mr. JOHN F. COMPTON, of Perrysville, is announced as a candidate for County Clerk. He is well and favorably known in this county, and needs no introduction or recommendation from us. He served his country faithfully during the war as a private soldier, and is a gentleman in every respect. He is entirely qualified for the important position to which he aspires, and would make an efficient and prudent officer.

Personal

GEORGE W. ODELL, of Hutchinson, KS, a former resident of this place, is lying dangerously ill.

JOHN COLLETT Jr., and a friend of his by the name of Mr. ORN, both students of Wabash College, are here spending vacation.

R.H. NIXON took a trip down to the Arkansas Hot Springs on Thursday last to visit his wife, who is there trying the virtues of the springs for rheumatism.

SIMPSON W. COFFIN, of Eugene township, is a candidate for County Treasurer. He was born and raised in this county, and has never lived any other place with the exception of one year he resided in Illinois. He is now 51 years old, in good health, a farmer by occupation, and a man of good business capacity.

Wednesday, April 5, 1882

Election Results

Clinton township

Justice of Peace	D.H. BIRT, Republican
Assessor	RICHARD M. RUCKER, Democrat
Trustee	GEORGE W. STULTZ, Republican
Road Superintendent	JOSEPH S. CLARK, Democrat
Constables	CHARLES VANNEST, Democrat
	SAMUEL DAVIDSON, Republican
	FRANK VANDUYN, Republican

Helt township

Trustee	JAMES OSBORN, Greenback National
Road Superintendent	PETE AIKMAN, Republican
Assessor	JOHN T. RICHARDS, Democrat
Justice of Peace	GEORGE W. SAXTON, Republican
	ALEX MURPHY, Republican

Vermillion township

Trustee	JAMES CHIPPS, Democrat
Assessosr	JOHN R. STAHL, Democrat
Road Superintendent	JACK DAVIS, Democrat
Justice of Peace	JOHN W. HARTMAN, Republican
	SAMUEL C. HOLLINGSWORTH, Democrat
Constables	SILAS HOLLINGSWORTH, Republican
	JOHN H. WIGLEY, Democrat
	R.H. MYERS, Democrat

Eugene township

Trustee	ANTHONY FABLE, Democrat
Assesssor	JOHN W. WILTERMOOD, Democrat
Road Superintendent	JOHN T. HIGGINS, Democrat
Justice of Peace	JAMES B. ILES, Democrat
	M.S. HARRIS, Democrat
Constables	WILLIAM STARKEY, Democrat
	MARTIN P. REID, Democrat
	LEWIS SIMS, Democrat

Highland township

Trustee	L.A. MORGAN, Democrat
Road Superintendent	THOMAS J. MITCHELL, Democrat

Justice of Peace	J.E. ROBINSON, Republican
Assessor	J.B. RICHARDSON, Republican

Drowned

On last Thursday morning while some timber men of Clinton were rowing up the river in a skiff, they discovered the dead body of a man lodged against a tree that had fallen in the river. When brought to town, someone recognized the deceased as being Rev. B.H. KINTRUP, the Catholic priest of Montezuma. His personal effects consisted of $10 in money and a silver watch, which had stopped running at 4:10. The Priest had told his lady the evening before that he was going to Terre Haute on the morning train. In crossing the bridge of the I.B. & W. RR, it is supposed he slipped and fell through the bridge into the Wabash, and was drowned. His overcoat was found on the bridge, and also his bible. There were no marks or bruises to indicate that he had been foully dealt with. On account of his coat being found on the bridge, and the fact of him having no shoes on when found, some advance the idea that he might have committed suicide. He was a man weighing over 200 pounds, and was addicted to the habit of drinking intoxicating liquors, but never to excess. He was between 45 and 50 years of age. The coroners' verdict was accidental death. The funeral took place on Saturday morning at Armiesburg Cemetery, Father LOGAN officiating.

Miss ALMA BLANCHARD closed her term of school in District No. 44 in Castleton township last Friday. Miss BLANCHARD commences a 3 months term of school next Monday in the district adjoining No. 44.

Hutchinson, KS, Courier

We hear it rumored that DAVE McBETH will soon retire from the hotel business and that Major J.S. STEPHENS, of Perrysville, will be the next proprietor of the Central House.

Clinton Herald

Montezuma

PHILLIP BIPUS and ANNA HOWARD were made one flesh by Rev. McMASTERS last week and are now enjoying the sweets of married life in their own home.

Montezuma township

Trustee	WILLIAM A. HENDERSON
Assessor	SEP VANLANDINGHAM
Justice of Peace	MINOR T. DAVIS, JAMES STEPHENSON, JAMES GLENN
Constables	CARLOS C. KING, THOMAS L. POLLARD, SCOTT WOODWARD

Final Settlement of Estate

Estate of JOHN PAYTON, deceased
April 1, 1882

JAMES ROBERTS, Clerk
By NORTH CRAIG, Deputy Clerk

Final Settlement of Estate

Estate of HENRY C. WRIGHT, deceased
March 30, 1882

JAMES ROBERTS, Clerk

Home News

B.F. BONHAM, of Ft. Dodge, IA, is here visiting his girl.

AL HAWORTH is the proud father of a new gal baby, which made its appearance on last Thursday night.

JOHNNY HENSON left here very suddenly on last Thursday night without informing his parents or friends of where he intended going. His folks became very much alarmed about his manner of leaving, and began a search for him by telegraph. A dispatch was received from him on Saturday morning stating that he was at Chamois, MO, and would write a letter the next day.

Obituary
JOHN W. CRAIG, of Eugene, died of lung fever on last Saturday night, after about one month's illness. The deceased was born in Ohio in 1837, and had been a resident of this county since 1866. Mr. CRAIG was a kind and generous hearted man, and had many warm friends who deeply regret his unexpected death. He was a member of the Grand Army of the Republic, and was buried according to the rites of that order.

Letter list

THOMPSON, Miss GLADIUS	WILSON, Miss KATE
THOMPSON, Mrs. JANE	THORNBURG, E.
WILLIAMS, HANNAH	WILSON, MAY
SPENNINGS, Madam	SLOSSON, M.H.
STEWART, I.M.	CARMACK, JOHN M.
CABBERS, Mrs. VICTOR	BOUSLER, DAN
BRINN, Miss ESTY	BROWN, WILLIAM
LONGWORTH, ZEBEDEE	TOUBE, JOSEPH
JACOBS, MOLLIE	FILES, KING
RUSSELL, Miss MATTIE	RUMPELLY, R.
FREEMAN, F.E.	SACRES, FEBEA

Personal
Mrs. JANE FRAZEE, of Perrysville, has been appointed administratrix of the Estate of Dr. LEWIS FRAZEE, deceased.

Miss MATTIE E. DAVIS was in town last week visiting her parents. She left on Monday for North Vernon, IN, where she is going into the notion business with another lady.

Perrysville
Died – on Wednesday, and infant child of WILLIAM CONNOR, of congestion of the brain and stomach.

Wednesday, April 12, 1882

Mr. JOSEPH M. RABB takes great pleasure in announcing that fortune has again smiled upon his household, and left him with a very small sized boy to raise. The event took place last Sunday evening.

Williamsport Republican

Montezuma
Died – On Wednesday morning of lung disease, Miss SUSAN FONCANNON. She was well known and highly respected.

JOE STILLWELL started for his home in Kansas Tuesday morning.

JACK CONNOR and his young wife arrived here last week. Mr. CONNOR thinks that he will go into the barber business in Dana.

Miss CRAFT, of Annapolis, spent a few days visiting her aunt, Mrs. WEAVER. Miss CRAFT says she would love to live in Montezuma.

Mrs. M.A. SIMPSON, mother of Mrs. WILLIAM WOOSTER, has been quite ill the past week, but is some better at present.

The many friends of Rev. M.L. GREEN, well known in Vermillion County, will be much pleased to learn that on last Monday week, he was elected as Assessor of Penn township, Parke County.

Perrysville
GEORGE WINTERS started for the western country where he has been for the past 2 years.

CHARLEY FLESHMAN started for the far west last week, perhaps to explore the country.

DAVID SANDERS, who emigrated to Wisconsin last summer, has returned to this place, the climate not being agreeable to his health.

BYARD STEVENS will sell his household goods this week, and will remove to Missouri in a few days.

HIRAM LAWLESS, a former citizen of this town, died at his residence about 6 miles W of town, on last Friday.

REZIN METZGER has moved back to his hotel, and is now running it again.

List of Real Estate Transfers for March 1882

GEORGE W. CLARK and wife to SAMUEL P. CLARK
30 acres in Vermillion township - $450

GEORGE W. CLARK and wife to SARAH CLARK
80 acres in Vermillion township - $1,250

ELIZABETH J. SCONCE etal to JAMES F. POLLARD
Lot in Eugene - $300

PERMELIA HEDGES to COLUMBUS C. HEDGES
10 acres in Clinton township - $250

JAMES A. BUSH and wife to LEANNA WILTERMOOD
2 acres in Vermillion township - $320

LETTA DINSMORE etal to JAMES A. DUGGER etal
---------- acres in Helt township - $5,137

ROBERT J. GESSIE etal to ELIZABETH HALL
Lots 22, 23, & 24, in Gessie – $75

JAMES M. McMEEN and wife to SILAS HUGHES
Lot 5, in Gessie - $22.50

MARGARET ABBOTT and husband to BEN BLANCHARD
2 acres adjoining Newport - $1,500

JOHN O'KEEFE to BAT McCARTY
23 acres in Helt township - $300

WILLIAM L. LITTLE and wife to JAMES M. NICHOLS
61.13 acres in Vermillion township - $1,200

NANCY J. PORTER and husband to ROBERT CLENDENING
-------- acres, in Eugene township - $1,200

WILLIAM NICHOLS Sr. to ELI BRINDLEY
90.75 acres in Vermillion township - $3,100

MARTHA J. TRADER to JOSEPH CROSS
S ½ lot 3, block 19, in Clinton - $200

MARY HELT etal to JAMES A. WHITE Jr.
15 acres in Helt township - $200

JAMES A. HAYS and wife to GEORGE A. CRABB
Lot 7, block 26, in Clinton - $800

JAMES CROZIER and wife to LOUISA E.A. JOHN
Lots 1, 4, 5, and part 2, 3, and 9, block 8, in Clinton - $1,000

MARY A. CONLEY and husband to JAMES ROBERTS
½ lots 5 & 8, block 31, in Clinton - $1,600

JOHN F. DUGGER and wife to JESSE RUNYAN etal
40 acres in Clinton township - $525

DANIEL W. GARDNER and wife to MARY J. OOSLEY
Part lot 7, block 11, in Clinton - $550

VIRGINIA JONES and husband to CHARITY AYRES
Lot 9, block 1, in Morey's addition to Clinton - $80

JAMES ROBERTS and wife to HUGH H. CONLEY etal
Lots 81 & 82, and outlot adjoining Newport - $1,600

SNOWDEN LUSADDER and wife to Highland township
Lands for Schoolhouse - $25

LUCINDA MOFFATT and husband to JOHN L. EGGLESTON etal
20 acres in Vermillion township - $1,100

JOSEPH W. MOREY and wife to ALONZO HOSTETTER
Part lots 7 & 10, block 29, in Clinton - $150

MARCUS CAMERON and wife to JOHN WHITCOMB
96 acres in Clinton township - $3,500

JOHN A. STRAIN and wife to ABEL B. WILSON
Part lots 7 & 10, block 11, in Clinton - $500

CYNTHA A. HURD to PATRICK FLYNN
¼ of block 1, in Hillsdale - $100

HENRY JORDAN and wife to TILGHMAN MALONE
20 acres in Helt township - $1,100

HENRY JORDAN and wife to RICHARD MALONE
20 acres in Helt township - $1,000

EDWIN S. McCOY and wife to JOHN J. McCOY
7.32 acres in Vermillion township - $1,700

JOHN W. DAVIS and wife to HANNAH J. THRIFT
Lot 1, block 2, in Clinton - $215

REASON SWINEHEART and wife to EARL B. -----------
Part lots 2 & 3, in Clinton - $125

ELLA BARNHART and husband to B.F. MOREY & Son
Lot 1, block 14, in Clinton - $550

PETER LAMB to NELSON C. ANDERSON
Lots 5 & 8, block 26, in Clinton - $500

NELSON C. ANDERSON and wife to PETER LAMB
Part of outlot 6, adjoining Clinton - $600

ANDREW CARMACK and wife to ALICE THOMPSON
Lot 3, block 11, in Dana - $50

JOHN E. BILSLAND and wife to JAMES W. MAXWELL
Lot 7, block 4, in Dana - $200

WAKEFIELD TWEEDY etal to ENGLAND OSBORN
Lot 8, block 1, and outlot adjoining Jonestown - $325

MARTHA AYE and husband to ANDREW J. OVERPECK
Outlot near Jonestown - $300

WILLIAM WRIGHT and wife to PHILO CURTIS
1 acre in Clinton township - $50

HIRAM J. FOLTZ and wife to WILLIAM H. JULIAN
10 acres in Clinton township - $500

Final Settlement of Estate
Estate of HIRAM HELT, deceased
April 4, 1882
JAMES ROBERTS, Clerk
By NORTH CRAIG, Deputy Clerk

Home News
JOHN R. STAHL, the newly elected Assessor, has appointed GEORGE VANDEVENDER as his Deputy.

LAURA WILLIAMS, nee NOYES, of Hutchinson, KS, has a new baby at her house. We did not learn the sex.

Mrs. MAGGIE RAMSEY celebrated her birthday on last Thursday by giving a grand turkey dinner to a few of her special friends.

JAMES DUZAN is putting up a new building for Uncle ROBERT STOKES, on the lot E of TRIPLETT's drug store, to be used by his son FIN STOKES for a meat market.

TOM TUCKER moved to Georgetown, IL, yesterday, where he has been furnished employment in a brickyard. TOM is a good, clever fellow, and industrious.

Obituary
The youngest child of NOAH and ANNA BROWN, of Eugene, died on Thursday last, aged 2 years and 8 months.

Married
Mrs. ANNA SLATER, widow of the late JOHN SLATER, was recently united in marriage to FRANK SLATER, brother of her former husband.

Death
JOHN CRAIG, Adjutant of Eugene Post No. 22, Dept. of IN, G.A.A., died in Eugene, IN, on Saturday evening, April 1, 1882. Comrade CRAIG was a member of Co. D, 11 IN Cavalry, and was a good and faithful soldier.

Clerk Roberts issued the following marriage licenses:
JOHN D. THOMPSON to NANNA HARKNESS
WILLIAM P. ROSS to OLLIE J. WRIGHT
ANDREW J. FOLTZ to NANCY A. WELKER
JENNETTA V. MOHANNON to HATTIE RADER
JAY M. MILLS to KINNIE DICKASON

Personal
PERRY THOMAS, a student of Wabash College, was at home visiting last week.

GEORGE W. ODELL, of Hutchinson, KS, who had a serious attack of erysipelas, has about recovered.

MARTIN SEELY was called to Danville, IL, on last Monday, by a telegram announcing his sister was lying dangerously ill.

B.O. CARPENTER, proprietor of a large flouring mill at Perrysville, was in our city on Friday last. If he could sell out his mill at that place, he would move here and erect one.

A Mr. GALLAGHER, of Highland township, called on us last week. He is talking of becoming a candidate for District Prosecutor. He says he has been studying law for several years, and intends to be admitted to the bar at the next term of the Circuit Court.

Wednesday, April 19, 1882

Clinton
Prof. CANADY, a graduate of Keokuk Business College, IA, was in town on Friday and Saturday prospecting for a writing class.

On last Friday, there was born to WILLIAM HAGENBAUGH and wife, a boy baby.

Highland
Mrs. MAY LEE, of Brazil, is visiting her mother, Mrs. BELL, of this place.

CHARLES McFALL, who left this place two years ago and went to Virginia, has returned to this township.

HORACE ANDREWS, of Dana, started with his family on last Monday for Sweet Water, TN, where he expects to reside.

FRANK JOHNSON has gone to visit his brother AB JOHNSON, who was recently married and is now living in Clay County, IL.

TAYLOR Bros., of Dana, has sold their lumber yard to LOWRY & FISHER.

Perrysville
JACK MITCHELL, who has been down with paralysis, is slowly improving.

PETER COSSEY, who has been sick a long time, is able to be out again.

ALBERT KERNS, who taught the Jordan School last term, had gone to Danville, IN, to attend school.

ED CHENOWETH, who formerly lived with his Uncle LEMON CHENOWETH and took French leave a couple of years since, has returned.

JOSEPH MILLER, 3 miles N of town, has sold his farm to JOHN LUSADDER, and will remove to town soon.

Montezuma
Miss BELL KEMP, daughter of Dr. J.W. and LOUISA KEMP, died on Thursday last of brain fever. She was 15 years old the day she died. Rev. CUMMINGS, of Rockville, and Rev. GRIFFITH, of our town, preached the funeral. Much respect was shown to her memory by her classmates of the public school.

Mrs. INDIA OSBORN, of Decatur, returned to her home on Thursday morning after a pleasant visit with her mother, Mrs. MARY BAILEY.

Miss ALICE LINN, oldest daughter of JOHN LINN, who has been in delicate health for a year, is very poorly at this writing.

Notice of Final Settlement of Estate

Estate of HENRY C. WRIGHT, deceased
March 30, 1882

JAMES ROBERTS, Clerk

Administrator's Sale of Personals

Estate of JOHN W. CRAIG, deceased
Saturday, May 6, 1882
Sale at Eugene
Personal property

11 horses, 2 mules, 2 cows, 4 top buggies, on double top carriage, 2 hacks, 1 buckboard, 1 spring wagon, 1 farm wagon, 3 lap robes, whips, 6 sets of double harness, 1 set of single harness, household and kitchen furniture, etc.

April 11, 1882

M.G. HOSFORD, Admr.

Home News
JAMES MALONE, of Eugene, has been appointed administrator of the Estate of JESSE SMITH, deceased.

Obituary
Miss SUSAN FONCANNON, of Montezuma, aged 43 years and 8 months, died of consumption on April 8, 1882. Miss FONCANNON was a very estimable lady, and had a host of warm friends in this county who will be pained to hear of her death.

Married
On last Monday evening, at the U.B. Parsonage, Rev. W.H. JONES officiating, JACOB BOST and Miss LIZZIE DUZAN were united in bonds of wedlock.

Heard From
BILL MASON, the white livered villain who so cruelly deserted his wife at this place about 2 years ago, has been heard from. He is now stopping in Terre Haute. It is reported that he has one or two other wives besides the one at this place. He is now talking of coming back here to pay the wife he wronged and deserted a visit. We hope she will give him a hot water bath if he attempts to enter her door.

Marriage
JAMES T. HARVEY and Miss CLARA BELL were united in wedlock at 8 o'clock yesterday morning, at the residence of the bride's mother, Rev. J.H. HOLLINGSWORTH officiating.

Personal
JOHN P. BRILES, of Clinton, the poet blacksmith, and the jolliest old soul in the county, was in town over Monday night.

Mrs. JASPER JAMES, of Missouri, a former citizen of this county, is back on a visit to friends and relatives in Helt township.

Miss TABITHA M. BOGART, of Perrin, MO, who has been visiting her many relatives and friends since September 6th, returned to her home on last Monday.

Administrator's Sale of Personals

Estate of JESSE SMITH, deceased
Saturday, May 13, 1882
At late residence of deceased 3 miles W of Eugene
Personal property (not taken by widow)

2 mules, 3 cattle, hogs, 1 two horse wagon, 1 new spring wagon, 2 sets of double harness, 300 bushels of wheat in granary, corn in crib, wheat in field, hay in stack, 1 reaper and mower, farming implements, etc.

April 17, 1882

JAMES MALONE, Admr.

Wednesday, April 26, 1882

CHARLES E. HOSFORD, of Terre Haute, the scoundrel who fleeced a number of farmers in this county out of large sums of money, and went west to avoid arrest, has returned home. He should be immediately arrested.

Clinton
SAM BRILES is now employed in VICTOR's blacksmith shop.

ELMER QUICK, of Michigan, is in town visiting his sister MAY.

Highland
PERRY MERRIWETHER has a newcomer at his house. It's a boy and weighs 8 pounds.

The two MIDDLEBROOKS, of this place, who are working at the tile factory on the I.D. & S., near Judson, have come home to make arrangements for moving their families.

Montezuma
MINOR T. DAVIS is now the heaviest grain buyer in this market. He shipped 9 carloads last week.

Miss ALICE LINN, who has been quite ill for about six weeks, is again recovering and will soon be able to be out.

Home News
S.R. WHITE, residing 7 miles W of here, has a new boy baby at his house.

PETER COSSEY, of Highland township, who has been confined to his room since late last fall, is now delirious at times and unmanageable. He gets wild and wants to kill members of his own family. He has to be guarded very closely to prevent him from doing someone an injury. It is probable that arrangements will be made to have him sent to the asylum.

Grand Jury
The following gentlemen compose the Grand Jury for this term of court:

Clinton township	GEORGE W. EDWARDS, foreman
	ALEX FONCANNON
	Mr. DEWEY
Vermillion township	RUFUS LITTLE
Eugene township	BENJAMIN DEARDOFF
Highland township	THOMAS W. STEPHENS

Personal
Mrs. REBECCA HOLLINGSWORTH is under the weather and confined to her bed.

M.H. STARK, of Clinton township, is going to Indianapolis to engage in the law business.

W.P. HENSON went out to Missouri last week, and persuaded his son JOHN HENSON to return home. They both arrived here on Friday morning.

Notice of Non-Residents

JOSEPH C. LYNN vs. HENRY SHANNON
Collect money due on account
HENRY SHANNON is not a resident of Indiana
Must appear before May 27, 1882
April 22, 1882

WILLLIAM F. KERNS, J.P.

Drowned
FRANK VANDEVENDER, a young man of this place, aged about 19 years, met a sad death on last Monday evening. He was plowing for JAMES HASTY in the river bottom, and had to cross the Little Vermillion in a ferryboat to get to his work. In the evening on his return home, there was no one at the creek to ferry him over, and he undertook to ford it with a wagon and 2 horses. The horses got tangled in the harness in the deep water, and FRANK drowned. He was found later tangled under the wagon. He was unable to swim.

A Difficult Surgical Operation
On Tuesday of last week, Prof. POWELL of Chicago, and HERBERT W. MOREHOUSE, M.D., of Danville, IL, removed a cystic tumor from Miss MOLLIE MAST, of Bono, Vermillion County, IN, weighing not less than 40 pounds. The above surgeons were aided by Drs. MOORE, BARTON, and LEAVITT, of Danville, and Drs. EATON and KEYES of this county. When last heard from, she was improving and all symptoms were favorable for a speedy recovery.

Clinton
AQUILLA WASHBURN of Greencastle, is in the city. He intends to establish a pill factory at St. Bernice soon.

WILL DUNCAN, the most dignified gentleman of town, now swings the razor in GEORGE HARRIS' barber shop.

M.H. STARK boarded the train at this place last week bound for Indianapolis where he intends to prosecute the study of law. His wife JOSIE, will make a short visit to her grandpa's in Helt township, after which she too will go to the capital.

Vermillion Circuit Court, April Term, 1882

State of Indiana vs. TAYLOR SIMPSON
Selling liquor to a minor – continued

State of Indiana vs. TAYLOR SIMPSON
Allowing a minor to play billiards – continued

State of Indiana vs. GEORGE WHITTED, JOSEPH HART, & JAMES RIDDLE
Murder – set for trial on 15th day of term

State of Indiana vs. WILLAM G. MERRILL
Appeal – affidavit quashed

State of Indiana vs. MITCHELL ALLEN & THOMAS ALLEN
Change of venue – set for trial on 15th day of term

HENRY S.S. FORD, SETH PEARMAN, MARCUS PEARMAN, by Z.D. JAMES, guardian vs. CLARA A. FORD, SARAH BAYMER etal
Petition – continued

SAMUEL REED, MOSES REED vs. ACHA REED, LEWIS REED etal
Partition – continued

Frankfort & State Line RR vs. JOHN GROENENDYKE
Petition for damages
JAMES B. ILES, CLAUDE MATTHEWS, JAMES R. DUNLAP appointed appraisers

MARY A. STANLEY vs. JESSE L. STANLEY
Divorce – continued for alias

MARY J. LOVE vs. ARTHUR C. LOVE
Petition

EDWARD W. JOHNSON, ROBERT FLYNN vs. LEONIDAS H. BELLUS, JAMES WILLS
Default – judgment for $233.31 and order for sale of attached property

Travelers Insurance Co. vs. C.E. HOSFORD, LIDA HOSFORD, MILTON SHOWALTER etal
Note & mortgage – proof of publication filed as to HOSFORD

ELAM S. McBROOM vs. I.B. & W. R.R Co.
Change of venue – set for 13th day of term

HELEN A. McKNIGHT vs. WILLIAM C. CLOVER
Quiet title – default as to unknown heirs
Disclaimer filed by Board of Commissioners

HARRY WHITCOMB, CHARLES WHITCOMB ex rel
HARVEY SHEPARD, RAY SHEPARD
Partition and sale – continued for report of sale

Sale of Indiana ex rel BALDWIN, Attorney General vs.
ELIAS PRITCHARD etal
Mandate – judgment on demurrer in favor of defendant

MARY J. RICKETTS vs. THOMAS H. SMITH, Exec. of JOSEPH STUTLER est.
Claim – dismissed by plaintiff

JOHN HETH vs. M.G. HOSFORD, exec. JOHN HEPBURN's estate
Claim – dismissed at plaintiff's cost

WILLIAM COLLETT vs. the F. & S.L. RR Co. & Western Construction Co.
Injunction – dismissed by plaintiff

GEORGE ANDREWS, MARY A. ANDREWS, vs. L.H. BELLUS, ANNIE E. BELLUS
Foreclosure – judgment for default, $514.85 plus $85 attorney fees

JAMES M. SAVAGE vs. FLORINDA SAVAGE
Divorce – granted to plaintiff, and plaintiff shall not marry for 2 years.

OLIVE WASHBURN vs. WILLIAM WASHBURN
Divorce – decree granted

ISABELLA KEYS vs. WILLIAM KEYS
Divorce – decree granted plaintiff, plaintiff shall not marry for 2 years.

JAMES M. MAXWELL vs. JOHN M. AMMERMAN
Note – dismissed by agreement

Harrison Machine Works vs. THOMAS J. NICHOLS, JACOB L. THOMAS
Note – judgment for $209.57

JULIA A. MARTENAS, admr. of JOSEPH MARTENAS Estate vs. JOHN HATHAWAY
Change of venue – set for trial on 14th day of term

JOHN R. SCONCE estate vs. ELIZABETH J. SCONCE, Widow
Petition under $500 law

JOHN COLLETT, S.S. COLLETT etal vs. AMOS CURTIS
Foreclosure – default – judgment for $140.90 – decree of foreclosure

PEYTON F. DOUGLAS etal vs. LUCY DICKEN
Petition – decree of sale

BENJAMIN JENKINS est. vs. HATTIE JENKINS
Widow's petition under $500

FRANCIS A. BOWEN vs. RUFUS H. WASHBURN etal
Personal property damages – dismissed by agreement

MARY DOUGLAS etal vs. WILLIAM L. LITTLE, Trustee
Petition

State ex rel JASPER A. MOORE vs. JAMES M. MOORE, WALTER G. CRABB
Guardians bond – judgment for $660

LUCRETIA FLEMMING vs. WESLEY FLEMMING
Divorce – continued

JOHN W. STODDARD, EDWARD STODDARD vs. AMOS CURTIS
Note – default – judgment for $74.75

JOSEPHUS COLLETT vs. JACOB L. THOMAS
Foreclosure – dismissed at plaintiff's cost

State of Indiana ex rel JASON W. HOWELL, admr. vs. ISAAC BOGART etal
On bond – order that suit abate at costs of Relator

Home News
Sheriff MYERS took PETER COSSEY of Highland township, over to the Insane Asylum.

Dr. HARRY JAMES has just received $2,500 arrears of pension, and is now the happiest man in Jonestown.

It is reported that GEORGE SWITZER, a prominent citizen of Eugene, is losing his mind. We are sorry to hear this.

CHARLEY DICKEN, of this township, and Miss REBECCA BASINGER, of Eugene township, were married by Esq. JOHN W. HARTMAN on last Monday evening.

Mrs. PETE STAATS, whose husband lost his life in the army, has been granted a pension. Her first draw, which included several year's arrears, amounted to $2,500.

JOHN D. GALLAGHER, of Highland township, was admitted to the Newport Bar last week. He proposes to quit teaching school for a living, and enter the profession of law.

Married
On last Friday evening, at the U.B. Parsonage, JOHN KERDOLFF and Miss BELLE THOMPSON were united in marriage by Rev. W.H. JONES, of the U.B. Church. Their courtship was of short duration, and but few suspected such an occurrence until the happy event took place. There were only a few invited guests present to witness the nuptials.

Death
Miss MINERVA ELLEN SUTTON, who has been making her home at Uncle ROBERT STOKES for some time, died of consumption at about 12 o'clock on last Sunday night, aged 35 years. When she was a babe, only a few months old, her parents passed through this county on their way to the west. The child was then in delicate health, and near where they camped one night the mother visited a farm house and the lady seeing the condition of the child, persuaded its mother to leave it with her, which she did, and this was the last ever heard of its parents. ELLEN SUTTON grew to be a woman, and finally went to live with an old lady who shortly died, and before dying, willed her property amounting to about $400, to Miss SUTTON. To this amount she added until at the time of her death, she had between $500 and $600. Miss SUTTON also made a will, and ordered all her funeral expenses, and purchasing 2 tombstones, one for herself, and one for the lady who had willed her the $400, to be given to B.F. ALDRIDGE of this township. M.G. RHOADS was appointed executor of the Will. The deceased was a member of the M.E. Church, and was respected by all her acquaintances. Her funeral took place on last Monday afternoon, Rev. J.H. HOLLINGSWORTH, of the M.E. Church, performing the last rites.

When the family of JAMES HADEN, who reside at ABBOTT's coal bank, woke up yesterday morning, they found their infant child dead in bed.

Personal
Mrs. ELIZA GILBERT, of Illinois, daughter of HENRY HOLLINGSWORTH, is here on a visit.

DAVID MEAD, of Danville, IL, was down last week settling up the JOE BOYD estate.

MAURICE HEGARTY and family went down to Terre Haute last Monday evening to attend the wedding of Miss ANNA BURNS.

Highland
The SOUTHARD boys, living N of here, have planted 50 bushels of potatoes and intend to plant more as the season advances. They are the "boss" potato raisers in this part of the country.

Perrysville
JOSEPH MILLER has sold his farm, N of town, and has bought the BENTON property in Long Hungry for which he paid $350 and will move into it as soon as he has some repairs made.

Wednesday, May 10, 1882

An Open Switch
A sad accident occurred on the C. & E.I. RR at West Newell, 4 miles N of Danville, on last Thursday morning through the carelessness of a freight conductor who had switched his train to a side track and left the switch open. In a few minutes a train came along and ran into the open switch, striking the other train with a fearful crash, killing FRANK BROWN, a brakeman, and seriously hurting the fireman.

Surgical Operation
A difficult and successful operation was performed by home talent a few days ago. GEORGE SKIDMORE of Helt's Prairie, has been suffering for a long time – but more especially during the last year – with a tumor, growing upon his lower jaw bone, hard and very painful, and lately tending to a rapid fatality. He had consulted a number of physicians and surgeons in various cities, but they hesitated to take his case. On last Wednesday, Dr. JAMES CROZIER, of Clinton, assisted by Dr. HENRY NEBEKER, after placing him thoroughly under the influence of chloroform, removed the tumor entire, which was firmly adhered to the bone on the side and under the surface, in close proximity to the large blood vessels of that region. It was a neat and very successful operation, and the patient is now free from pain and doing well. Mr. SKIDMORE's many friends will be glad to hear of this good news.

Montezuma
JAMES BAILEY has returned home from Ohio, where he has been with the engineer corps of the I.B. & W. eastern extension.

WILLIAM DERRINGTON has returned from Pecatonica, IL, having disposed of his property there. We understand he will try farming again on his place, south of Hillsdale.

Quite a number of our older people went over to Helt township on Sunday to attend the funeral of their late esteemed friend, JOHN FORD.

While the trainmen on the westbound local freight were switching at Dana on Wednesday last, WILLIAM FOSS, one of the brakemen, falling, was run over and received such severe injuries as to cause his death the same evening. He was about 20 years of age, well known here and was shortly to have been married to an esteemed young lady of Montezuma.

Highland
JOHN BROWN and SAM AIKMAN, students of Dayton Biblical Seminary, returned home last week.

Perrysville
ART KILPATRICK is learning the carpenter's trade with SAM SHANER.

NED SPOTSWOOD is able to be out on the streets again after a severe illness of 3 weeks.

J.H. BENTON has resumed his old place as clerk for E.T. SPOTSWOOD & Sons.

CHARLEY FLESHMAN has returned from Nebraska where he moved. After a stay of 3 or 4 weeks, he didn't like that climate worth a cent.

Home News
Mrs. MAGGIE HARSHAW, of Savanna, IL, is here on a visit to her parents.

FRANK DICKEN and Mrs. PHOEBE RICHARDS were married on last Friday evening.

ALBERT FONCANNON and Miss CORA COLE, both of Helt township, were united in wedlock on Thursday last.

JAMES D. WADE, of Big Stone City, Dakota Territory, a former resident of this township, has been appointed clerk of the new Board of Commissioners of his county.

Miss MOLLIE MAST, of Bono, who was operated on and relieved of a 40 pound tumor week before last, is rapidly recovering, and was able to sit up in bed on last Saturday and write a letter.

Death
Mrs. JOE RABB, of Williamsport, died on last Sunday night from childbirth. She was a very estimable lady, and leaves a large host of friends to mourn her loss and unexpected death.

Death
Uncle TILLY JENKS, an old and esteemed citizen of Bono, died at about 3 o'clock on last Friday afternoon. Uncle TILLY had lived beyond the time usually allotted to man in this world. He was born in Vermont in 1800, and consequently was 82 years old. He had been a citizen of this county since 1848, and was respected by everybody. He was not a member of any church organization, but was a firm believer in the Universalist faith.

Obituary
At about 9 o'clock on last Saturday morning occurred the death of Uncle JOHN FORD, of Helt township. His disease was lung fever. Mr. FORD was born in Ohio in 1809, and emigrated to this county with his parents in 1818, when a mere boy. He lived upon the farm on which he died for over 50 years. When his parents came to Helt township, this county had not been organized, and was one vast wilderness, Indians being quite numerous in the county at that time. His funeral, which took place on last Sunday, was very largely attended by relatives and friends, attesting the high esteem in which he was held by his neighbors. He had no enemies in this county. Everybody loved and respected Uncle JOHN FORD. He was a generous a hearted man as ever lived, and was ever ready to help the distressed and unfortunate. His kindness and many noble deeds will live in the minds of the people for many years to come. He was a member of the M.E. Church, and tried to live an honorable and upright life.

Personal
AB V. HOLMES, of Warren County, a former citizen of this place, was elected Justice of the Peace at the recent election.

JOE COLLETT, of Terre Haute, has gone to the Arkansas Hot Springs.

List of Real Estate Transfers for April 1882

MARY GIBSON to PATRICK FLYNN
¾ of block 1, in Hillsdale - $150

ANDREW KOCHO and wife to JOSEPH WESTER
Lots 1 & 2, block 16, in Clinton - $200

THOMAS PATRICK and wife to Eugene township
½ acre in Eugene township - $25

JOSEPH MILLER and wife to JOHN LUSADDER
113 acres in Highland township - $2,600

GEORGE H. McNEILL and wife to SUSAN BRYANT
Part lot 50, in Perrysville - $150

LORENZO D. HOLD etal to WILLIAM D. PASKELL
Part lot 27, in Perrysville - $40

SARAH E. JONES etal to FRANCIS DAVIS
21 acres in Vermillion township - $225

JOHN NORRIS and wife to F.M. DAVIS
40 acres in Vermillion township - $400

NANCY A. STRAIN and husband to HENRY VOLKEL
19 acres in Highland township - $425

BARTON S. AIKMAN to PETER AIKMAN
24 acres in Helt township - $694

DANIEL CASTLE to G.W. CAMPBELL
2 acres in Helt township - $75

HARRIET C. DALLAS to R.H. NIXON
300 acres in Helt township - $10,500

SAMUEL AIKMAN etal to O.B. LOWRY
Lots 2, 3, & 4, block 4, in Dana - $150

SAMUEL E. KAUFMAN etal to GEORGE H. FISHER
Lots 13, 14, & 15, block 14, in Dana - $150

JOHN W. REDMAN and wife to O.B. LOWRY
S ½ lot 20, block 4, in Dana - $550

JESSE HOUCHIN and wife to O.R. JOHNSON & Bros.
Lots 10, 12, 13, 14, 15, 16, 17, & 18, in Alta - $120

ROBERT B. STOKES and wife to ROBERT H. NIXON
Part lot 73, in Newport - $100

ALFRED R. HOPKINS and wife to JAMES CHIPPS
40 acres in Eugene township - $130

CHARLES E. HAYS etal to RICHARD MAUGILDER
Lots 25 & 26, block 4, in Jonestown – $225

JAMES A. SMITH and wife to JAMES A. LEWIS
Outlot adjoining Gessie - $325

JOHN H. BOGART and wife to ROBERT D. PATTERSON
Lot 6, in Clinton - $80

SAMUEL KAUFMAN etal to HORACE F. ANDREWS
Lot 4, in Dana - $50

JOHN J. THORN and wife to FRANK P. THORN
15 acres in Helt township - $341.25

CHARLES WIGLEY etal to STEPHEN CRANE etal
80 acres in Helt township - $3,200

ANDREW J. PITTS and wife to PETER AIKMAN
½ acre near Bono - $260

MARCUS DYER and wife to JOEL DYER
60 acres in Clinton township - $2,700

HENRY A. ANDREWS and wife to WILLIAM D. McFALL
40 acres in Helt township - $1,000

HENRY C. WRIGHT's estate to ROBERT MOUDY
25 acres in Highland township - $200

STEPHEN WRIGHT's estate to ROBERT MOUDY
87 acres in Highland township - $1,700

GEORGE W. ANDREWS to HENRY ANDREWS
33 acres in Helt township - $900

DANIEL E. STRAIN and wife to SAMUEL H. VANNEST
Lot 9, block 32, in Clinton - $600

THOMAS L. COMMONS and wife to SETH HAWORTH
Interest in 43 acres in Vermillion township - $100

ROBERT J. GESSIE and wife to AMOS FLESHMAN
Outlot 1, adjoining Gessie – $200

JOSEPHUS COLLETT to ELIZABETH SIMS etal
7.15 acres in Eugene township - $429

PLATT Z. ANDERSON and wife to WALTER G. CRABB
Lot 5, block 16, in Clinton - $26

JOHN T. PONTON and wife to WILLIAM J. LAKE
Lot 27, in Alta - $12

ELIZABETH GROVES to HORACE O. PERRIN
20 acres in Helt township - $500

WILLIAM W. FULTZ and wife to ALBERT F. FULTZ
5 acres in Eugene township - $506

Wednesday, May 17, 1882

Verdict
The trial of GEORGE WHITTED, JOSEPH HART, and JAMES RIDDLE for the murder of EVAN THOMAS on February 26, 1882, was commenced at that place on May 10. After a jury was impaneled, the two sides argued. After receiving testimony and performing closing arguments, the case was closed. After about 17 hours, a verdict was made. GEORGE WHITTED received 20 years in the State Penitentiary at hard labor. JOSEPH HART received 3 years for his role in the murder. JAMES RIDDLE, having received immunity from all punishment, was discharged.

Perrysville
Dr. J.W. SMITH has sold his property here to JOHN R. McNEILL, and contemplates emigrating to Colorado in a few weeks.

Highland
JAMES WRIGHT has bought half interest in MORRIS JONES' grocery store.

A Surprise
On the evening of the 10th instant, many friends, young and old, of our esteemed fellow citizen, DANIEL STRAIN Jr., of one accord happened in at his residence with baskets filled with rich viands and a general good time was enjoyed by all present. The occasion was to impress DANIEL that he was past 45 years old, and had been sailing in safety, with his present partner over life's rough sea for 25 years.

JAMES C. TUTT, of Eugene township, has bought the old Dr. BRICKER estate, at Highland. He paid $4,000, and takes possession the first of August.

Wedding
ALONZO HOSTETTER, an old bachelor of Clinton, came to the conclusion that it was not best for man to live alone, and accordingly on last Monday morning, he stuck his head in the matrimonial noose. His victim is Miss EMMA E. WILEY, a bright and beautiful young lady of that city. The happy event took place at the Central House, Rev. H.L. DICKERSON performing the ceremony.

Home News
Miss FLORA HASTY does not intend to teach the coming fall and winter. It is reported that she has her eyes on a Kansas youth, and that the two will be made one shortly.

Clinton
Miss NELLIE HENDERSON, who had been visiting her classmates at this place, left last Friday for Marshall, IL.

WILLIAM BRADSHAW, aged about 60, was buried on last Saturday. Few were the mourners who followed him to the grave, yet he will sleep calmly and serenely as if his remains had been followed by an immense cortege.

The public schools of this place closed on last Friday. Miss NELLIE DAVISON will begin a subscription school on next Monday. She has 52 pupils engaged.

RICHARD PARKER and ALICE BOND, GEORGE BASS and ROSA BROWN, all colored, passed under the hymeneal yoke last Thursday evening, Esq. McDOUGALL adjusting the matrimonial noose. This was done in the M.E. Church, which was crowded and jammed with curious spectators.

Wednesday, May 24, 1882

Perrysville
B.C. GLOVER has been appointed roadmaster for this township.

JOHN HAIN has bought a tract of land of CALVIN HUGHES, lying just east of his farm.

CALVIN HUGHES has bought the farm of his brother-in-law, Rev. KAUFMAN, two miles SW of town.

Miss NETTIE MINSHALL is teaching a primary school here. There will be no higher grade of school here this summer.

Dr. POLAND has bought Dr. SMITH's stock of medicines, and will take possession of the office when Dr. SMITH retires.

Highland
Mrs. DOGGETT went out to Broadland last week to visit her sister, Mrs. CONLEY.

Montezuma
W.A. LUTES, formerly of the I.D. & S. was here over Saturday and Sunday on his way to Illinois, where he goes railroad building. R.P. LUTES and family are still in Indianapolis, all in good health.

LAMB & HISE have dissolved partnership; LAMB keeping the saloon and HISE the lumber business.

JOE FICKLIN and JUD ROSS, the rear guard of those who went to help build Mexican railroads, returned home on Friday looking well, but inclined to think, there is no place like home.

Mr. JUSTIN O. FOSS, whose son WILLIAM FOSS was killed at Dana by the cars, desires me in his behalf and that of his family to return thanks to the people of Dana, and especially to Mr. HAYES and family of the Dana Hotel for their kindness to the unfortunate sufferer on that occasion.

Sheriff's Sale on Decree
ISAAC B. HEDGES vs. EDMOND D. JAMES, SARAH JAMES, ELIZABETH JAMES
$3,078.70
Saturday, June 17, 1882
At courthouse between 10 and 4
Real estate
Part of S ½ SE ¼ Sec 21, T 15 N R 9 W – 77 acres
113 acres in NW ¼ Sec 28 T 15 N R 9 W
SE ¼ NW ¼ Sec 20 T 15 N R 9 W – 10 acres
Total of 210 acres
May 24, 1882
JUMP& WARD & ANDERSON attorneys
WILLIAM C. MYERS, Sheriff

Home News
M.G. RHOADS has been appointed administrator of the Estate of ELLEN SUTTON, deceased.

The father of C.M. PARKS of this place, died at Georgetown, IL, at about on Saturday last. He was 83 years of age, and had been in feeble health for a long time.

JAMES H. VANNICE has been notified that he has been allowed back pension amounting to $3,400. From 1863 to 1873 he was allowed $8 per month. Since 1873 he was allowed at the rate of $24 per month.

Crawfordsville Journal

DAVID HUNTER, the most popular stock dealer in this State, purchased 16 head of fat cattle last Friday from Mr. FRANK RILEY, of Gessie, IN, that averaged 1400 pounds, and only two years old at that, paying a fancy price for the same, 6 ½ cents per pound.

Covington People's Paper

For Sale
I have 17 head of yearling cattle for sale. Call soon if you want a bargain.

J.M. SAVAGE

E.F. DAVIS has rented the west room in the London block for his son OLIVER DAVIS, who is coming back here to go into the dry goods business. It is also reported that the young man is going to provide himself with a housekeeper, and her name is Miss ELLA JAMISON, of Ellettsville, IN. They will occupy the house vacated by Mrs. L.E. ZENER.

Mrs. L.E. ZENER is now one of the happiest women in town. She has just moved into her neat and tasty new residence, which is a model of beauty and finish. The carpenters who erected this elegant little mansion are E.D. WHEELER and CAL ARRASMITH. Hon. E.L. CANADY is the artist who put on the finishing touches with the paintbrush.

LOUIS BARTH, a well known hotel clerk in Indianapolis was found dead last Friday morning in the old Merrick House, that city. He was a hard case, and a few years ago lost an arm in a drunken fight at a German picnic, near that city. He was formerly a resident of Opedee, this county, and was well known by a number of our citizens. Excessive drinking is supposed to have caused his death.

Wednesday, May 31, 1882

Crystal Wedding
One week ago last Friday evening, Mr. and Mrs. R.M. WHITE, of Helt's Prairie, were permitted to witness their crystal wedding celebrated in magnificent style. About 150 of their friends and relatives from their own neighborhood and Clinton, assembled at their residence. The Clinton Cornet Band, of which Mr. R.M. WHITE is a member, was an important feature of the occasion.

Birthday Party
Surprise parties being the order of night in this locality, the people of Helt's Prairie seized upon Tuesday evening, May 23, 1882, as a favorable time to play a joke on our minister, Rev. J.F. McDANIEL, it being the 59th anniversary of his birth. The minister and his wife had gone to Clinton on business, and when they returned they were completely surprised. Everyone had a wonderful time.

Perrysville
JAMES B. COOK is clerking in a grocery store in Danville, IL.

Home News
HAL WHEELER has bought out a barber's outfit at Ridge Farm, IL, and is going to move there.

JOHN H. KERDOLFF and THOMAS C. MOFFATT have bought out FIN STOKES' kit of tools and gone into the butchering business. FIN having made a sufficient amount of money at the business has retired to the shades of private life.

GEORGE SKIDMORE, of Helt's Prairie, who had a tumor removed from his under jaw a few weeks ago, is not recovering very fast, and is reported to be suffering a great deal from the operation. We hope to hear of his speedy recovery.

Highland
JAMES WICKENS has a new boy at his house. It came in on the Friday night train.

JAMES SMITH, OL SHEPARD, LAFE DOGGETT and LEM SNYDER were baptized in the Wabash last Sabbath.

JOHN MIDDLEBROOK, of Russellville, came home last Saturday to visit his family.

Personal
JOHN COLLETT Jr. of Wabash College spent last Sunday in town.

Dr. J.C. HARRISON, of Highland, was taken into the G.A.R. on last Friday night.

E.F. DAVIS and family arrived here last week, from Goodland, and intend to make Newport their future home.

B.K. DICKEN Sr. will leave tomorrow morning for Alma, WI, on an extended visit among relatives. He expects to be gone until the first of September.

Clinton
Mrs. JOHN WHITCOMB gave her little girl, NEMA WHITCOMB, a birthday party on last Wednesday evening.

Wednesday, June 7, 1882

Candidates
JOSIAH CAMPBELL, the Republican nominee for Representative, served 4 years and 3 months in the Union Army. He went out in 1861 and stayed until the last shot was fired. He has always been a resident of this county.

A.R. HOPKINS, the Republican nominee for Clerk, was born and raised in this county. He has always borne a good reputation as an honorable and upright citizen.

F.M. RILEY, the nominee for Treasurer, was born and raised in this county. He was a Union soldier during the late rebellion. He stands well among his neighbors.

WILLIAM C. MYERS, the nominee for Sheriff, was a good and faithful soldier during the late war. He has always been a resident of the county, and has made a good officer thus far, and should be re-elected.

C.S. DAVIS, the nominee for Recorder, enlisted in the army in the winter of 1863, when only 18 years of age, and served until the close of the war. He has served one term and wants to serve the people another.

P.Z. ANDERSON, of Clinton, the nominee for Surveyor, is an efficient officer, and we predict will be re-elected by a good round majority.

GEORGE W. CAMPBELL, the nominee for Commissioner from the first district, was a soldier in the Sixth Indiana Cavalry. He is a farmer by occupation, is well posted, and will make a good guardian of the people's interests.

JOHN B. WRIGHT, nominee for Commissioner from the second district, was also a soldier in the late war, and is a good selection for the position to which he has been chosen. He will undoubtedly be elected by a good big majority.

THOMAS BRINDLEY, the candidate for Coroner, need no recommend. He is a good coroner, and has filled the position acceptably to everybody.

Clinton
JASPER MOORE and his young wife moved to Chrisman, IL, last week. JASPER expects to go into the tile business out there.

Mrs. STAATS was taken seriously ill with the pleurisy last Wednesday evening. At present writing she is convalescing.

CARL HELDING received a serious injury last week from a horse falling on him. It was reported that two or three ribs were fractured. We are glad that his condition is improving at present.

Montezuma
ALEX McCUNE Sr., an old and much respected citizen of Rockville, and father of our Dr. G.W. McCUNE, died there last week. The deceased was 76 years of age.

SIMON COX has on account of his health, sold out his shoe shop, and will try huckstering. He is one of our best citizens, and deserves success.

The town board, at its regular meeting last Friday night, elected JAMES STEPHENSON as school trustee for the ensuing 3 years, in place of B.F. HUDSON, whose term has expired. JIM has lots of energy, and will make a good officer.

Grandma DOWNIN, relict of the late WILLIAM J. DOWNIN Sr., died at her home here on Saturday morning at 10 o'clock. She was much respected, and leaves many friends to mourn her loss.

JOHN SWINDELL, while working on a trestle near Scotland, IL, on Wednesday last, fell there down 14 feet, and received quite severe injuries. He was brought home, and has since been confined to his bed.

Home News
EVAN THOMPSON, of Helt township, has been appointed administrator of the Estate of TILLY JENKS, deceased.

Retail liquor licenses were granted to GEORGE W. EDMONDS of this place, and ED EDMONDS of Eugene, on Monday last.

We were slightly mistaken in stating that GEORGE SKIDMORE, of Helt's Prairie, had been suffering intensely from the surgical operation performed a few weeks since in removing a tumor from under his jaw. His suffering seems to have originated from tumorous developments that have been making their appearance since the operation. His physical system has improved very much, and we still hope to hear of his early recovery.

JOE S. McCORMICK has bought out the butcher shop at this place, and will furnish his customers with first-class beef on Tuesdays and Saturdays of each week.

F.N. AUSTIN, of Bono, is closing out his stock of Ladies and Children's Shoes. He will give you a bargain in all notions and overalls.

OL DAVIS, of this place, was married at 10 a.m. yesterday to Miss ELLA JAMISON, of Ellettsville, this state. Miss JAMISON is a sister to Mrs. Z.T. GALLOWAY of this place.

Personal
Mrs. NELLIE SOUDERS, of Hillsdale, and her niece, Mrs. MOLLIE TERPIN, of Greenfield, OH, were in town visiting yesterday.

Mrs. N.E. WEAVER, of Emporia, KS, is visiting her parents, Mr. and Mrs. A.J. ADAMS.
Danville, IL, Saturday Opinion

Mrs. ELLEN JONES returned home last week from Washington City where she had been for several weeks visiting her daughter, Mrs. MORTON C. HUNTER Jr. Her little grandchild came with her.

Real Estate Transfers for May 1882

LEWIS NORRIS and wife to JANE DAVIS
16 acres in Vermillion township - $35

MARY SOUTHARD to IRA SOUTHARD
Lots 4 & 5, block 6, in Clinton - $80

MILTON M. McNEILL and wife to LOUISA E. D. MOUDY
Part lot 51, and outlot adjoining Perrysville - $750

WILLIAM T. FERGUSON and wife to WILLIAM BEAUCHAMP etal
20 acres in Highland township - $325

CALVIN HUGHES and wife to JOHN HAIN
60 acres in Highland township - $3,000

JOHN L. WEBB and wife to RICHARD MORRIS and wife
Lot 15, in M. & H.'s addition to Perrysville - $100

JOSEPH HANN and wife to JAMES CHIPPS
Part lot 55, in Newport - $400

JOHN C. JOHNSON to JAMES CHIPPS
Lot 96, in Newport - $800

JOHN C. JOHNSON to CATHERINE J. JOHNSON
295 acres in Vermillion township - $1

FIELDING RABOURN's estate to JAMES R. DUNLAP
57 acres in Highland township - $1,764.50

JAMES T. DUGGER etal to JOHN OSBORN
---------- in Helt township - $1,800

JOHN H. BOGART and wife to PLATT Z. ANDERSON
Lots 8 & 9, block 2, and part of lot 4, block 11, in Clinton - $800

SAMUEL K. TODD etal to WILSON ZURMELY etal
Interest in Eugene Mills - $2,000

PLATT Z. ANDERSON and wife to JOHN WRIGHT
Part lot 4, block 11, in Clinton - $300

JOHN WRIGHT and wife to NELSON C. ANDERSON
Part lot 4, block 11, in Clinton - $300

RICHARD MALONE to WILLIAM UNDERWOOD
10 acres in Helt township - $150

WILIAM K. McNEILL to ARCHIBALD NICCUM
24 ½ acres in Highland township - $161

ARACHIBALD NICCUM to JOHN BENSINGER
24 ½ acres in Highland township - $245

WILLIAM WOODALL and wife to MILTON BRODOCK
Lot 4, in Clinton - $360

NEIL J. McDOUGALL etal to HARRY B. DUDLEY
Outlot adjoining Clinton - $75

JAMES E. KNOWLES etal to JOSEPH R. UTTER
Outlot adjoining Clinton – $160

CHARLES B. JONES to HIRAM CHENOWETH etal
Lot 12, and outlots 42 & 43, in Perrysville - $16

BARBARA A. McCALLA to JAMES C. TUTT etal
100 ¾ acres in Helt township - $4,000

BARTON S. AIKMAN to LEVI H. AIKMAN
6 ¾ acres in Helt township - $206

HARRISON PAYTON etal to ELSON J. SIMS
5/9 of 80 acres in Helt township - $700

LEWIS NORRIS and wife to JOHN E. MILLER
40 acres in Vermillion township - $800

JAMES S. ROGERS to WILLIAM E. FULWIDER and wife
20 acres in Vermillion township - $700

WILSON ZURMELY and wife to MONROE G. HOSFORD
Interest in Eugene Mills - $1,100

WORTH W. PORTER and wife to JOHN COLLETT
4 acres in Eugene township - $400

ISAAC F. SANDERS to HARRIS E. SANDERS etal
33 ½ acres in Highland township - $800

WILLIAM JENNING to ANN NICHOLS
22 acres in Vermillion township - $680

ANN NICHOLS and husband to JOSEPH A. SANDERS and wife
20 acres in Vermillion township - $500

RICHARD MALONE to MORRIS H. RANDALL
20 acres in Helt township - $450

Wednesday, June 14, 1882

Highland
Mrs. MILLER, of Paris, IL, is visiting her sister, Mrs. MOLLIE SHOWALTERS of this place.

Clinton
JAMES ALLEN and wife split the blanket last week.

The BELLUS Saloon was sold last week to Mrs. CAL TUCKER.

HARRY EDMISTON, our gentlemanly young merchant, who has been visiting relatives over at Bainbridge, OH, returned home last Friday.

Dr. AQUILLA WASHBURN started for Pittsburg, PA on last Thursday. If the business outlook is good, he intends to locate there.

Montezuma
JOSEPH BURNS Esq. is confined to the house with inflammatory rheumatism.

Mrs. L.R. YOUNG went on Tuesday last to East St. Louis, IL, to visit her sister, Mrs. FRANK SMITH. She took her little granddaughter LOUIE PECK, now a bright and beautiful little cherub of 4 months.

WILLIAM DARRINGTON and family are again residents of Montezuma and from his spryness he bids fair to outlive many younger folks.

Home News
L.C. ALLEN, a former resident of this place, has moved out to Kansas City, MO.

MEL B. DAVIS, of Clinton, was admitted, last week, to practice in the Superior Court of Terre Haute.

Personal
Miss EMMA SHARP, of Waveland, is here on a visit, the guest of her brother, WILLIAM SHARP.

JAMES ASBURY left on last Monday morning for Eugene, Ringgold County, IA, on a three months visit to one of his brothers.

Removal
Mrs. C.B. GALLOWAY has removed her millinery store into the new building just erected by ROBERT STOKES, where may be found all the latest and most fashionable millinery goods. Also pianos, organs, all kinds of musical merchandise, sewing machine needles, repairs of all kinds, oils, and numerous other things.

Letter List

ROSS, W.F.
McDANIEL, S.A.
JULIAN, GERROLD
HAWKINS, JAMES C.
RITEBURG, S.A.
MOFFATT, JOHN
JOHNSON, JAMES
GOODWIN, W.A.

EPPERSON, Dr. C.G.	CHEZUM, JOHN C.
BROWN, CHARLES D.	BENNETT, Mrs. NANCY
COAL, MINNIE	FERN, Miss MARY B.
OWELL, Miss IDA	McMILLAN, Mrs. MARY

Wednesday, June 21, 1882

Highland
A Mr. GIBSON, who mysteriously disappeared from this place about 22 years ago, is reported to be running a store in Columbus, this State. It was thought by his wife and friends he was dead.

LEVI BONEBRAKE and VINAL AYE have gone into the butcher business.

DAVID DOUGLASS and BENSON JAMES have leased the coal mine just west of here and are rolling out plenty of coal.

Uncle JOHN PEARMAN, who left this place for Kansas about 2 years ago, returned on a short visit last week. He gives a glowing account of that state.

DAVID DINSMORE's daughter, CLARA DINSMORE, and her husband living in the north part of this state, are visiting in this neighborhood.

BUSH JONES is quite proud over being called father. It is a good sized boy and is doing well.

Clinton
A bland smile was perceptible on the countenance of AL FRESSEL on last Monday morning. It is needless to say, a boy.

Mrs. ANNA PITMAN, of Evansville, is in town visiting her parents, Mr. and Mrs. C.B. KNOWLES.

Mrs. MAY PRATT, nee STAATS, who was married in this place last summer, and then moved to New York, is down sick with the quick consumption. Her many young friends will be sorry to hear this.

Mrs. E.H. HAYS and her daughter HATTIE, left this place on the train last Monday night, for Michigan, where Mr. HAYS, who went there some time ago, has received employment. A social was given them at Mrs. DAVID McBETH's on the evening before their departure.

Home News
J.W. GREEN of Boswell, Benton County, was in town last week.

R.F. CHURCH, of Helt township, is going to move back to Missouri again, shortly.

Mrs. KATE W. CARPENTER, of Indianapolis, daughter of THOMAS CUSHMAN, is here on a visit.

EDAH BOYER, of Ashmore, IL, is now on a protracted visit to Helt township, the guest of her cousin, JESSE HOUCHIN.

OL STAATS and lady, of Helt township, spent last Sunday in town, the guests of his sister, Mrs. L.E. ZENER.

Mrs. JESSIE MORGAN, of Helt township, has been confined to her bed for 9 weeks. Her recovery is considered doubtful.

A dispatch was received here last week from Hutchinson, KS, stating that Mrs. GEORGE W. ODELL was lying dangerously ill.

Mrs. VIOLA TARRANCE, of Terre Haute, was in town last week, visiting her father, WALTER J. PLACE, and relatives.

Miss MAMIE LITTLE and Miss ELLA PARRETT attended the State Sunday School Association, at Crawfordsville, last week.

JOHN HEGARTY, of Missouri, is here on a visit to his brother MAURICE HEGARTY.

E.B. BROWN, of Opedee, has just been granted a pension of $6 per month on account of a disability received in the service. He is afflicted with varicose veins. His first draw, which will include arrearages, will amount to nearly $800.

Matrimony
Rev. R.V. HUNTER, a Presbyterian minister of Philo, IL, who was pastor of the Presbyterian Church at this place a few years ago, and well known by many of our citizens, will be united in wedlock this evening, at 8 ½ o'clock, at Waveland, to Miss ESTELLA KRITZ, the beautiful and accomplished daughter of Prof. KRITZ, of Wabash College. M.G. RHOADS and lady, of this place, are invited to attend the tying of the nuptial knots.

Commissioners Court

Poor	
JOSEPH CONRAD, poor asylum	577.72
R.H. NICHOLS, keeping pauper	15.00
JAMES CHIPPS, Trustee Vermillion township	176.58
ANTHONY FABLE, Trustee Eugene township	177.60
GEORGE W. STULTZ, Trustee Clinton township	140.95
JAMES OSBORN, Trustee Helt township	155.24
J.A. BARNES, Physician Highland township	25.00
JAMES WALLACE, Physician, Vermillion township	48.75
H.H. JAMES, Physician, Helt township	21.25
DANIEL SEARS, keeping paupers	30.00
H.C. SMITH, Trustee Highland township	86.25
Roads and Highways	
R.B. DUKEN, viewer	1.50
L.H. AIKMAN, viewer	1.50
S.G. MALONE Jr., viewer	3.25
HENRY JORDAN, viewer	3.00
N.H. SMITH, viewer	1.50
JAMES BUSH, viewer	1.50
W.C. MYERS, viewer	7.90
County Board of Health	
M.L. HALL	49.75
WILLIAM B. BUFORD	14.10
Attorneys	
H.H. CONLEY	5.00
Assessing	
IRWIN LAMB	20.00
PHILO CURTIS	26.00
JOHN R. STAHL	84.00
GEORGE W. VANDEVENDER	16.00
JOHN W. WILTERMOOD	84.00
N.M. TUTT	58.00
JOHN T. RICHARDSON	64.00

JOHN T. BOREN	66.00
JAMES B. RICHARDSON	120.00
JOSEPH H. NICHOLAS	120.00
THOMAS H. SMITH	2.50
R.M. RUCKER	104.00
R.H. NIXON	2.50
Repairs of Public Buildings	
THOMAS BRINDLEY	50.00
W.C. ARRASMITH	4.50
THOMAS FOSTER	25.97
Bridge Repairs	
PETER AIKMAN	30.75
WILLIAM L. PORTER	177.27
JOHN O. WRIGHT	117.00
County School Superintendent	
H.H. CONLEY	176.00
Criminals	
F.M. BISHOP	100.00
W.C. MYERS	126.00
W.L. LITTLE	2.90
Printing	
S.B. DAVIS	3.00
Courts	
JAMES R. DUNLAP	42.00
JAMES A. ELDER	63.00
JACOB L. THOMAS	24.50
W.C. MYERS	33.10
Ditches	
W.C. MYERS	14.10
Fees and Salaries	
H.O. PETERS	200.00
ELIAS PRITCHARD	695.95
Books and Stationary	
W.B. BURFORD	4.50
C.W. BROWN	7.00
County Offices	
M. HEGARTY	2.45
R.H. NIXON	6.70
Free Gravel Road Repairs	
GEORGE W. STULTZ	363.87
Copying Records	
ELIAS PRITCHARD	90.00

Perrysville
Dr. J.W. SMITH started Thursday for Billings, a town in Montana, where he will practice his profession.

Dr. SPOTSWOOD is closing out his stock of goods here, and contemplates going into the drug business in Crawfordsville.

CALVIN HUGHES and his son CHED HUGHES returned last week from Kansas, where they went to purchase a farm.

Montezuma
Wealthy men receive riches and poor men babes. MILES DAVIS and wife received a brand new boy on last Sunday morning.

Dr. CANNON and his son FRANK CANNON, who went to the Hot Springs for health, write that their health has much improved.

Wednesday, June 28, 1882

Highland
JOHN PEARMAN, after visiting a few days, returned again to Northern Kansas, taking with him his son ADAM PEARMAN and wife.

FRED LINDSEY and ADDA SIMPSON were married on last Friday evening by Esq. G.W. SAXTON.

Clinton
Mrs. MYRTLE BASSETT is lying very sick at Hot Springs, Arkansas. Her recovery is considered doubtful.

Mrs. ED KNOWLES departed this life on last Thursday night. Her funeral was preached by Rev. A.W. WOOD at the residence of the deceased on Friday at 5 o'clock p.m., after which her remains were laid away in the Cemetery at this place.

WILLIS HEDGES, who has been attending school at Greencastle during the past year, returned home last Thursday.

JIM ALLEN and wife, after a short separation, have commenced living together again. JIM says the second honeymoon is lots sweeter than the first.

HARRY STAATS, who has been clerking in a store for his uncle at Brazil, is in town visiting his mother who has been sick with the pleurisy. He can work harder at nothing than anyone we ever saw.

Mr. WILLIAM MAIL, who has been in town during the past week visiting, left for his home at Vincennes last Saturday.

Home News
JOE C. DAVIS returned from Asbury College last week.

Miss HATTIE ELDER and Miss BELLE FISHER, of Bono, Helt township, left on Wednesday last for Sparta, Wisconsin, to spend the summer.

E.B. BROWN, of Opedee, received $900 instead of $800 as reported by us in our last issue.

R.H. CARPENTER, of Indianapolis, spent last Sunday in town visiting his sick wife, the daughter of THOMAS CUSHMAN, who came here a few weeks ago on a visit to her parents.

Mrs. REBECCA HOLLINGSWORTH, wife of HENRY HOLLINGSWORTH, is lying dangerously ill, but her physician still has hopes for her recovery. She has been confined to her bed for a long time.

JOHN E. NAGLE, who was committed to jail at Danville, IL, sometime ago on the charge of incest, has been released and gone to Kansas City, MO, where he is working in a large flouring mill. He says he will never live with his family again.

Obituary
Mrs. EBER HOLLINGSWORTH, residing a few miles SW of town, died on Friday last, after a lingering illness. Her remains were interred in the Wimsett Cemetery on Saturday. The deceased was a noble and kind hearted woman, a Christian lady, and esteemed by all her neighbors and acquaintances. She leaves a husband, son, and a daughter, and numerous friends to lament her death.

Matrimony
ANDY CURTIS and Miss ELLA CARTER, both of this township, were married on Sunday last, Esq. J.W. HARTMAN tying the connubial knot.

OLIVER KNIGHT has left Hutchinson, KS, and gone to Garden City, 180 miles further west, where he and another gentleman propose to start a paper. Three months at farthest will satisfy him that there is no money to be made in publishing a paper in a county with only a few hundred inhabitants.

Sheriff's Sale on Decree

Travelers Insurance Co. vs. CHARLES E. HOSFORD, LIDA HOSFORD, MILTON SHOWALTERS, MARY E. SHOWALTERS, SIDNEY B. DAVIS, assignee of CHARLES E. HOSFORD
$4,572.58
Sale to be held at courthouse between 10 and 4
Saturday, July 22, 1882

NW fraction of Sec 35 T 16N R 9 W – 117.81 acres
NE ¼ NE ¼ Sec 34 T 16 N R 9 W – 33 acres
Total 150.81 acres

June 28, 1882
LEVERING, BLANCHARD, & CUSHMAN, Attorneys
WILLIAM C. MYERS, Sheriff

Wednesday, July 5, 1882

Montezuma
JAMES BARNES and wife start for Central Iowa next week to visit relatives. They will be absent for 2 months.

WILLIAM H. and STEVE SYLVESTER started on Monday last on a visit to their relatives in Green and Davis Counties, Wisconsin.

ED BURNS returned home from Ann Arbor, Michigan, College on Thursday last looking well and hearty.

Prof. WILLIAM TRUEBLOOD will be our School Superintendent next scholastic year. Miss BELLE FORD, grammar room, Miss DORA MOFFATT, intermediate room, and Miss SARAH MOTTE, primary, will be our teachers. All excellent selections.

Clinton
Rev. JESSE HILL, formerly pastor of the M.E. Church of this place, was in town last Thursday, the guest of his daughter, Mrs. CHARLES WHITCOMB.

The Misses BELLE and LILLIE CRANE, of Dana, were in town a couple of days last week visiting their brother JIM CRANE.

SAM WEBB, after a business experience of about 3 months, sold out to his partner, F.D. NEWHOUSE. WEBB has been chiefly engaged in speculating in livestock. He retires from the field with a rich, full and delicious experience.

An Unfortunate Family
A 9 year old boy, the only child of Mr. and Mrs. J.M. HAYS, of Clinton, was drowned in the Wabash on last Wednesday evening. The little fellow, by permission of his parents, had gone down to the river with another boy to help wash a buggy, and was wading out when he stepped off into a deep hole and drowned before help could arrive. His body was recovered about 2 hours after the accident. It is an old adage that misfortunes never come singly. Some two months since they lost their only daughter, a bright and beautiful young Miss, about 15 years of age. The grief stricken parents have the sympathy of their many friends in their sad bereavement.

Home News
ED SPRAGUE and family, of Kansas, arrived in Eugene last week to spend a few days visiting his brother, HARRY SPRAGUE.

Mrs. SUSA ROBINSON has moved back to Newport to engage in the dressmaking business.

H.S. CADY, who is working on a bridge in Freedom, Owen County, spent last Sunday at home with his family.

ELMER HENSON went out to Hinesborough, IL, on Monday last to see his girl, whom he has been corresponding with for sometime but never met.

Mrs. MARY MILLER, a sister of A.J. and FRANCIS DAVIS, residing west of here, was taken over to the Insane Asylum by Sheriff MYERS, last week. It is supposed her derangement was caused by the death of her husband, which sad event occurred about 3 months ago. She is 48 years old and has a child, a little girl, 9 years old.

Sad Accident
On last Saturday afternoon, HARRY BLUNK, EDDIE HOLLINGSWORTH, QUINCE GRUBB, and FRED DAVIS, all small boys between the ages of 8 and 11 years, went to the Little Vermillion River, which courses by our town, to take a bath. Neither of the boys could swim very well. HARRY BLUNK, who was 10 years old last November, ventured out on a log in the creek and slipped and fell into deep water. The other little boys tried to rescue him, but HARRY was so frightened he could not reach the ladder that they pushed to him. Early the next morning his body was found near where he went down for the last time. His remains were taken to his distraught mother, a widow lady, on East Extension Street, where they remained until 5 o'clock in the evening when they were followed to the Cemetery by a large concourse of sympathizing friends.

Highland
Mrs. MARGARET NORRIS, well known in this township, died last Saturday night at Terre Haute at the residence of her sister, Mrs. GEORGE CRETZ. She was buried at this place on Monday in the Trowbridge Cemetery.

Wednesday, July 12, 1882

A Serious Accident
On last Thursday morning a number of our citizens, among them FRANK ARRASMITH, went up to Danville to have a jolly time and see the races. FRANK, and nearly all the other boys decided to get a farewell drink, and missed the last train. He started up the Wabash track for the junction, thinking he could overtake it at that point. In crossing the bridge, he slipped and fell a distance of 30 feet, his right leg striking a timber and crushing the bone in his thigh. He dragged himself up the grade to the track where he lay quite awhile before he could attract the attention of anyone to come to his assistance. Finally a woman residing nearby, who had gotten up to wait on a sick child, heard his distress cry, woke her husband up and sent him over to see what was the matter. He was taken to the junction where he took the morning train home and Dr. M.L. HALL set his broken limb. He is getting along fine. He was lucky he was not instantly killed.

Highland
NEL TEMPLE, of Dana, who broke his leg last winter or spring, was able to attend the 4th at Montezuma.

Perrysville
RUHL and CONNOR, barbers of this place, have dissolved partnership, and are now running separate shops.

SIMP STEPHENS Jr. is proud and happy – a little girl now calls him papa.

MILT STEVENS will leave here in a few weeks, and talks of engaging in the grocery business at Veedersburg.

Obituary
Mrs. MARIA B. DUZAN, widow of CHARLES W. DUZAN, died at DAVISON FILSON's near Camargo, IL, on June 10, 1882, of malarial fever. Mrs. MARIA B. DUZAN was born in North Carolina, March 29, 1818. She came to Indiana with her father at the age of 14 years, where she resided until 1871, and the greater part of that time being a resident of Newport. She had been a member of the M.E. Church for 40 years and lived a consistent Christian life.

Home News
W.H. HASKELL, of Clinton, left on Tuesday night of last week for Colorado.

E.G. WILSON and JAMES JACOBS of Montezuma, and JOHN CONNELLY, of Annapolis, were over here on last Thursday night and organized an Odd Fellows lodge.

Mrs. EDDIE KAUFMAN of Dana, after spending several days in town visiting relatives and friends, left on last Monday afternoon for Danville, IL, to spend a few days in that city visiting her cousin, ANDREW FILLINGER.

Mrs. CHARITY DAWSON, of Cameron, Warren County, IL, arrived here last week to visit her sick mother, Mrs. HENRY HOLLINGSWORTH, who has been lying very low for sometime, but at present is thought to be gaining slowly.

CHESTER RALSTON, of Helt township, is the proud father of twins. At present his wife is stopping out in Illinois.

MEL JORDAN and Miss LILLIE CRANE, both of Helt township, are making arrangements to work in double harness.

Terrible Accident
THOMAS McMASTERS, a wealthy young farmer, residing in Parke County, near Bloomingdale, was taken to the Surgical Institute yesterday, for amputation of his left leg, and to have some serious wounds attended to. He was found lying unconscious beside the I.D. & S. road yesterday morning at 2 o'clock, a train having severed his left foot, crushed his left arm, and terribly mangled the right side of his head. He says he had some trouble with the trainmen, and from that time he can't remember anything else. He was under the influence of liquor. Owing to the loss of blood, the probabilities of his recovery are not very encouraging.

Real Estate Transfers for the Month of June 1882

WILLIAM JENNING to ANN NICHOLS
22 acres in Vermillion township - $880

ANN NICHOLS and husband to JOSEPH A. SANDERS
20 acres in Vermillion township - $500

RICHARD MALONE to MORRIS H. RANDALL
20 acres in Helt township - $450

JOHN SLATER's estate to ANNIE SLATER
Lot 5, block 14, part of lot 6, block 3, in Clinton - $1,100

JOHN SLATER's estate to JOHN WRIGHT
Part lot 6, 7, & 10, block 11, in Clinton - $150

JOHN L. DEEG and wife to RICHARD PARKER
Lot 11, block 6, in Clinton - $300

NELSON C. ANDERSON and wife to MORGAN J. TUCKER
Part lot 7, block 3, in Clinton - $600

JOEL JARED and wife to JOHN BRIGHT
40 acres in Clinton township - $850

JOHN A. BRIGHT and wife to JACOB W. SHIRLEY
40 acres in Clinton township - $800

LYSANDER SHEW and wife to FRANCIS M. WRIGHT
34.55 acres in Clinton township - $423.25

EMILY BALES etal to CALEB BALES
1 acre in Helt township - $50

OSCAR B. LOWRY to ABIGAIL THOMPSON
Lot 2, block 4, in Dana - $400

JACOB W. MILLER and wife to HENRY O. PETERS
Lots 87 & 88, in Eugene - $65

JAMES C. STUTLER and wife to WILLIAM H. STUTLER
Lots 13 & 14, in Gessie - $65

L.B. FLEMING to JONATHAN CARITHERS
2 ½ acres in Highland township - $62.50

PERMINTER P. NOEL and wife to JOHN F. DUGGER
54 acres in Clinton township - $1,000

JOHN F. DUGGER and wife to MANGUS JOHNSON
54 acres in Clinton township - $480

NATHANIEL BENSON etal to JOSEPH HANSON
Lot 8, block 1, in Morey's addition to Clinton - $125

JOHN F. NICHOLS and wife to JAMES P. FULWILDER
11 acres in Clinton township - $275

WILLIAM GIBSON and wife to JOHN F. NICHOLS
5 acres in Clinton township - $20

ELIZABETH J. MONTGOMERY and husband to JANE FORD etal
1/9 of 240 acres in Helt township - $1,100

JOSEPH W. FOLER to HENRY C. NICHOLS
Lots 28 & 29, in G. & C.'s addition to Perrysville - $2.67

ADALINE V. JONES to JOEL H. BENTON
Lot 86 in Perrysville - $75

ELLEN GROENENDYKE to SAMUEL W. MALONE
Lot 7, and part lot 8, in Eugene - $900

ALEXANDER T. PATTERSON to PETER M. STOKESBERRY
Lots 2, 3, & 6, block 28, in Clinton - $608.33

ROSA J. UNDERWOOD and husband to SOLOMON CARPENTER
40 acres in Helt township - $1,200

DIANA LAUDSDOWN to MARY A. FONCANNON
Outlot adjoining Jonestown - $135

WILLIAM P. THOMPSON and wife to W.P. ANDREWS
Part lots 5, 8, & 9, block 1, in Clinton - $600

JAMES M. MOORE and wife to NELSON C. ANDERSON
1/8 of lots 1, 4, 5, 8, & 9, block 29, in Clinton - $430

Wednesday, July 19, 1882

Highland
FRANK JOHNSON will return to his home in Ashmore, IL, next Friday.

Home News
LEN NAGLE moved over to Lodi, Parke County, on Sunday last.

JIM BLANCHARD is now foreman of a country newspaper office in Missouri.

TOM MOFFATT has got a job, and is working for some railroad company at Topeka, KS.

Mrs. EMMA KITCHEN, of Danville, IL, daughter of WILLIAM GIBSON, spent last Sunday with her father.

CHESTER RALSTON, of Helt township, denies being the father of twins. He says it is all a mistake, and furthermore he is not married.

GEORGE SKIDMORE and wife, of Helt's Prairie, and his son SAM SKIDMORE, of Dana, were in town on Thursday last. GEORGE came up to try the virtue of a faith doctor in removing a fibrous tumor from his neck. Mr. SKIDMORE is quite poorly at present, but we hope to hear of his change for the better before many days. He was getting along nicely until about 3 weeks ago when he overheated himself in running hogs out of his wheat field, which gave him a back-set. We hope he will be more careful in the future.

JOHN ETTER has been employed to tend bar for HARRY SPRAGUE at this place, Mr. SIMPSON's health not permitting him to remain in business longer.

JAMES HASTY has leased JOHN C. JOHNSON's old homestead farm, east of town, and will move on to it in a short time.

Mrs. EMMA PATTON, nee WELLER, of Ridge Farm, a former citizen of this place, is the mother of a bright little boy, only a few days old.

Sheriff MYERS took HENRY HOLLINGSWORTH's wife over to the Insane Asylum yesterday for treatment. She has been in poor health for a long time, and for several weeks has been unable to recognize her own children. She will not eat anything only as it is forced down her.

Wednesday, July 26, 1882

Highland
Miss ELLA SMITH, of New Goshen, is visiting her sister, Mrs. SHOWALTERS of this place.

Clinton
MONT L. CASEY has been employed by the conductor of the passenger train to wait on ladies at the depot. He made quite a display of his gallantry last Friday evening.

Home News
STRATT HOLLINGSWORTH, of Fontanet, Vigo County, was up and spent last Sunday with his relatives and friends.

An infant child of JOE M. RABB, of Williamsport, died on last Saturday week.

ELMER HENSON left on last Friday evening for Hutchinson, KS, where he has been employed to clerk for GEORGE W. ODELL & Sons.

Prof. G.L. WATSON, of Eugene, will have to furnish catnip tea for one more at his house. It is a girl, and will be old enough to marry in 18 years from last Thursday night.

GEORGE TRUITT and Miss CELIA JACKSON are keeping it quiet, but we understand they are making arrangements to marry at an early day. It is pretty hard to keep secrets from a newspaper.

Heavy Weights
Three of our corpulent citizens were weighed on Saturday last and kicked the beam at 722 pounds. Their weights are as follows: Mrs. MARGARET RAMSEY, a modest widow, 254 pounds; SILAS HOLLINGSWORTH, the town Marshall, 242 pounds; JOHN GIVENS, landlord at the Newport Hotel, 226 pounds.

Death
GEORGE SWITZER, a retired farmer of Eugene township, died between 12 and 1 o'clock on last Friday morning, aged 64 years. The deceased was born in Virginia in 1818, and had been a resident of this county for many years. Some 3 or 4 months ago, he lost his mind, and from that time, gradually began to fail in health. He had always been a stout, vigorous man until this last sad affliction. He had been a prosperous farmer and had laid up sufficient of this world's goods to keep him and his wife comfortably during their declining years. They were never blessed with any children. The funeral took place on Saturday and was largely attended by is many acquaintances and friends. The deceased was a good citizen and very highly respected. He leaves a wife to mourn his loss.

Married
On Sunday July 23, 1882, Mr. GEORGE NASON, of this place, to Miss LOU PALMER, living one mile north of here.

SCOTT HELT, a son of THOMAS HELT, of Helt's Prairie, has just been sent to the penitentiary for 15 years, in Missouri, for helping to rob a bank in that state the first of last month. He had two accomplices. One of them a school teacher by the name of MILLER, who use to teach school on Helt's Prairie.

Arrangements have been made for one more teacher and a higher grade to be taught in our school at this place the coming fall and winter. There are to be 4 teachers. Prof. J.W. PERRIN, of Eugene, is to be principal, and J.J. PADRICK of the same town, teacher in the grammar department. No one has yet been employed for either the intermediate or primary departments.

Wednesday, August 2, 1882

Death

It becomes our duty this week to record the death of Mrs. MARY A. CUSHMAN, of this place, which sad event occurred at about 9:15 o'clock on Wednesday night of last week. She had been ailing for about two weeks, but was not considered dangerously ill. At about 6 o'clock on that evening she had a hemorrhage of the bowels, which medical skill failed to check, and which soon ebbed her life blood away.

Her maiden name was MARY A. GLANTON. She was born in Kentucky in 1822; was married to Dr. JOHN S. BAXTER in 1840, and moved to Perrysville in 1842, where Dr. BAXTER died in 1853. She was married to THOMAS CUSHMAN in October 1863, and came to Newport with him after he was elected County Auditor in the fall of 1873, where she resided until her death. She left surviving two surviving children; one the daughter of Dr. BAXTER, who is now married to Prof. SHAFER of Thorntown, IN, and GLANT, the daughter of THOMAS CUSHMAN, whose name was taken from her mother's maiden name, GLANTON. Her only son, Dr. L.S. BAXTER, died at Perrysville 6 or 7 years ago.

The funeral services were conducted at the family residence on last Thursday evening, Rev. J.H. HOLLINGSWORTH and Rev. J.W. PARRETT officiating. On Friday morning her remains were taken by train to Perrysville, accompanied by the relatives and a large circle of friends, where they were quietly laid away to rest in the peaceful city of the dead.

For us to undertake to write the many noble traits of character with which the deceased was possessed, would be a matter of impossibility. There was not a more noble hearted woman lived in Vermillion County. She had the esteem and confidence of all her neighbors and acquaintances, and was beloved and respected by everybody. She was a Christian woman and had been a member of the M.E. Church for many years. In her death a husband has been deprived of a noble companion, the children a kind and generous hearted mother, and society of one of its best citizens.

Highland
JIM RALSTON is owner of a fine large baby boy.

WAKEFIELD INGRAM, we understand, has bought the OSBORN farm west of here. The amount paid was $7,000.

The McCALLA family will leave this place soon for Salem, OH.

JESS KAUFMAN, of this township, who is the best hostler in Vermillion County, is the owner of the best stallion in this part of the country.

JOHN COMPTON has a new boy baby at his house.

Clinton
Mr. PRATER, with his family, moved down near Vincennes on last Saturday where he expects to engage in the business of farming.

Bono
THOMAS AIKMAN, of Nebraska, is visiting J.A. MAST.

JAMES TILLOTSON is here visiting his mother. His home is in Kansas.

H.M. THOMPSON is going to move to Bloomingdale, Parke County, the first of September.

HENRY JENKS' twin babies have been very sick, but are getting better.

L.O. BISHOP of the Clinton Herald, has purchased at his own expense, a brand new printing outfit, including steam power press capable of printing 1200 pages per hour. He will start a new page paper at Clinton early this month. It will be devoted to the success of the Republican party, the industrial interests of Vermillion County, and the bettering of humanity everyway. Plucky boy.

Letter List

WELLS, JESSIE B.	WIDNER, AMOS
TURNER, MORDECIA D.	MILLER, N.D.
SHAW, DAVID	CANRI, E.E.
CAMPBELL, JAMES P.	CRAIG, OTIS B.
CARPENTER, GEORGE W.	BUTLER, CASSIUS
ARISK, WILLIAM	DANISE, Mrs. J.
SMITH, Mrs. PERMELIA	

Home News
WILLIAM J. CUSHMAN, of Danville, IL, came down last week to attend the funeral of his step-mother, and remained here until Sunday.

Mrs. CATE CARPENTER, of Indianapolis, daughter of THOMAS CUSHMAN, who has been here on a visit for several weeks, is in very poor health and is confined to her bed. Her husband R.H. CARPENTER came over last Saturday to see her.

The "Saturday Argus" is the title of L.O. BISHOP's new paper. Argus means a hundred eyes. LUTE says that the Argus will look sharp. We hope he will be encouraged in his undertaking.

GEORGE SKIDMORE, of Helt's Prairie, who is suffering from a cancer on the side of his face and neck, is now in rather a critical condition and is suffering intense misery. GEORGE has the full sympathy of his many friends in his sad affliction.

THOMAS AIKMAN, who left this county some 8 years ago, and who has since resided in Western Nebraska, returned to his old home near Bono last Wednesday. He brought with him his family, consisting of a wife and 2 children. After paying his relatives a short visit, he will return to that State where he is traveling as a Methodist circuit rider. His present home is at Cozad, Dawson County, NB.

JESSE GIBSON leaves this morning for Danville, IL, to visit her sister, Mrs. EMMA KITCHEN.

Wednesday, August 9, 1882

Highland
HENRY VERBRICK is proud over a youngster. It is a girl and made its appearance last week.

W.F. KERNS, of Bono, received a few days ago, a check for $900 from "Uncle Sam" for injuries received during the rebellion.

Dr. HARRISON moved to Alta one day last week where he expects to settle. Highland is now without a physician, for the first time in a number of years.

WILLIAM HARRIS and Miss IDA LANE were made one on last Sunday week.

Clinton
Mrs. SARAH WILLIAMSON, who has been visiting her cousins, DOLLIE and MINNIE HAGENBAUGH during the past two weeks, left on last Monday.

Mrs. PHOEBE STAATS has bought the property now occupied by JOHN HOWARD, and will move into it shortly.

Mrs. MAY PRATT, nee STAATS, of New York, returned to this place on a visit to her mother last week. MAY's health has been very poor since she left here one year ago, and she now has symptoms of the consumption.

CLARA SMITH departed last week to spend a few days in visiting her "country cousins" near Tuscola, IL.

Miss BELLE CAMPBELL left the first of this week for Terre Haute, where she has secured a position as clerk in a dry goods store. BELLE is a jolly girl and we hate very much to see her leave our town. Miss MIAMI BLACK succeeds her in the store of ROBB & EDMISTON.

CHAUNCEY RYNERSON, of Tuscola, IL, was in town last Saturday shaking hands with his old friends. CHAUNCEY has an offer of a place as traveling salesman of a Cincinnati house, which he will probably accept.

Notice of Final Settlement of Estate
Estate of JOHN HINES, deceased
July 31, 1882

JAMES ROBERTS, Clerk
By NORTH CRAIG, Deputy Clerk

Home News
Mrs. ELIZABETH SWITZER, of Eugene, has been appointed administratrix of the estate of GEORGE SWITZER, deceased.

BOB MYERS is going to move out to Kansas sometime next week. He intends to locate on a farm 4 miles south of Hutchinson, in Reno County.

Obituary
At 4 o'clock on last Thursday afternoon, Mrs. JONATHAN MERRIMAN, of this place, died of consumption. The deceased had been in poor health for a long time, and death was undoubtedly a relief to her. Her funeral occurred on Friday afternoon and was very respectably attended. Her remains were interred in the Zener Cemetery, a short distance east of town. She leaves a husband and two daughters, ANNA and LUCY, to mourn her death.

Real Estate Transfers for Month of July 1882
JOHN WRIGHT and wife to GEORGE W. HUNTER and wife
Lot 4 and ½ of lot 5, block 32, in Clinton - $1,000

JASPER A. MOORE and wife to NELSON C. ANDERSON
½ of lot 1, 4, 5, 8, & 9, block 29, in Clinton - $400

WILLIAM P. ANDREWS to FRANK ANDREWS
Part of lots 5, 8, & 9, block 1, in Clinton - $500

JOEL DYER to ISAAC N. DYER
177 acres in Clinton township - $4,095

JOEL DYER to WINFORD DYER
51.86 acres in Clinton township - $2,075.75

JOEL DYER to MARCUS DYER
80 acres in Clinton township - $3,200

HENRY NEBEKER and wife to JOHN WRIGHT
Part lot 7, block 4, in Clinton - $500

JASPER A. MOORE and wife to JAMES M. MOORE
1/3 lot 10, block 3, in Clinton - $350

LEONIDAS H. BELLUS and wife to JAMES B. LYNE
Part lot 10, block 3, in Clinton - $221.35

JOHN WRIGHT and wife to HENRY NEBEKER
Part lot 4, block 11, in Clinton - $350

ENOCH L. CANADY etal to MARY F. HASTY
2/5 of lots 21, & 22, in Newport - $200

JENNIE M. SNOW to Newport Coal Co.
40 acres in Vermillion township - $3,970

MARGARET G. ABBOTT and husband to Newport Coal Co.
20 acres in Vermillion township - $4,000

ADALINE V. JONES to LIDA A. BENTON
Lots 83, 84, 85, and part lot 36 & 37, in Perrysville - $3,000

SAMUEL H. VANSANT and wife to MATTHEW SCOTT
Lot 9, block 32, in Clinton - $874

JACOB W. SHIRLEY to SILAS WEESE
12 acres in Clinton township - $275

NELSON C. ANDERSON and wife to ANZALETTA WEESE
6 acres in Clinton township - $50

Notice of Final Settlement of Estate
Estate of JOHN HEPBURN, deceased
August 1, 1882
JAMES ROBERTS, Clerk
By NORTH CRAIG, Deputy Clerk

Administrator's Sale
Estate of GEORGE SWITZER, deceased
Saturday September 2, 1882
Sale at residence, personal property not taken by widow
Horses, cow, agricultural implements, household and kitchen furniture, etc.
ELIZABETH SWITZER, admr.

Application for Liquor License
THOMAS STEPHENS – Perrysville
HENRY D. SPRAGUE - Eugene

Wednesday, August 16, 1882

Highland
Mr. TEAGARDENER, of Laporte, is visiting her sister, Mrs. McCALLA.

BEN DOSS and wife are making arrangements to start to Oregon soon.

Clinton
OTIS PERRIN returned home from Texas last week. OTE is amply satisfied with his experience as a cowboy and the fiery courser of the equestrian race has greater charms for him than ever.

Mrs. HYNDSHAW, of Chicago, was down last week visiting her husband of the firm "BROWN & HYNDSHAW".

Miss BELLE CRANE, of Dana, was in town on last Sunday, visiting her sister ALICE and her brother JIM.

JAMES QUINLAN has bought the saloon stock and fixtures heretofore belonging to B.F. LAMB, and has transferred them to his old stand, where he will still carry on the business as usual.
Montezuma Era

Home News
CHARLEY HASTY, of Lafayette, is in town visiting his grandfather, JOHN HASTY.

Miss NELLIE GAYLORD, of Knoxville, IL, is here visiting her sister, Mrs. R.A. PARRETT.

JOE GRIFFIN is dangerously ill with typhoid fever. There is very little hope for his recovery.

FRANK MUSSON, of Opedee, is as happy as a bumble bee in clover time. It is a girl, and the very image of its good looking mother.

JAMES CRANE, druggist of Clinton and a former citizen of Newport, was in town on Friday last shaking hands with his many young friends.

W.A. DUNCAN and his wife, a daughter of T.S. HOOD, of Helt township, are in from Oskaloosa, IA, on a visit to her parents. Mr. DUNCAN is a photographer, and attended the National Photographers Convention held at Indianapolis last week.

Miss KATE GASAWAY is seriously ill.

WILLIE HALL, son of MARTHA HALL, is quite sick.

Mrs. MARY CRAIG, was taken down quite ill on last Monday morning.

MIKE CASEY, of Clinton, drew $1,600 arrears of pension the other day.

Esq. W.F. KERNS, of Bono, Helt township, drew over $900 back pension a few days since.

BRENTON NICHOLS left yesterday for Kansas, in which State he intends to locate and teach school this winter. BRENTON is a model young man, and we are sorry he has left us.

NOAH BROWN, of Eugene township, has rented the HENSON property, north of the harness shop, and is going to move to Newport sometime next week to work on the new gravel road.

J.A. MOORE of Chrisman, IL, was in town on Friday last, and gave the Hoosier a short call. He was a former resident of Clinton, this county, and is now working in a tile factory at Chrisman.

PERRY DeHAVEN, MERRITT LAMB and GEORGE DOUGLASS have the Kansas fever and are going to move to that State. Joy go with them, but we are of the opinion that some of them will be wending their way back to old Vermillion before many years.

Obituary
ISAAC NICHOLS, of Dana, who has been ill for some time, died on last Saturday morning, aged 60 years. He had been a resident of this county since a child. His parents were old settlers of this county. He was a member of the Methodist Church.

Obituary
Mrs. SARAH ANDERSON, wife of ELIJAH ANDERSON, of Newman, IL, died August 9, 1882, of typhoid fever. She was born June 15, 1831, and was married to E. ANDERSON September 3, 1848. Mrs. ANDERSON was a member of the M.E. Church and was a consistent Christian. The remains were interred in the Albin Cemetery. The following brothers and sisters were present: E.D. ANDERSON, JOSEPH ANDERSON, H.C. JAMES, Mrs. MARY JENKS, of this county. The funeral was preached by Rev. J.R. REASONER.

Obituary
WALTER B. MOFFATT of Perrysville died on last Sunday night, aged 60 years. The deceased had been a resident of this county since 1838. A year ago or more, he had a severe attack of typhoid fever from which he never fully recovered. He has suffered much in the last 12 months but bore it patiently. He was a warm and genial hearted citizen, and had many good traits of character. His funeral occurred yesterday, and was very respectably attended by neighbors and acquaintances.

A Cozy Boarding House
Mrs. MARGARET RAMSEY has thoroughly renovated her boarding house, east of the public square, and is now prepared to entertain boarders in first-class style. Persons wanting board by either the day or week can do no better than to give her a call. Prices reasonable. Schoolteachers will find it a pleasant stopping place during the Institute.

Wednesday, August 23, 1882

Tired of Life
ELLA DAVIS, who has been living a dissolute life, premeditated suicide last night. She procured a vial of laudanum and repaired to SLUSSER's garden for the purpose stated. Before swallowing the poison, she told someone of her intentions. Officer LOUTZENHEIZER and DUNKIN were summoned and convinced her not to carry out the act. They succeeded in getting the poison. Her age is about 17 years, and her father and mother are both dead. She is terribly distressed, and steps have been taken to place her at the poor farm, where she can have medical treatment.
Danville, IL, Daily Commercial

Clinton
Mrs. BRUCE with her bevy of buxom daughters has moved into the property lately purchased of Mrs. BELLE ANDERSON.

Mr. NOURSE, father-in-law of P.Z. ANDERSON and JAMES WILSON, is among us on a visit to relatives and friends.

The contract for building the new M.E. Church has been let to Mr. MATER, of Danville, IL.

BOB WISHARD is noted for his regular attendance at church; L.O. BISHOP for his early rising; BILL HAGENBAUGH for truthfulness; FINLEY D. for the time of his birth; JOE UTTER as a teller of moral stories.

Mr. and Mrs. E. RANKIN have lost their youngest child. It was buried at 10 a.m. Tuesday.

Home News
BILL REED, residing a short distance south of town, is going to sell out and move to Kansas.

BOB JAGGERS has bought the ANDY DICKEN property and there is talk that he is going to get married.

WILLIAM L. TRIPLETT has sold his stock of drugs and building to HARRY RHOADS, of Tower Hill, IL, consideration $1,000. Mrs. RHOADS is a nephew of M.G. RHOADS.

W.H. WOOSTER, a son of H.M. WOOSTER of Montezuma, aged 22 years, died at Arcanum, OH, on the 14th instant. He was a model young man, a Christian and very highly esteemed by all his neighbors and friends. His remains were brought back to Montezuma and interred in Oak Hill Cemetery.

Mrs. IVA A. SEARS is down sick.

AL MILLER, of Helt's Prairie, has ordered a new organ.

JAMES CHIPPS' little boy is now in a fair way to getting well.

Mrs. CRAIG don't seem to be improving to any considerable extent.

LINK SANDERS, of this township, took down suddenly ill on Monday last.

BOB MYERS and family start for Hutchinson, KS, on Saturday next, where they expect to make their future home.

LINK SANDERS, residing 5 miles west of town, has a new baby at his house. We did not learn the gender, but understand it arrived here on Friday.

ROBERT WRIGHT, of Parke County, father of WILLIAM P. WRIGHT of this place, has bought Dr. LEWIS SHEPARD's property in the west part of town. Consideration $1,650.

FIN STOKES is talking of moving back to the farm. He is tired of town life. We think he has come to conclusion, town is a poor place for a farmer.

We are glad to learn that GEORGE SKIDMORE, of Helt's Prairie, who is afflicted with cancer of the face and neck, is reported to be getting better. Hope he will get well.

The two additional teachers for the Newport School are Miss RENA RUGAN, of Terre Haute, IN, for the intermediate department, and Miss MATILDA HOLMES of Delphi, the primary department. Both are strangers, but we understand come well recommended.

The wife of JACK HARRIS, the colored woman who eloped from Clinton with a barber by the name of SMITH, and located at this place, has made application in the September term of Circuit Court for a divorce. She intends to marry the gentleman she eloped with.

Personal
BILL SWINDELL, of Highland, is going to move to Kansas the first of next month.

FRANK H. MUNSON, of Opedee, is going back to Onargo, IL, to engage in the drug business.

Mrs. LOU ALDRIDGE and children, of Onargo, IL, are visiting her brother, FRANK H. MUNSON, of Opedee.

Our old friend, W.B. FOLAND, and his good looking wife, of Troy, OH, are in town visiting his parents.

FRANK COFFEEN, of Homer, IL, is here on a visit, the guest of OL DAVIS. It is reported that he is sweet on Miss JENNIE ADAMS.

POLK HOOD, of Eugene, the most successful fisherman on the Wabash, was in the city on Friday.

ELMER HENSON has returned from Hutchinson, KS, and intends to remain here. He has got enough of the grasshopper country.

Miss IDA ROBERTSON, of Bartholomew County, IN, a former citizen of Newport, is here on a two weeks visit. She is as good looking and jovial as ever.

D.C. JOHNSON, of Clinton, was in the city on Friday last talking up life insurance to our citizens. He represents one of the best companies in the United States.

Mrs. C.W. WARD, Mrs. J. JUMP, and Miss EVA COLLETT left on last Monday morning for Crawfordsville, to be gone one week, on a visit to their cousin, Miss MINNIE H. CAMPBELL.

Matrimony
HENRY FABLE and Miss SALLIE HIGGINS, both of Eugene, were united in wedlock on last Sunday evening, Rev. J.H. HOLLINGSWORTH performing the ceremony.

Obituary
JOE GRIFFIN, aged about 17 years, died at 5 o'clock on last Sunday evening at the residence of Mrs. HARRIET TURPENING, of typhoid fever. His funeral took place on Monday. He was interred at the Highfill Cemetery, 3 ½ miles south of town.

Executor's Sale of Personal Property
Estate of SETH HAWORTH, deceased
Sale to be held at residence of the deceased at 1 p.m.
Wednesday, September 13, 1882
Personal property not taken by widow
Horses, cows, sheep, hogs, agricultural machinery, corn, wheat, oats, hay, household and kitchen furniture, etc.
AMOS COOK, Executor of Will

Wednesday, August 30, 1882

Highland
A little child of HENRY VERBRICK died on last Thursday.

A Mr. WHETSON, living at Alta, died on last Wednesday night.

TOM HELT, of this township, has gone to Missouri State Penitentiary to see his son SCOTT HELT.

JOHN HEAVY, of Parke County, who is to teach our school this winter, was here last week.

Departed this life on last Sunday morning, August 20, 1882, at 3 o'clock, Mrs. VALENTINE CONLEY, formerly Miss VALENTINE TAYLOR, a step daughter of JOHN RUSSELL. She was married about a year ago to JAMES CONLEY, of Newman, IL, where she died. Her remains were brought to this place for burial on Sunday night and on Monday a large number of friends and relatives followed her to her last resting place. She was about 22 years of age, and leaves an infant child, loving husband, a mother, and brothers and sisters to mourn her loss. She was loved by all her acquaintances and associates and many were tears shed by them at her burial.

Accident
On last Saturday, FERDINAND BAILEY, a young man of Eugene township, aged about 24 years, was instantly killed by a giant powder explosion while engaged in blowing up stumps for SAMUEL MALONE, an old farmer of that township. He had just put a charge in a stump and stepped back a safe distance to await the result. As the charge seemed to be slow, he concluded the fuse had gone out, and he started up to the stump with a basket of percussion caps and ten pounds of powder. When he got in 30 feet of the stump, the charge went off, and the concussion exploded the caps and powder in his basket, blowing Mr. BAILEY at least 30 feet from where he was, and killing him instantly. The explosion blew off both his arms, stripped him of his clothing, and mashed him to a jelly. Coroner BRINDLEY was notified and held an inquest.

Rescued
One week ago Tuesday, water burst into the mines of TRUNKEE Bros., imprisoning WILLIAM CUBIT in his room, where he has since remained without food or water. Since that time his fellow miners, believing him to be alive, have worked day and night bailing out water, and did not cease their efforts until yesterday when he was rescued alive. He was brought to his brother's house, where he now is very weak and delirious, being cared for by many kind hands. For 9 long days and night, his fellow miners worked without pay to rescue him. Later – WILLIAM CUBIT died at 7:30 last evening.

Covington People's Journal

Clinton
Mrs. BASSETT, of El Paso, TX, is lying very low at N.C. ANDERSON's. Her husband is with her.

JOHN E. RYAN has closed the trade with B.F. MOREY and will soon leave for the State of Kansas. We wish him success in his new location.

Gen. HUNTER has traded his residence to McBETH for the hotel furniture, and will take possession of the hotel this week. The Gen. is a genial and businesslike gentleman, and we predict for him a liberal patronage.

Home News
JOHN NICHOLS has been appointed executor of the Estate of ISAAC NICHOLS, deceased.

A five months old child of JOE GARRETT, residing west of town, died on last Monday evening.

JOHN E. RYAN has sold his farm of 270 acres, 3 miles south of Clinton, to BENJAMIN F. MOREY & Son for $9,000.

JOSEPH JAMES, WHITE JAMES, and WRIGHT JAMES, have bought the GASKILL farm at Summit Grove. $60 per acre was the price paid.

GEORGE BASINGER's wife, of this township, took down suddenly ill on last Monday morning and died at 9 o'clock the same day.

Obituary
Little WILLIE HALL, aged 9 years, a son of MARTHA HALL of this place, died on last Monday afternoon. WILLIE was a bright and intelligent little boy and his death will be deeply regretted by his young playmates. The funeral occurred yesterday afternoon.

Death
FRANK STURM, a young boy of about 14 years old, was smothered to death in the wheat elevator at the Eugene Station on last Monday evening. We did not learn any of the particulars. It is supposed he was playing in the chute, when a load of wheat was being emptied into the elevator and was smothered down before he was able to extricate himself.

Teacher's Institute
The Teacher's Institute is now in progress at this place. Teachers attending are:

WILSON, A.J.
PARKER, A.A.
PERRIN, JOHN W.
McMEEN, JAMES M.
McNEILL, CHARLES G.
DEALAND, GEORGE W.
JAMES, HATTON
CAMPBELL, RALPH
SMITH, JOHN L.
STURM, GEORGE W.
NEAL, S.H.
BROOKBANK, J.W.
WATSON, GEORGE L.
HEATON, E.M.
ATWOOD, R.J.
CAMPBELL, D.M.
WOODY, C.A.
WILTERMOOD, J.A.
DON CARLOS, ORA
NIXON, VICTOR
WATSON, MARION
JONES, FRANK
KERNS, W.A.
HOLMES, M.L.
McCREA, W.C.
PADRICK, J.J.
CAMPBELL, J.
JACKSON, C.B.
LEWIS, JAMES A.
JAMES, MILTON
HEAVY, JOHN
MEADE, DAVID
MORGAN, B.A.
PERRIN, JAMES R.
MERRIMAN, ANNA
CADY, LENNA
WINANS, IVA
PORTER, MARY
MALONE, EVA
JORDAN, CARRIE
WALKER, ANNIE M.
RUSH, ALMA
McDONALD, CARRIE
STRAIN, LIZZIE M.
McMEEN, ALICE
KILPATRICK, LILLIE
HENDERSON, NELLIE
GAYLORD, NELLIE
KEYES, S.L.
STOKESBERRY, EUGENE
RUNYAN, RENA C.
THOMPSON, ALICE
AIKMAN, HATTIE
WELLS, JESSIE B.
MITCHELL, IRENA A.
STONE, EMMA
MURPHY, MARY E.
DUFFY, MAGGIE
EGGLESTON, FLORA
FRENCH, LIZZIE
DOWELL, EMMA
MINSHALL, NETTIE
MOFFATT, IDA
FINNEY, ALICE
McROBERTS, ALDA
ELLIS, FLORA
MOODY, D.W.

Perrysville
Mrs. J.C. McKIBBEN started last week for Dakota, to visit her husband at the Indian Agency, near Yankton.

ALLEN LANGLEY has got tired of hotel keeping after a month's experience, and quit the business and the Wabash Hotel is vacant again.

THOMAS GLOVER and wife, of Ash Grove, MO, former residents of this township, are visiting relatives here at present.

CHARLEY CHEZUM, who recently sold part of his farm, sold his personal property at public sale last Saturday. He talks of going west in a short time.

Wednesday, September 6, 1882

Personal
Mrs. R.A. DAVIS arrived here yesterday morning from Kansas to see her mother, Mrs. MARY CRAIG, who is lying at the point of death.

J.M. GUILLIAMS, a teacher of Latin, Greek and German languages in the Danville, IL, Normal College, was in town on Thursday last.

Home News
CAL HUGHES has been appointed administrator of the Estate of WALTER B. MOFFATT, deceased.

Married
At the U.B. Parsonage on August 29, 1882, by Rev. W.H. JONES, Mr. WILLIAM PEER and Miss ELIZABETH BRADBURY, all of Dana, IN.

Married
On September 1, 1882, at the residence of SAMUEL PILES, in Helt township, WILLIAM H. RANDALL was united in marriage to FLORA BEYMER, Rev. J.A. MAST officiating.

The Board of County Commissioners met in Regular session on Monday last. Present – JAMES A. ELDER, JACOB L. THOMAS, and JAMES R. DUNLAP. Retail liquor licenses were granted to HARRY SPRAGUE of Eugene, and THOMAS W. STEPHENS, of Perrysville. There were remonstrances against MORGAN TUCKER and FRANK SLATER, of Clinton. Their cases were put off until Friday of this week.

Death
We are called upon this week to record the death of Mrs. MARY CRAIG, who departed this life at 11 o'clock on last Thursday morning, after a few weeks illness. The deceased was born in Lawrence County, IN, and had she lived until next month, would have been 66 years of age. She moved to this county in 1830, and was united in marriage to OWENS CRAIG in 1837, whom she lived with happily until June 27, 1862, when her husband was taken from her by death. OWENS CRAIG was a prominent and influential citizen of this county, having served the people of this county as sheriff for two terms, being elected to the first term in 1846, and then re-elected again. Mrs. CRAIG was a noble and generous hearted woman, and was respected and esteemed by everybody. Her funeral occurred on last Friday afternoon from her late residence, one building north of the Hoosier State office, and was very respectably attended by her neighbors and friends. Rev. W.H. JONES, of the U.B. Church was the officiating minister. After the short services her remains were followed by her grief stricken friends to the Wimsett Cemetery, and there quietly laid away to moulder back to mother dust. Although not a member of church, there were no better Christian women than Mrs. MARY CRAIG. She was the mother of 7 children, 6 of whom survive her.

L.R. HENDERSON, of Fremont County, IA, is visiting his cousin, JESSE HOUCHIN of Helt township. Mr. HENDERSON was born in this county, and is now a member of the Legislature from his county. SAM CHANDLER, another Vermillion County boy, is Sheriff of Fremont County.

Miss DORA MOFFATT, an attractive school madam, was in town last week at her uncle's, THOMAS CUSHMAN's.

Personal
W.F. FORD, of Helt township, and his brother-in-law, THEOPILAS AMMERMAN of Parke County, were in town on Saturday.

Mrs. L.E. ZENER left on last Saturday for Jacksonville, FL, where she intends to remain with her sister for one year. Her residence will be occupied by J. JUMP and lady during her absence.

Highland
PERRY MERRIWETHER has rented the old BRICKER farm and will move here in a few weeks.

CALE JACKSON, of this township, starts on Wednesday for Purdue University.

LELIA KERNS, MOLLIE MAST and SCOTT AIKMAN, of Bono, and SAM JACKSON, of Dana, and quite a number of others will start to the State Normal the beginning of this term.

It is reported that IRA ANDREWS, of this township, and Miss KOONSE, of New Goshen, will be married before long.

WILLIAM RANDALL and FLORA BEYMER were united in matrimony on last Tuesday by Rev. J.A. MAST.

CHARLES BROWN and NELLIE RUSSELL are about to step over the broomstick. Also ENOCH JACKSON and LUCY GARRETT. Time will tell.

Clinton
Mrs. MAY PLATT and her mother PHOEBE PLATT were on a visit to Terre Haute last week. MAY's health has greatly improved. She finds this climate to be more salubrious than that of the State of New York.

Perrysville
CHED HUGHES and family started last week for Kansas, where he intends to locate.

CHARLEY FLESHMAN started again last week for the grasshopper state.

D.C. SMITH will this week remove his family to Crawfordsville, where he has been engaged in business for sometime.

ART G. ELBERSON of this place, who is engaged in a carriage shop in Covington, spent last Sunday with friends here.

ALBERT KERNS, of this place, has been engaged to teach the Jordan School two miles southwest of town.

Dr. J.W. SMITH is about to remove to and locate in Crawfordsville.

Mrs. JOHN SHAGLEY, of Kansas, is visiting relatives in this township.

SAM DUNLAP will start this week with his household goods for Kansas, whither his wife has already gone.

A number of Odd Fellows of this place, attended the funeral last Sunday of a Mr. PRESCOTT, an old and prominent citizen of Covington.

CHARLEY AYERS Jr., who recently bought JAMES COOK's house and lot, was married last week, and now has a bird to put in his cage.

Wednesday, September 13, 1882

The Mound
Mr. WILLIAM HOOD has his little son CHARLIE under the care of Dr. SPAIN, in Terre Haute. We hope soon to hear of his recovery.

WILLIE GROVES and his mother, of Terre Haute, have returned to their old home to spend a few weeks. WILLIE is in very feeble health.

Miss SALLIE KEYES has been employed to teach in the Dana School. She is a teacher that has given good satisfaction wherever she has taught.

Montezuma
The 76th birthday of old father KERNS was duly celebrated by his children on Monday last. All the former except one son were present while the remembrance of the happy faces of some 20 of his grandchildren has made the old veteran feel good ever since.

Mrs. M.A. SIMPSON is from old age and general debility lying very low at her daughter's and will not long survive.

The many friends of Mrs. WILLIAM DERRINGTON will be sorry to learn of her very poor health with no immediate prospect of recovery.

Eugene
Misses HATTIE, FANNIE, and ANNIE TOWLE started Monday morning for Evanston, IL, to attend the school at that place.

N.B. MACK has been employed to teach the school at Lodi. MELVIN STURM, the former teacher at that place, has bought an interest in a dry goods store there.

The following persons have been employed to teach the school in this township: GEORGE L. WATSON and Miss LACIE EDMONDS in town; MARION WATSON at Shelby's; Miss ALICE McMEEN at Whipple's; JOSIAH CAMPBELL at Sproules; DAVID CAMPBELL at Malone's; and DAVID MEADE at Porter's. No teachers have been employed for either Lindsay or Patrick Schools.

Dr. RICHARDSON has opened a drug store in HEIDBREDER's building.

Dr. W.C. EICHELBERGER will leave in a few days for Philadelphia, where he will pursue studies on the eye and ear.

Home News
W.J. PLACE supports a gold headed cane, the gift of his son, L.J. PLACE.

NORTH CRAIG has sold his farm, consisting of 97 acres, to JOHN W. PARRETT for $1,750.

A.L. SCONCE, a former resident of Eugene, is running a blacksmith shop in Mattoon, IL.

There is a report that CHARLEY DUNLAP and Miss ZILLA CADY will be united in wedlock tomorrow.

Miss CELIA JACKSON has moved down to Dana, where she intends to engage in dressmaking.

Our public school opened here on Monday last with 130 pupils in attendance. The teachers are J.W. PERRIN, principal; J.J. PADRICK, grammar department; Miss RENA RUGAN, intermediate; and Miss MATILDA HOLMES, primary department.

Accident
LEVI COOK, who resides at Elwood, Vermilion County, IL, was married on last Sunday week, and on the Monday morning following, had an arm torn off by a threshing machine. He was attempting to put a belt on while the machine was in motion when his arm caught in the fanning wheel and was torn off in an instant.

Personal
JOE DAVIS left for Greencastle yesterday to attend the Asbury University School.

PERRY THOMAS and JOHN COLLETT Jr. left yesterday morning for Wabash College.

Mrs. EMMA DAVIS left yesterday for her home in Kansas. She was accompanied by her brother, NORTH CRAIG.

Dr. JOE WHITE, of Helt township, and Dr. FRANK DAVIS of Clinton, left yesterday for Indianapolis to attend medical college.

H.C. SMITH and W.T. FERGUSON have dissolved partnership by mutual consent.

CHARLEY DAVIS, EDDIE WHITE and SEIGEL ALDRIDGE, of Helt's Prairie, and ELMER DAVIS, of this township, left on last Saturday for Paxton, IL, to attend school at that place.

HENRY HOLLINGSWORTH being desirous of retiring from the grocery business, will sell his stock of goods on favorable terms to the right man. Call and see him if you want to secure a bargain.

Owing to my disability, I am compelled to go out of the business. I will sell my entire stock, or a part of it, to suit the purchaser. It is a number one location for a harness shop.
W.P. HENSON

Real Estate Transfers for Month of August 1882
SAMUEL E. KAUFMAN etal to CLINTON WATSON
Lot 18, block 13, in Dana - $100

JAMES OSBORN and wife to WAKEFIELD INGRAM
215 ½ acres in Helt township - $7,000

MARY GIBSON to CHARLES A. BROWN etal
Lot 21, in Hillsdale - $50

JOHN H. FINNELL to JOHN H. BOGART
40 acres in Clinton township - $775

JOHN W. REED and wife to WILLIAM D. McFALL
40 acres in Helt township - $800

JOHN G. BRYSON and wife to WATKIN DAVIS and wife
Lot 9, block 26, in Clinton - $2,500

United States to JAMES W. HEPBURN
42.49 acres in Eugene township – patent

ROBERT J. GESSIE and wife to JOHN H. KRESS
Outlots 6 & 7, adjoining Gessie - $100

ANDREW M. DICKEN and wife to ROBERT S. JAGGERS
W ½ of lots 19 & 20, in Newport - $175

SARAH MORRIS and husband to LINDSAY BURTON
Lot 6, block 29, in Clinton - $60

ADDISON L. WHITCOMB and wife to JOHN KINSLEY
Undivided ½ of 80 acres in Clinton township - $1,000

MARY J. MOORE to ANNIE E. COOK
Lot 71, in Perrysville - $375

JAMES B. COOK and wife to CHARLES W. AYERS
Lot 71, in Perrysville for $375

ISAAC B. HEDGES and wife to JOHN DEEG
Lot 10, block 9, in Clinton - $100

WINFIELD P. THOMAS and wife to CHRISTOPHER TRUMP
40 acres in Vermillion township - $250

JOHN E. RYAN and wife to BENJAMIN F. MOREY and Son
270 acres in Clinton township - $9,000

E.T.H. & C. RR Co. to WASHINGTON KING
Lot 4, block 1, in Morey's addition to Clinton - $60

JOHN H. BOGART to JOSEPHUS COLLETT
40 acres in Clinton township - $775

WILLIAM L. TRIPLETT to MARTIN G. RHOADS
Part lot 72, in Newport - $2,000

JOSEPH UNDERWOOD and wife to LOUIS HOLLINGSWORTH
20 acres in Helt township - $500

RICHARD MALONE to LOUIS HOLLINGSWORTH
20 acres in Helt township - $400

ALBERT HENDERSON and wife to JONATHAN DILLON
30 acres in Vermillion township - $900

Obituary
Mrs. TABITHA POWERS, wife of Dr. JESSE L. POWERS, departed this life on last Saturday morning at 2 o'clock. She was stricken with paralysis on Thursday morning. She was born in Kentucky in 1802, removed to this county in 1834, and has ever since resided on the same farm in Helt township. The departed was a woman of more than ordinary intelligence. She was a member of the Christian Church and lived a very consistent life. She was loved and respected by all who knew her. Although being blind for 30 years, she had born her lot with patience and resignation. The funeral services which were very appropriate, were conducted by Rev. THOMAS GRIFFITH on Sabbath at 11 o'clock. Her remains were interred at the Cemetery near her late residence. The aged husband and family have the sympathy of all.

Notice of Administration
Estate of WALTER B. MOFFATT, deceased
September 1, 1882
CALVIN HUGHES, Admr.

Notice of Administration
Estate of ISAAC NICHOLS, deceased
August 26, 1882
JOHN NICHOLS, Admr.

Administrator's Sale of Personal Property
Estate of WALTER B. MOFFATT, deceased
Sale at residence in Perrysville at 10 a.m.
Thursday, September 28, 1882
Personal property not taken by widow
Household and kitchen furniture, corn in field, agricultural machinery, dental tools, etc. The corn is on decendent's farm in Fountain County.
CALVIN HUGHES, Admr.

Notice of Attachment and Garnishment
P.C. BULLINGTON vs. W.P. HARRIS & Co.
August 14, 1882
ALEX MURPHY, J.P.

HUGH H. CONLEY
Attorney at law
Newport

MARTIN G. RHOADS
attorney at law
Newport

BEN BLANCHARD
Attorney at law
Newport

JOHN D. CUSHMAN
Attorney at law
Newport

J.C. SAWYER
O.B. GIBSON
Attorneys at law
Newport

J. JUMP
C.W. WARD
Attorneys at law
Newport

F.S. CUMBERLAND
Furniture
Montezuma

T.J. GROVES
Shorthorns, Berkshires
Dana

G.W. McCUNE
Flour exchange depot
Montezuma

Wednesday. September 20, 1882

The Mound
The finest peaches that we have eaten this season grew on JAMES OSBORN's old farm.

Montezuma
GEORGE W. MOORE has sold his bakery to the KEMP Bros., and has gone on a prospecting tour to Kansas, wither he talks of emigrating.

JOHN H. LINN's family have all joined him at Dana, except their daughter ALICE, who on account of her severe illness remains here with her uncle, Mr. KAYLER.

This weeks changes of residence include Mr. SITES to the HUGHES property on Jefferson Street, Mr. SCHOOLCRAFT to the LINN property, Mrs. MOFFATT, late of Perrysville, to the LAVERTY property next to Mrs. LAVERTY's residence.

School opened here on the 18th instant with an excellent corps of teachers. Prof. WILLIAM TRUEBLOOD principal, Miss BELLE FORD teacher of grammar room, Miss DORA MOFFATT of intermediate room and Miss SARAH MOTTE, the primary room.

The society event here on Tuesday evening of last week was the marriage of OL AKINS and Miss HATTIE VANLANDINGHAM by Rev. GRIFFITH. The young couple are general favorites. They left the same night for a bridal tour to Cincinnati and other Ohio points from when they will return to Chrisman, IL, where Mr. AKINS is the agent for the I.B. & W.

Highland
JONES & WRIGHT have dissolved partnership and have been trying to settle for the last few weeks.

MAURICE JAMES, while working on a house last week, fell, severely injuring himself.

Mrs. SALLIE AYE has gone on a visit to Noblesville, her old home. Her father, of Watseka, IL, accompanied her on her trip.

A man by the name of GARLINGHOUSE is putting up a sawmill in Alta.

ISAAC WALLACE, of Huffmansville, IL, has been visiting here within the past week.

Rev. Mr. CONLEY, of Newman, Il, a Presbyterian minister, preached on last Sunday the funeral of Mrs. VAL CONLEY, who died some weeks ago and was brought here for burial. It was the best funeral discourse we have listened to for many years.

BENJAMIN DOSS and wife and Miss NELLIE RUSSELL will start on next Monday morning for Oakland, OR, where they expect to make their future home.

Home News
J.J. PADRICK has a new baby at his house. It's a boy.

Mrs. ELSIE EFAW, of Larchland, IL, is in Helt township visiting her father, JOSEPH JONES.

Senator O.P. DAVIS and his daughter, Mrs. ALICE ODEKIRK, spent last Saturday and Sunday at Onarga, IL, visiting his daughter, Mrs. FRANK MUNSON.

JONATHAN THORNTON and wife, and his son CHARLEY, spent last Friday, Saturday, and Sunday in town visiting his son WILLIAM F. THORNTON, who is a compositor in this office.

Rev. Mrs. M.L. GREEN, of Annapolis, is here visiting her daughter, Mrs. J.J. PADRICK.

GEORGE SKIDMORE, of Helt's Prairie, who is suffering from a cancer of the face and neck, is reported worse.

Married
JAMES ASBURY and Mrs. SARAH WISE, both of this township, were united in matrimony yesterday evening by Esq. JOHN W. HARTMAN.

Married
CHARLEY DUNLAP and Miss ZILLA CADY were united in wedlock, at the residence of the bride, this place, on last Wednesday evening, Rev. J.W. PARRETT officiating. Only a few invited guests were present.

Circuit Court September 1882

State of Indiana vs. TAYLOR SIMPSON
Selling liquor to a minor – judgment for defendant

State of Indiana vs. TAYLOR SIMPSON
Allowing minor to play billiards – judgment for defendant

HENRY S.S. FORD etal vs. CLARA A. FORD etal
Partition – final report and discharged

SAMUEL REED etal vs. ACHA REED etal
Partition – continued for full payment

MARY A. STANLEY vs. JESSE L. STANLEY
Divorce – continued for alias summons – decree granted

MARY J. LOVE vs. ARTHUR C. LOVE
Petition continued
CHARLES P. POTTS appointed guardian for child

HARRY WHITCOMB etal vs. HARVEY SHEPARD etal
Partition – continued for report of sale

PEYTON F. DOUGLASS etal vs. LUCY DICKEN
Petition – continued

MARY DOUGLASS etal vs. WILLIAM L. LITTLE, trustee
Petition for order to pay debts – continued

LUCRETIA FLEMMING vs. WESLEY FLEMMING
Divorce – continued – decree for plaintiff

State of Indiana, JASON W. POWELL, admr. vs. ISAAC BOGART etal
On bond – trial and decree

HENRY C. SMITH vs. LEWIS A. MORGAN
Appeal from Commissioners court – continued

ROSA BREWER vs. W.L. RABOURN, admr. of FIELDING RABOURN
Claim – dismissed

JOHN Q. VILLARS vs. W.L. RABOURN, admr of FIELDING RABOURN
Claim – judgment by agreement for $20

JABEZ B. OSMAN vs. JAMES D. HUNT
Attachment – dismissed

JOHN CLARK vs. JOSEPH CLARK
Appeal – dismissed

SUSANNA M. SMITH etal vs. JAMES A. REDINGER etal
Partition – decree for plaintiff

MARY A. SWAN vs. WILLIAM SWAN
Divorce – decree for plaintiff

MARTIN L. PIERCE vs. ENOS NEBEKER etal
Change of venue – dismissed

CAROLINE E. JONES vs. BEN BLANCHARD
Money converted – venue changed to Vigo County

MALISSA CORRY vs. WILLIAM CORRY
Divorce – decree for plaintiff

NELSON C. ANDERSON vs. JASPER A. MOORE etal
Partition – decree for plaintiff

MARY BELLE THOMPSON vs. ALEXANDER THOMPSON
Divorce – decree for plaintiff

JAMES M. MOORE vs. EMMA MOORE etal
Petition – decree for plaintiff

MARY A. SWAN vs. JOHN YOUNGER, JAMES WATSON
Foreclosure – demands $800 – dismissed

WILLIAM JONES vs. EMMA R. JONES
Divorce – continued

JENNIE HARRIS vs. JACKSON HARRIS
Divorce – decree for plaintiff

JOHN SUMMER vs. EMMA J. SUMMER
Divorce – decree for plaintiff

CORA E. IKE vs. MORGAN R. IKE
Divorce – continued

WILLIAM J. HENDRIX vs. I.B. & W. RR Co.
Appeal – dismissed

WILLIAM R. FINNEMORE vs. THOMAS W. STEPHENS
Note – dismissed by plaintiff

Singer Manufacturing Co. vs. DANIEL C. JOHNSON
Note – default – judgment for $80.51

JOHN COLLETT etal vs. ISAAC VANNEST etal
Note – default – judgment for $360.75

JOHN COLLETT etal vs. WALLACE MOORE etal
Note – dismissed

SARAH BOGART etal vs. JAMES SHAW etal
Partition – commissioners appointed to report next term

WILLIAM GIBSON vs. ROBERT FINLEY STOKES
Default – judgment for $95.80

Board of Commissioners September term 1882

Allowances

CLIFT, WILLIAMS & Co., repairs public buildings	10.40
WILLIAM L. TRIPLETT, public buildings	16.55
THOMAS CUSHMAN, public buildings	56.00
M. HEGARTY, public buildings	3.01
E.M. WALMSLEY, public buildings	91.18
W.C. MYERS, public buildings	10.50
THOMAS CUSHMAN, assessing	100.00
S.B. DAVIS, printing	162.00
W.B. BURFORD, stationary	66.25

Poor

JOE CONRAD, county asylum	781.20
ANTHONY FABLE, Eugene township	191.45
H.C. SMITH, Highland township	155.98
GEORGE W. STULTZ, Clinton township	183.38
JAMES CHIPPS, Vermillion township	337.95
DANIEL SEARS, Vermillion township	30.00
R.E. NICHOLS, Vermillion township	15.00
H.H. JAMES, Helt township	21.25
JAMES A. BARNES, Highland township	25.00
E.A. FLAUGHER, Eugene township	18.50
JAMES WALLACE, Vermillion township	48.75
C.S. DAVIS, county newspapers	3.50

Chunn's Gravel Road

R.D. MOFFATT	21.00
JOHN R. McNEILL	13.70
AMOS FLESHMAN	10.55
M.G. RHOADS	10.00
M.L. CASEY	20.00
P.Z. ANDERSON	105.00
W.C. MYERS	4.55

Perrysville and Southwest Gravel Road

S.B. DAVIS	16.00
CLAUDE MATTHEWS	5.70
B.F. MOREY	5.70
W.L. PORTER	9.05
M.G. RHOADS	10.00
P.Z. ANDERSON	166.00
W.C. MYERS	5.50

Newport and Quaker Point Gravel Road

S.B. DAVIS	14.00
W.C. MYERS	4.95

Clinton and Paris Gravel Road

H.O. PETERS	315.00
H.O. PETERS	140.70

Dana and Lebanon Gravel Road

GEORGE R. HICKS	14.50
H.E. CADE	14.50
MILTON WRIGHT	14.50
M.G. RHOADS	10.00
P.Z. ANDERSON	48.00

Feather Creek Gravel Road

S.B. DAVIS	16.00
W.C. MYERS	5.00

Bridges

JOHN T. HIGGINS	241.85
P.Z. ANDERSON	30.00
P.Z. ANDERSON	15.00
JOE HANN	2.50

Salaries

H.H. CONLEY, School Superintendent	195.00
M.L. HALL, County Board of Health	32.25
H.O. PETERS, Salary	200.00
ELIAS PRITCHARD, Salary	348.60
H.O. PETERS, Hazel Bluff Gravel Road	108.03
H.O. PETERS, County bonds	1000.00
H.O. PETERS, Interest on county bonds	804.75
W.C. MYERS, Criminals	132.80
W.C. MYERS, Courts	38.05
JAMES R. DUNLAP, account	21.00
JAMES A. ELDER, account	31.50
W.C. MYERS, account of dishes	10.85
P.Z. ANDERSON, account	19.50
THOMAS BRINDLEY, Janitor	50.00

Liquor license granted

H.D. SPRAGUE – Eugene
T.W. STEPHENS – Perrysville
MORGAN J. TUCKER – Clinton
FRANK SLATER – Clinton

Physicians appointed

JAMES WALLACE – Vermillion township and poor asylum
ERASTUS MACK – Helt township

Wednesday, September 27, 1882

Clinton

Dr. CROZIER suffered a severe attack of the ague the latter part of last week.

CHARLES WHITCOMB now has a new jeweler. He hails from Illinois.

MIRT H. STARK, who moved to Indianapolis last spring to engage in the practice of law, has returned, and will again wield the birch at Frog College in Helt township this winter.

Montezuma

AKINS & DAVIS have again got into business, this time as lumber dealers in consequence of which Dana has lately sold us considerable lumber, loses a customer.

GEORGE W. MOORE returned home last week from Kansas where he has bought him a farm, paying $800 therefore. He will remove thither about November 1st.

DAVID FENDER went to Indianapolis on Monday morning where he will go to work in the Bee Line Shops.

O.P. BROWN is having some elegant monuments erected in our Oakland Cemetery to the memory of the members of his family, which he will shortly remove there from other cemeteries.

Home News
Mrs. ANN DILLOW has been quite sick for several weeks.

Little FRANK BLUNK, down on Extension Street, is seriously ill.

PARK HUNTER, son of M.C. HUNTER Jr., is seriously sick with some kind of fever.

Mrs. MARGARET RAMSEY, who has been sick for six weeks, is still confined to her bed.

GEORGE MAHAN, residing 1 ½ miles southwest of here, pulled out on last Sunday to leave for Kansas.

Mrs. GEORGE W. ODELL, of Hutchinson, KS, a former resident of this place, is seriously ill.

GEORGE ELDER and Miss MATTIE TEMPLE, of Helt township, are to be married today. Also IRA ANDREWS and Miss NOLAN of the same township. They intend to go over to Indianapolis and take in the State Fair this week, and then settle down to business.

Mrs. ELIZABETH GRIFFIN has been brought home from the Insane Asylum, and is pronounced cured.

Wedding
ED SMITH and Mrs. JENNIE HARRIS, who was divorced from her husband at the last term of circuit court, were united in wedlock on Sunday last, Esq. SAMUEL C. HOLLINGSWORTH performing the ceremony with the dignity becoming an officer of his rank. Both the contracting parties are colored. The nuptials were witnessed by JOE HANN and a few other town sports.

Marriage licenses were issued yesterday for WILLIAM H. JACKSON and ELIZABETH ANN STEELE, of Clinton township.

Personal
JOHN W. GALLOWAY has gone down to Ellettsville, his old home, on a short visit.

Mrs. THOMAS McPHERRON, of Jacksonville, IL, daughter of H.S. CADY, is here on a visit.

Uncle BEN HARRISON, of Clinton township, now 78 years of age, was in town on Monday last and is nearly as spry as a young man.

Wednesday, October 4, 1882

Home News
QUINCY MYERS, son of Sheriff MYERS, is down with the typhoid fever.

It is rumored that FRANK TURNER and Miss LISSA HASTY are arranging for a journey together down the stream of time.

Married
At the U.B. Parsonage, on September 28, 1882, by Rev. W.H. JONES, Mr. CHARLES A. BROWN of Highland, and Miss NELLIE V. RUSSELL, of Hillsdale.

W.P. HENSON and son have bought out HENRY HOLLINGSWORTH's stock of groceries on the west side.

GEORGE DOUGLAS who moved to Kansas a couple of weeks ago, is dissatisfied with the country and is going to move back here.

Mrs. ELIZABETH DALLAS and her son WILBER DALLAS, of St. Paul, Minnesota, are in town visiting, the guests of J.W. PARRETT and family.

BOB VAUGHN and Miss ALICE JAMES, of Helt's Prairie, are making the necessary arrangements to be spliced on the 15th of this month. Both have our consent.

Rev. W.H. JONES, pastor of the U.B. Church at this place for the past year, left with his family on Friday last for Kentland, Newton County, IN, his new field of labor. Brother JONES is a conscientious man, and while here we believe he tried to do his duty.

Married
At the residence of the bride, in Helt township, at 8 o'clock on last Wednesday evening, by Rev. THOMAS AIKMAN, a M.E. minister of the Nebraska Mission Conference, Mr. GEORGE ELDER and Miss MATTIE TEMPLE. Both have the best wishes of their many friends.

Rev. THOMAS AIKMAN, of the Nebraska M.E. Conference, who has lately located in Bono, this county, his old home, was in town on Monday. He has been given the Howard, Parke County, circuit for this coming year by Elder BUCKLES.

Sick List
A.R. HOPKINS and two children; Mrs. MARGARET RAMSEY; Mrs. JOE DILLOW; Miss FANNIE NAGLE; FRANK FORTNER; Mrs. SALLIE ASTON. Mr. HOPKINS has about recovered, but his son MYRT is dangerously ill and the chances of his recovery are slim.

At latest accounts, Mrs. HENRY HOLLINGSWORTH, who is undergoing treatment at the Insane Asylum, is no better and is not able to recognize anyone.

JAMES A. LEWIS, who resided near Gessie, Highland township, died of consumption on last Sunday evening. He was a member of the M.E. Church, and a kind hearted, Christian gentleman. His funeral took place yesterday.

Death
Mrs. MYRTLE BASSETT, daughter of the late AQUILLA NEBEKER, of Clinton, died of consumption in that city on Tuesday of last week, aged 25 years, 8 months, and 10 days. The deceased was an estimable lady and had a host of warm friends in this county. The funeral occurred on Thursday last and was very largely attended. The funeral discourse was preached by Rev. MARTIN, President of Indiana Asbury University.

Tricky Husband
JOHN FRAZIER, of Terre Haute, who was united in wedlock to MALINDA MALONE, WILLIAM L. MALONE's widow of Helt township, about one year ago, has proved to be an uncomfortable husband. On Tuesday of last week, he sent her down to Clinton on business, and during her absence, sold about $1,000 worth of property and lit out for tall timber. His whereabouts are unknown, but a part of the property he sold has been reprieved and the purchasers will have to lose it as he was not her authorized agent. It is believed he was headed east.

Highland
A Mr. CHAMBERLAIN, of Cincinnati, is visting his nephew, SAMUEL PEARMAN.

IVA GARRETT, aged 11 years, daughter of Mr. and Mrs. GARRETT, died on last Wednesday evening of typhoid fever.

CHARLEY BROWN and NELLIE RUSSELL were married on last Thursday by Rev. W.H. JONES, of Newport.

Wednesday, October 11, 1882

Montezuma
GEORGE W. MOORE has sold his house and lot to O.P. BROWN for $1,000, and will next week move to Cherokee County, KS, to engage in farming.

Married
By the Rev. THOMAS GRIFFITH, on Wednesday, October 4, 1882, Mr. FRANK WATKINS, Junior member of WATKINS Bros., to Miss CARRIE WALMSLEY, all of Montezuma.

The family of THOMAS WILLIAMSON, who moved from Hillsdale to Hendricks County last year, returned here on Friday last, and have rented a house in the south part of town. TOM failed to come, and Mrs. WILLIAMSON is left to struggle and support her family the best she can.

Home News
Senator O.P. DAVIS and his daughter, Mrs. ALICE ODEKIRK, went out to Onargo, IL, last week to visit his daughter, Mrs. FRANK MUNSON.

OTIS ODELL, of Hutchinson, KS, one of our former townsmen, arrived here last week. He came back after his girl and is going to take her home with him.

Mrs. COLBY BUSH, of Junction City, KS, daughter of JOHN HASTY, is here on a visit to her parents.

MYRT HOPKINS, son of A.R. HOPKINS, is lying at the point of death, and cannot possibly get well.

JACK MITCHELL, of Highland township, was in town on last Monday on his way to the Arkansas Hot Springs. He is in poor health, and thinks the waters of that noted resort will do him good.

VICTOR NIXON is down with the typhoid fever.

NORTH CRAIG and E.Y. JACKSON Jr. talk of selling out and moving to Kansas.

F.M. BISHOP and his new wife are going to move out to Garden City, KS, the first of next month, where he is talking of buying property and locating. We regret to lose such a valuable and public spirited citizen.

Obituary
PETER COSSEY, an old and respected farmer of Highland township, who had been suffering from a partial alienation of mind for several months, died at his home on Wednesday last, aged 70 years. The deceased was honest and industrious, and one among the wealthiest farmers in the county. He was born in Maryland in 1812, and settled in this county in 1832, where he had resided ever since. His funeral occurred on Thursday last and was very largely attended by his old neighbors and acquaintances. He made a will, and divided his large estate equally among his 7 children. He appointed JAMES COSSEY as executor of the estate.

Real Estate Transfers for Month of September 1882

CHARLES CHEZUM to AMOS FLESHMAN
80 acres in Highland township - $4,000

JOHN S. KIRKPATRICK and wife to LEWIS A. MORGAN
Lots 6 & 7, in Perrysville - $25

CAROLINE E. MILLIKIN and husband to T.H. SHELBY etal
-------- acres in Eugene township - $100

WILLIAM J. LAKE and wife to JOHN W. CASEBEER
Lots 19, 20, 21, & 22, in Alta - $500

LAURETTA PEARMAN heirs to SAMUEL PEARMAN
70 acres in Helt township - $640

JOSEPH S. STUTLER's estate to SILAS GOUTY
80 acres in Highland township - $4,000

SAMUEL AIKMAN etal to JOHN E. BILSLAND
Lots 10, 11, & 12, block 11, in Dana - $250

DANIEL W. GARDNER and wife to PHOEBE A. STAATS
Part of lot 10, block 11, in Clinton - $725

PETER S. MOUDY and wife to CHARLES R. TATE
Lot 13, in Gessie and Cushman's addition to Perrysville - $35

JOHN YOUNGER and wife to MARY B. ANDERSON
50.16 acres in Clinton township - $1,000

BENJAMIN HARRISON and wife to ADDISON L. WHITCOMB etal
2 acres in Clinton township - $200

PERRY DAY and wife to ROSA A. CANADY
------- near Eugene - $150

GEORGE ELDER etal to JOSIAH H. MERRIWETHER
3 ½ acres near Bono - $613

WILLIAM H. LANGLEY and wife to GEORGE E. WATT
Lot 28 and outlot in Perrysville - $175

ROBERT J. GESSIE and wife to JAMES C. STUTLER
Lot 34, in Gessie - $30

ELIZA J. JOHNSON to GEORGE F. CLAYTON
Outlot 5, in Perrysville - $250

ELLEN GLOVER to THOMAS D. GLOVER
Lot 3, in Stephen's addition to Perrysville - $200

PETER S. MOUDY and wife to JOHN TATE and wife
Lot 12, in G. and C's addition to Perrysville - $225

SAMUEL AIKMAN etal to OTIS M. KEYES
Lot 7, 8, & 9, block 11, in Dana - $200

MARGARET J. RUHL and husband to POLLY HIBBS
Lot 2, of McNeill's addition to Perrysville - $165

THOMAS S. HOOD and wife to OLIVER P. MARTIN
75 acres in Helt township - $3,000

GEORGE R. FINLEY and wife to JESSE DONEY etal
60 acres in Clinton township - $1,000

SARAH C. LEWIS and husband to JOHN F. DUGGER
1/9 of 7 acres in Helt township - $130

GEORGE W. HUNTER and wife to DAVID McBETH
Lot 4, and part lot 5, block 32, in Clinton - $1,200

SAMUEL AIKMAN Jr. to PETER AIKMAN
11 ½ acres, in Helt township - $340

PETER AIKMAN and wife to SAMUEL AIKMAN Jr.
8 acres in Helt township - $240

RICHARD A. CLEARWATERS to JAMES A. CLEARWATERS etal
10 acres, in Vermillion township - $200

WINFORD M. TAYLOR and wife to JOHN F. DUGGER
1/9 of 76 acres, in Helt township - $130

SAMUEL E. KAUFMAN and wife to THOMAS W. LADSON
Lot 13, block 13, in Dana - $100

JAMES GASKILL and wife to JOSEPH JAMES
115 acres in Helt township - $8,700

JOSEPH JAMES and wife to E. WHITE JAMES etal
100 acres in Helt township - $5,000

THOMAS HALL and wife to JABEZ B. OSMON
43 acres in Vermillion township - $1,475

ALFRED C. DEPUY and wife to JAMES H. BURNSIDE
19 ½ acres in Helt township for $565

JOHN E. RYAN and wife to EARL B. NOURSE
Part lots 2, 3, & 6, block 8, in Clinton - $1,000

SARAH A. McDANIEL to SAMUEL NAYLOR
36 acres in Eugene township - $800

HORACE O. PERRIN and wife to JOSEPHUS COLLETT
20 acres in Clinton township - $600

JOHN F. LANGSTON etal to JAMES KAUFMAN
20 acres in Helt township - $600

JOHN S. MILLER and wife to TAYLOR ADAMS
40 acres in Vermillion township - $800

F.G. IRWIN and wife to MICHAEL CONAWAY
Lot 63 in Eugene - $500

DAVID JONES and wife to ABRAHAM SOEY
10 acres in Vermillion township - $200

MATILDA M. KAUFMAN and husband to ALFRED SPURGEON
12 acres in Helt township - $300

Notice of Non-Residence
CUTHBERT F. KEYS and HIRAM SHEPARD vs. WILLIAM BOREN
Complaint 2244
J.C. SAWYERS attorney
WILLIAM BOREN is not a resident of Indiana
Must appear before third Monday of November, 1882
October 10, 1882
JAMES ROBERTS, Clerk
By NORTH CRAIG, Deputy Clerk

Notice of Non-Residence
MALINDA FRAZIER vs. JOHN FRAZIER
Complaint 2238
JUMP & WARD attorney
JOHN FRAZIER is not a resident of Indiana
Must appear before December 6, 1882
October 10, 1882
JAMES ROBERTS, Clerk
By NORTH CRAIG, Deputy Clerk

Wednesday, October 18, 1882

Perrysville
WILLIAM P. SMITH has bought the old Presbvterian Church, near his residence, and is tearing it down.

EDWARD SHEWMAKER and DORA LYONS, of this place, were married in Danville, IL, last Thursday.

WILLIAM DUNLAP, of this place, has gone down to the Hot Springs for the benefit of his health.

ALBERT KERNS, who has been teaching the Jordan School, has been confined to his bed nearly 3 weeks with intermittent fever.

SHELBY PARKE and JACK PATTERSON are each running a bus between town and the railroad station.

Hon. J.F. COMPTON has gone to Dakota to take charge of the Indian School at the agency near Yankton, where J.C. McKIBBEN and family are located. He expects to be gone about 6 months.

ALLEN LANGLEY has retired from the Hotel De Wabash for the second time.

Highland
CHUTE and CLARENCE HOOKER, of Helt township, started to Kansas last week.

MOLLIE MAST, who is in attendance at the State Normal, spent Saturday and Sunday at home and returned on Monday.

CALVIN CRAIG, of this township, died of typhoid fever on last Sunday morning. He was buried at this place on Monday. Rev. JOHNSON, of Summit Grove, preached the funeral.

Dr. ROBERT HARRISON, of Kansas, is stopping at present with his brother, Dr. J.C. HARRISON of Hillsdale. He thinks of locating here.

Mrs. McCALLA and her son DAVID left this place on last Friday for Salem, OH, where they expect to make their future home.

An infant child of JAMES CONNELLY died and was buried on last Tuesday. The child's mother died only a few weeks ago.

Home News
It did not take GEORGE DOUGLAS long to get all he wanted out of Kansas. He arrived here on last Thursday morning, and intends to stay here now.

Letter List

DAVIS, W.B.	GODDIN, HENRY
HAYS, CHARLES E.	McGUIRE, HUGH
WRIGHT, ANNA	SLATER, SARAH
McCLARAM, ELIZA	HARE, MARY

Notice of Settlement of Estate
Estate of JOHN SMITH, deceased
October 14, 1882
JAMES ROBERTS, Clerk
By NORTH CRAIG, Deputy Clerk

Notice of Settlement of Estate
Estate of ALFRED CARMACK, deceased
October 14, 1882
JAMES ROBERTS, Clerk
By NORTH CRAIG, Deputy Clerk

Obituary
MYRT HOPKINS, son of A.R. HOPKINS, of this place, died at 20 minutes before 8 o'clock on last Wednesday morning, aged 17 years, 10 months, and 5 days. He was the oldest child and only son. He was a bright young man, and had many warm friends who sadly grieve over his loss to them. His disease was typhoid fever, with which he lingered for 4 weeks. His funeral took place on Thursday and was very largely attended.

Matrimony
On last Thursday evening, at about 8 o'clock, at the residence of the bride's mother, in this place, OTIS M. ODELL, of Hutchinson, KS, was united in marriage to Miss FLORA HASTY, the ceremony being performed by J.H. HOLLINGSWORTH, pastor of the M.E. Church. About 25 or 30 relatives and special friends witnessed the tying of the nuptial knots. In about 10 days the happy pair will start for their new home in Kansas.

Matrimony
JOE McCORMICK of this place, and Miss SALLIE CONAWAY, of Eugene, were united in wedlock on last Wednesday evening at the residence of the bride's parents. There were a very large number of invited guests present, who showered them with many presents.

Notice of Final Settlement of Estate
Estate of JAMES M. PAYTON, deceased
October 14, 1882
JAMES ROBERTS, Clerk
By NORTH CRAIG, Deputy Clerk

Executor's Sale of Personal Property
Estate of PETER COSSEY, deceased
Sale on Thursday, November 9, 1882
Sale at late residence one mile east of Gessie in Highland township
Personal property
31 three year old steers, lot of cows and calves, 25 hogs, 8 horses and colts, one self binding reaper, several hundred bushels of wheat in bin, lot of corn in field and crib, wheat in field, wagons, harness, household furniture, etc.
Dated October 10, 1882
JAMES COSSEY, executor

Notice of Sale of Real Estate
IRENA HAWORTH, SARAH HAWORTH, LAURA M. HAWORTH, IVA J. HAWORTH vs. MARTHA J. HAWORTH, ANNA LULU HAWORTH
Case No. 2237
Sale Thursday, November 16, 1882 on premises
N ½ NW fraction ¼ Sec 7 T 16 N R 10 W – 35 acres
NE ¼ Sec 7, Fraction – 2 acres
SE corner of NE ¼ Sec 7, Fraction – 9.84 acres
Total 46.84 acres
At the same time 46 acres in Edgar County, IL, will be sold the same day;
4 tracts were recently owned by SETH HAWORTH, deceased
M.G. RHOADS, Commissioner

Sale of Personal Property
Sale on Friday, October 20, 1882
Personal property
Horses, cattle, sheep, two farm wagons, one spring wagon, one set of double harness, two wheat drills, one corn drill, plows, and other farming implements, hay, 27 colonies of bees, two Cotswold bucks, books, and household goods, etc.
JESSE HOUCHIN
HENRY HOLLINGSWORTH, Caller
FRED HELT, Clerk

Wednesday, October 25, 1882

Highland township
Miss SHUMAKER, of Terre Haute, is visiting her uncle, D.B. DINSMORE.

CLIFTON DAVIS and ADDA FLEMMING, of this township, were married on last Thursday by Rev. WAINSCOTT.

Mrs. GARRETT is not expected to live at this writing.

Montezuma
Rev. Father SWAGERS is the Catholic Minister here now instead of Father BOEVER who has been transferred to Tell City, IN.

Mrs. JAMES TROWNSELL, of Tuscola, IL, who had been here for medical treatment here for some weeks for consumption, was taken home on Monday last. She died there on the 19th and was buried on the 22nd.

Mrs. MARTHA A. SIMPSON died of old age at the residence of her daughter, Mrs. WOOSTER, on Friday last. She had been a member of the Methodist Church for 59 years.

The wife of Mr. J.L. SWIFT died here on Sunday the 15th, of typhoid fever. She was much esteemed and her funeral was largely attended. She was in possession of a fine canary bird of more than usual intelligence. The little thing pined for her love and care, and dying within a few hours of its protector, was buried in the coffin with her.

Mrs. WILLIAM DARRINGTON died at the family residence here on Sunday after a long and severe illness. Her interment took place on Monday at New Discovery, east of Rockville.

The many friends of our popular and progressive merchant, E.G. WILSON, will be sorry to learn that the inability to make collections has forced him to make an assignment of all his property to W.N. ADKINS. It will be remembered Mr. WILSON was burned out here some 5 years ago, at which time he lost a large stock of goods. This severely crippled him, but he has manfully struggled, and now forced to take this unpleasant step, he does with, it is believed, assets more than sufficient to pay all his liabilities. Mr. WILSON has the heartfelt sympathy of all his fellow citizens who regard him a thoroughly honest man.

Home News
WILLIAM HERBERT and wife, OTIS M. ODELL and wife, and R.H. NIXON left for Kansas yesterday.

Mrs. MARGARET RAMSEY has been down sick for 10 or 11 weeks, and there seems to be no indication of her speedy recovery.

S.D. PEARMAN, of Helt township, was in town yesterday. He is going to sell off his personal property at public sale on the 4th of next month.

Matrimony
PETER COSSEY Jr. and Miss MARY BELLE HARRIS, both of Highland township, will be united in wedlock tomorrow.

The wife of HENRY HOLLINGSWORTH, who was taken to the Insane Asylum several months ago for treatment, was brought home on last Monday evening, and although not entirely cured, she is in a fair way to get well.

VICTOR NIXON was able to walk into the dining room yesterday for his dinner.

Sheriff MYERS' wife has been confined to her bed with affliction for over 2 years, and there is no probability that she will ever again be restored to health.

Death
GEORGE SKIDMORE died of cancer at 12 o'clock on Thursday last, aged 58 years. The deceased was a resident of Helt's Prairie, where he was born and raised. His father was one among the first settlers of this county, having located on Helt's Prairie in the early day when the Indians and wild beasts of the forest were quite numerous. The deceased was a worthy and enterprising citizen, esteemed and respected by everybody, and a consistent member of the M.E. Church. The funeral took place on Friday last at Salem Church and was very largely attended. The services were conducted by his pastor, Rev. E.R. JOHNSON, assisted by Rev. J.F. McDANIEL.

Valuable Farm for Sale
ADAM B. LITTLEPAGE advertises a valuable farm for sale. The farm is situated near Lodi, in Parke County, and residence is only 1 ¼ miles from the depot of the Toledo, Cincinnati, and St. Louis Railroad. It is one of the finest grain and stock farms in Parke County, and is underlaid with a thick vein of splendid coal.

Wednesday, November 1, 1882

Perrysville
W.T. FERGUSON and wife celebrated the 20th anniversary of their marriage one evening last week.

Mrs. HENRY CADE has gone to visit relatives at Baxter Springs, KS.

J.L. WEBSTER has removed to the farm of FRED BOLLA, one mile N of town.

WILLIAM McCRARY, who emigrated to the west several years ago, has emigrated back to this neighborhood.

J.M. HAIN will remove in a few days to Baraboo, WI, where he will engage in the saloon business.

JOHN COLLINS and ANN BRINKRUFF, residing in the west part of the township, were married here on last Thursday night.

TOM CLARKSON, who has been the chief moulder in COMINGORE's foundry for the last few years, will pull up stakes and leave here in a few days.

Home News
Mrs. MAGGIE HARSHAW, of Fontanelle, IA, daughter of JOSEPH A. MOREHEAD, is in here on a visit.

IKE AMBROSE, of Helt township, is down with a severe attack of the kidney disease, and it is thought to be doubtful whether he will recover.

Mrs. ABE THOMPSON, a daughter of T.S. HOOD, of Helt township, died on Thursday last.

Notice of Settlement of Estate
Estate of FIELDING RABOURN, deceased
October 30, 1882
JAMES ROBERTS, Clerk
By NORTH CRAIG, Deputy Clerk

Application for Liquor License
W.B. SIMPSON – Newport

Wednesday, November 8, 1882

BOB VAUGHN and Miss ALICE JAMES of Helt's Prairie, will be united in wedlock on Thursday evening of this week.

Notice to Non-Residents
GEORGE YOUNG vs. COLUMBUS PIERCE
Attachment of collection of money on account
COLOMBUS PIERCE is not a resident of Indiana
November 3, 1882
WILLIAM F. KERNS, J.P.

Montezuma
Miss RACHEL DOUGHERTY died at Mr. TURNER's on last Monday evening. The funeral took place on Tuesday. She was 54 years of age.

Obituary
At half past 8 o'clock on last Thursday morning, November 9th, the death angel summoned to her eternal home, CORALEE FILLINGER, daughter of J.B. and K. FILLINGER. She was taken with a sore throat about 2 weeks before her death, which was the cause of her, so soon, having to leave all that was dear to her by the strong ties of affection and love. For 13 years had she with feeble constitution braved the angel of death, and now, in her 14th year, with bright prospects awaiting her, she is beckoned and passes to the other world. She conversed freely with her parents about dying, and said when she was taken sick that she must die. She requested that her books be laid carefully away, and her little sister who was not at home, be told that she so much wished to see her. The bereaved family has the sympathy of all who knew her.

Home News
JOE M. RABB will probably preside as Judge of our next term of Circuit Court.

Rev. S.C. ZOOK, pastor of the U.B. Church, moved his family to this place last week.

JAMES F. WELLER, of Ridge Farm, IL, a former merchant of this place, has sold out and is going to locate at Veedersburg, IN.

ALEX FUQUA, of Vigo County, who shot and dangerously wounded one of his neighbors a short time since, on account of too close an intimacy with his wife, committed suicide last week by hanging himself in his own barn.

We omitted to state in our last issue, that D.R. GRAY, our station agent at this place, had a new girl baby at his house. It arrived here at 2 o'clock on Friday afternoon, November 3, 1882.

WILLIAM B. SIMPSON has leased the SPRAGUE saloon at this place and applied for license. He will take possession December 5th. The building is owned by SPRAGUE & ADAMS.

JAMES HASTY has moved to the country, on JOHN C. JOHNSON's farm, east of town.

Nuptials
On last Thursday evening, at Salem Church, Helt township, BOB VAUGHN and Miss ALICE JAMES were united in wedlock by Rev. E.R. JOHNSON, pastor of the M.E. Church of that place. Notwithstanding the inclemency of the weather, there was a large crowd assembled to witness the tying of the nuptial knots. The young couple has our many thanks for a box of wedding cake.

A Cheap Farm
A nice little farm of 32 acres, 9 miles N of Terre Haute on the Rockville Road for sale. The soil is black loam, very fertile, and adapted to any kind of grain or vegetables. There is a good log house and stable on the farm and the land is enclosed with good fences. Good well of never failing water and pump therein. This farm is well worth $50 per acre.

M.B. DAVIS
Clinton, IN

Wednesday, November 22, 1882

Judge THOMAS F. DAVIDSON authorizes us to say that he will practice law in the Warren County circuit.

Perrysville Gossip
Dr. B.I. POLAND will leave next Wednesday for Chicago where he will enter Bennett's Medical College. He will return next April and resume his practice.

Clinton
On last Friday, a little child, aged about 5 years, of JOHN CUTLER, who resides about 1 ½ miles northwest of here, was buried in the Cemetery at this place. There was a strong suspicion that the little child came to its death by cruel treatment; in other words that it was the victim of the relentless savagery of an inhuman stepmother. Accordingly the Coroner was sent for, and the body was disinterred for the purpose of holding an inquest. Dr. SHEPARD and Dr. BOGART conducted a post mortem, but with what result, we have not learned. Rumors are afloat, greatly exaggerated of course, that the little child has been the subject of most brutal treatment. Now that the matter has been taken in hand, it is to be hoped that it will be ferreted out, that suspicion may be removed from the accused if innocent, and due punishment meted out to her if guilty.

Real Estate Transfers for October 1882

HARRIET A. MURPHY and husband to WILLIAM B. INGLE
23 acres in Helt township - $812

JOHN F. SMITH and wife to WILLIAM HINES
60 acres in Highland township - $1,900

SPENCER MACK and wife to JOHN F. LANGSTON
Lots 6 & 7, in Summit Grove - $400

JOSEPH S. BUSKIRK and wife to JENNIE M. DAVIDSON
Lots 3 & 4, in Clinton - $550

BENJAMIN WITTENMYER's Estate to AMOS FLESHMAN
80 acres in Highland township - $2,390.85

BENJAMIN WITTENMYER's Estate to ELHANAN STEVENS
55 acres in Highland township - $2,200

ALICE M. STEPHENS and husband to GEORGE W. MOSBARGER
Lots 1 & 2, in Lacey's addition to Perrysville - $300

TILGHMAN FONCANNON and wife to PETER AMMERMAN
10 acres in Helt township - $500

JOSEPH M. MOREY and wife to NELSON C. ANDERSON
Part of lots 7 & 10, in Clinton - $800

WILLIAM HUNTER and wife to ALBERT HENDERSON's children
30 acres in Clinton township - $675

NORTH CRAIG etal to JOHN W. PARRETT
90 acres in Vermillion township - $1,800

SAMUEL E. KAUFMAN etal to DANIEL W. FINNEY
Lots 16, 17, & 18, in Dana - $150

SAMUEL AIKMAN etal to HORACE WELLS
Lot 23, in Dana - $50

HORACE WELLS and wife to WILLIAM E. FULWIDER etal
Lot 23, in Dana - $58

WAKEFIELD INGRAM and wife to JAMES QUINLAN
40 acres in Helt township - $1,600

DANIEL E. STRAIN Jr. and wife to JOSHUA M. HARPER
½ acre, in Helt township - $20

WILLIAM N. HOSFORD and wife to EVALINE CRAIG
Lots 9, 10, 89, 90 in Eugene - $1,100

AARON MILLS to SUSANA BECKETT
1.15 acres in Vermillion township - $175

SARAH J. FREEMAN and husband to THOMAS J. SKIDMORE
80 acres in Helt township - $1,800

TYLA V. BALLAH to JOHN P. LONG
25 acres in Highland township - $800

ISAAC J. LAMB and wife to JOHN P. LONG
30 acres in Clinton township - $700

MARGARET E. RAMSEY to AUGUST JENKS
Part lots 9, 19, & 11, in L. and A. addition to Newport - $250

OLIVER LINDSEY to JAMES W. ELLIS
1 acre in Vermillion township - $160

EMMA KOCH to NELSON HANSON
Lots 3 & 4, in Clinton - $100

PETER AMMERMAN and wife to W.D. McFALL
5/8 of an acre, near Jonestown - $112.50

MARY B. ANDERSON to MARY A. SWAN
Lots 2, 3, & 6, in Clinton - $700

HIRAM BUSBY and wife to LEANDER M. CRAYCRAFT
29 acres in Vermillion township - $420

JOSEPH HOWARD and wife to PETER COSSEY
40 acres in Highland township - $400

THOMAS C. BROWN and wife to GEORGE HOWLETT
10 acres in Vermillion township - $240

PLATT Z. ANDERSON and wife to CHRISTIAN PETERSON
Part lots 1, 4, & 5, block 1, in Clinton - $450

Notice of Administration
Estate of GEORGE SKIDMORE, deceased
N.T. LEITON, Executor

Home News
Postmaster STEPHENS, who is not in the best of health, went up to Chicago last week to consult a prominent physician of that city.

BILL SHARP, of this place, is now Dad. It is a boy, and arrived here one week from Monday last.

Rev. M.L. GREEN, former pastor of the M.E. Church at this place, is located here. The 40th anniversary of his marriage occurs on the 23rd of December, and we have been thinking if it would not be the proper thing for our citizens to make him a nice donation on that day. He is now broken down in health, and is not able to earn a living in the pulpit, or at any other employment.

Next Saturday is school teachers' examination for licenses. As Superintendent H.H. CONLEY has resigned to accept the office of Circuit Prosecutor, it is probable there will be no Superintendent elected in time to hold the examination. The Auditor has notified the Trustees to meet here in a special session today for the purpose of electing a school superintendent to fill the vacancy. We understand that Prof. GEORGE L. WATSON of Eugene, and Prof. JOHN R. STAHL of this place are candidates for the job. Both are good men.

Obituary
ALBERT HEWITT, aged about 35 years, died at St. Louis, MO, on November 16, 1882, of inflammation of the bowels. His remains were buried at Bellefountain on November 17th, with Masonic honors. The deceased was favorably known to many of the citizens of this county. He was raised by Esq. WILLIAM L. NAYLOR, of Eugene. He was an honest, sober and industrious young man, and had many warm friends among the young people when he was a resident of this county. He went to St. Louis a few years ago with a capital of $3,060, and from this he accumulated a fortune of $75,000. His death is a misfortune to society. Such enterprising men are worth considerable to the community they live in. He leaves a young wife whom he married about one year ago.

Sheriff's Sale on Decree
ISAAC B. HEDGES vs. EDMOND D. JAMES, SARAH JAMES, & ELIZABETH JAMES
$3,078.70
Sale to be held Saturday, December 16, 1882
Sale at courthouse between 10 and 4
S ½ SE ¼ Sec 21 T 15 R 9 W – 77 acres
NW ¼ Sec 28 T 15 R 9 W – 113 acres
SE ¼ NW ¼ Sec 20 T 15 R 9 W – 10 acres
Total of 210 acres
JUMP & WARD attorneys
WILLIAM C. MYERS, Sheriff

Application for Liquor License
PATRICK FLYNN – Hillsdale
JAMES HAIN, SAMUEL HAIN – Perrysville

Notice of Administration
Estate of JAMES A. LEWIS, deceased
October 24, 1882
JAMES A. LEWIS Jr., admr.

Wednesday, November 29, 1882

Circuit Court, November Term 1882
State of Indiana vs. SAMUEL MOREHEAD
Assault with a deadly weapon – trial by jury – not guilty

State of Indiana vs. WILLIAM, JOHN LANDSAW
Assault and battery – plea of guilty as to WILLIAM - $5
Trial by jury as to JOHN – 30 days in jail - $325

State of Indiana vs. THOMAS BLAIR
Appeal from J.P. Court – set for trial on December 14th

SAMUEL REED, MOSES REED vs. JOHN REED etal
Partition – final report, commissioner discharged

PEYTON F. DOUGLASS, LOLA M. CHURCH etal vs. LUCY DICKEN
Petition – set for December 14th

MARY DOUGLASS, PEYTON F. DOUGLASS etal vs. WILLIAM L. LITTLE, Trustee
Petition – trial – account of trustee filed and trustee discharged

HENRY CLAY SMITH vs. LEWIS A. MORGAN
Appeal – venue changed to Fountain County

SUSANNA M. SMITH etal vs. JAMES A. BEDINGER etal
Partition – final report filed and commissioner discharged

NELSON C. ANDERSON vs. JASPER A. MOORE etal
Petition – final report of commissioner filed and commissioner discharged

WILLIAM JAMES vs. EMMA R. JAMES
Divorce – continued

CORA E. IKE vs. MORGAN IKE
Divorce – continued

SARAH BOGART etal vs. JANE SHAW etal
Partition – report of commissioner filed

IRENA HAWORTH etal vs. MARTHA J. HAWORTH etal
Partition – report of sale filed and approved

ALVA WATSON vs. CHRISTIAN HOLD
Appeal from survey – resurvey directed

MALINDA FRASIER vs. JOHN FRASIER
Attachment – dismissed at plaintiff's costs

GEORGE MADDEN vs. ISAAC COOK's estate
Claim – judgment against claimant for costs

JOHN F. LACEY vs. ISAAC COOK's estate
Claim – judgment against claimant for costs

D.W. HUNT vs. ISAAC COOK's estate
Claim – judgment against claimant for costs

MALINDA FRASIER vs. JOHN FRASIER
Divorce – set for December 15th

CUTHBERT F. KEYS, HIRAM SHEPARD vs. WILLIAM BOREN
Attachment – set for December 15th

SYLVANUS MOORE vs. JOHN G. PENNTENNY
Change of venue – judgment in agreement against defendant for costs

JAMES KAUFMAN etal vs. JOHN HENDERSON etal
Board of Commissioners of Vermillion County, appeal from Commissioners court
Construction of Dana and Lebanon free gravel road – set aside

JAMES CHIPPS vs. JAMES A. ELDER, JACOB L. THOMAS, JAMES R. DUNLAP
Board of Commissioners
Appeal from Commissioners Court – judgment for $342.95

THOMAS BASINGER vs. JOHN LANDSAW
Damages – continued by agreement

SAMUEL REED vs. LEWIS E. REED, JAMES ROBERTS
Garnishment and attachment – dismissed at plaintiff's costs

PETER L. WRIGHT vs. HENRY C. HANSICKER
Note and mortgage – continued for publication

State of Indiana ex rel ELMIRA C. LAMB vs. JOHN E. WILSON
Bastardy – trial by jury – found defendant father of child – judgment for $100

JAMES W. MILLER vs. ALEXANDER LEMON
Change of venue – dismissed by plaintiff at his costs

SAMUEL C. HOLLINGSWORTH vs. WILLIAM D. VANNEST, ISAAC VANNEST
Note – default – judgment for $170

MAURICE HEGARTY vs. SAMUEL SANDERS
Note and mortgage – default – judgment for $160

HENRY F. KEITH vs. LEWIS M. CHECK
Replevin – dismissed at plaintiff's costs

JACOB R. DORING vs. SNOWDEN LUSADDER
Damages – changed to Fountain County

JOHN COLLETT vs. C. & E.I. RR Co.
Damages – set for December 15th

WILLIAM C. GRIFFITH vs. THOMAS W. STEPHENS
Note – default – judgment for $53.25 and attorney fees

WILLIAM M. JONES vs. JAMES M. WRIGHT
Accounting and on award – judgment by agreement for $74.27

EMMA STULTZ vs. ALFRED STULTZ
Divorce – set for December 15th

SARAH KEIGER vs. JOHN BOSER, JEREMIAH V. PENSON
Change of venue – continued by agreement

CYRUS M. McCORMICK, SAMUEL J. McCORMICK vs. JOHN J. SMITH, GEORGE R. HOPKINS
Note – set for December 15th

Clinton
REUBEN DAVIDSON departed this life on last Friday morning. He was a man of industry and morality and respected by all. He leaves a wife and two small children.

Miss TILLIE CAMPBELL returned home last Thursday after a two months' visit at her sister's, Mrs. SARAH REYNOLDS, of Plainfield.

St Bernice Items
The sawmill owned by PITTS & BEEMER, formerly located at JACKSON's Switch, has lately moved near the residence of Mr. JOHN ANDREWS, where it is doing good business.

B.F. SPICER will open up a confectionary stand at Jonestown next week.

Dr. WATKINS, of St. Bernice, will take up his residence in the city of Indianapolis in a short time. He leaves a good practice and many friends who wish him success.

Mr. POWERS, living 2 miles NW of town, while away from his home last week, his house took fire from some unknown cause, and burned down. All the household goods went with it.

THOMAS PAYNE, a resident of Kansas, who formerly resided in Helt's Prairie, made a flying visit to old Hoosierdom last week, and while here took to himself one of its fair sex. We wish the two a happy and long life in the grasshopper state.

Highland
The GARRETT family will start for Nebraska next week.

Mrs. MARY CHADD has been confined to her bed for 2 weeks with typhoid fever.

DAVID WOLFE and BELLE THOMPSON were married at Alta last Friday night by Rev. E.R. JOHNSON.

JAMES COMPTON, who was sent to the Illinois State Penitentiary from Edgar County 2 years ago, has returned home. His mother is at present not expected to live.

Bastardy Case
In the case of Miss ELMIRA C. LAMB against JOHN E. WILSON, for bastardy, the jury found a verdict of guilty, and the Judge assessed a judgment of $100 against the defendant. Not being able to pay or give bail for this amount, he was remanded back to jail, where the law compels him to remain for one year. He doesn't seem to have any rich relatives who are willing to come to his relief.

The new School Superintendent is A.J. JOHNSON, of Gessie. He is a man of fair education, now having an 18 months teacher's license, and we predict that he will make a good Superintendent.

WILLIAM LAMB, who was elected Auditor of Fountain County at the late election, has been fortunate in running for office. He was elected Auditor of that County in 1840, and held the office continuously until the fall term 1860. In 1867 he was elected County Treasurer, which office he held 2 terms. When his present term expires, it will make 32 years he has held County offices.

Matrimony
Married, in Montezuma, at the residence of the bride's mother, by the Rev. H.M. OGDEN, of Goodland, IN, on Tuesday, November 21st, Hon. P.C. STEWARD, of Nashville, TN, to Miss ORLANTHA C. MOFFATT, of Perrysville, IN. The attendants were ERNEST STEWARD and Miss DORA MOFFATT, LUTHER and Miss BERTHA STEWARD. Their future home will be in Nashville, TN.

Home News
Go to JOHN McMINIMY for your Thanksgiving turkey.

DICK GREER, of Eugene, is slowly dying of consumption. He cannot last many weeks.

NATHAN KIGER and LEOTA NEVINS, of Eugene township, were spliced by Esq. J.W. HARTMAN on Thursday last.

Mrs. LUCINDA GREEN, dressmaker, patronage respectfully solicited.

WILLIAM L. LITTLE returned from Kansas last week. While out there he purchased 520 acres of land, and a $1,600 residence in Hutchinson. 400 acres of the land lies in one body, for which he paid $8 per acre.

Commissioner JACOB L. THOMAS united with the M.E. Church, at Lebanon, on last Saturday night.

Letter List

PITMAN, HENSON D.
JONES, ALBERT
CONRAY, N.L.
FRINDLEY, SEXTON
ATWOOD, RUBY J.
BUTTE, ISAAC F.
FORTUNE, Miss GERTIE
THOMAS, W.T.
WELLS, MARTIN M.
EVERTSON, JOHN
GIBSON, WILLIAM H.
PATTERSON, JAMES
BOOHER, JOHN

Estray Notice

Taken up on October 23, 1882, one mile N of Dana
One heifer, 2 years old past, white all over except red border on ears
November 17, 1882

MARY O. MILLER

Estray Notice

Taken up November 1, 1882, 3 miles W of Perrysville
One red and white spotted heifer with red neck and ears, 2 years old past, has calf
November 20, 1882

McCLIN TUTTLE

Attachment

EDGAR L. REID vs. THOMAS REID
$200, writ of attachment – promissory note
THOMAS REID must appear for trial December 23, 1882
November 28, 1882

JOHN W. HARTMAN, J.P.

Wednesday, December 6, 1882

Matrimony
On last Thursday evening, at the residence of Mrs. MARY HARRISON, of this place, JOHN MILLER and Miss MARTHA HALL, both of Newport, were united in wedlock by Esq. JOHN W. HARTMAN.

New Store

FLYNN & JACKSON
Dry Goods, groceries
Hillsdale, IN

Elopement
DEWARD BARKER and Miss LAVICA BRINDLEY, a daughter of ELI BRINDLEY, residing 1 ½ miles SW of town, planned an elopement to Danville, IL, where they expected to procure license and get married. Both are under age, Miss BRINDLEY only 16. The romantic young lady was attending school, and started off on last Thursday morning for country schoolhouse as usual, but instead of going there, she and her lover came to town and took the train for Danville, where they attempted but failed to procure the necessary papers to make them one. They then took the afternoon train for Newport, and when they arrived here they found the indignant father of the girl on the hunt of them. They informed him of their determination, and seeing that it was useless to object, he finally consented to the match, procured the legal documents and had Esq. JOHN W. HARTMAN to join them in holy bonds of wedlock, the ceremony being performed at the residence of Mrs. MARY HARRISON. The next day they hired a livery rig and went to her parents, where they are now living as happy as king bees.

Death
At about 8 o'clock on last Wednesday morning, the wife of WILLIAM C. MYERS, who had been suffering upon a bed of affliction since the 10th of last June, a year ago, took her leave of all things earthly and her spirit passed to that better world. She had suffered long and much, and death was certainly a relief to her. She was a noble and kind hearted woman, an affectionate wife and good mother. Everybody was her friend, and when the sad news of her death was whispered on the breeze, although having long been expected, everyone seemed to lament that the community had lost so good a citizen. A short time before she was taken sick, she united with the M.E. Church, and about 3 weeks ago was received into full membership by the pastor and a few members who collected at her bedside for that purpose. Her funeral occurred on Thursday, the day following her death, and although a cold and disagreeable day, there was a large number turned out to pay that last respect and honor due the dead.

Death
Mrs. CHRISTIAN JORDAN, of Asbury Chapel neighborhood, died on Saturday last. She was born November 6, 1804, and was 78 years and 3 days old at her death. In the year 1832 she united with the M.E. Church, and for nearly 50 years has been a faithful Christian lady, consistently discharging the duties of mother and neighbor. Funeral services were held on Sabbath morning in Asbury Chapel, conducted by Rev. E.R. JOHNSON, assisted by Rev. WAINSCOTT. Her body was interred in the Helt's Prairie Cemetery.

New Commissioner
JOHN B. WRIGHT, of Eugene township, the newly elected Commissioner, took his place as one of the Board on Monday last. Mr. WRIGHT is a solid and substantial farmer, and a man of more than ordinary education, and it is the general opinion that he will make a most excellent Commissioner. He takes the place of JACOB L. THOMAS, who has made a faithful and honest guardian of the people's interests for the last 6 years.

Judge B.E. RHOADS and lady, of Terre Haute, and his brother M.G. RHOADS and family, of this place, ate Thanksgiving turkey with their father-in-law, R.D. MOFFATT, of Perrysville. They had a pleasant time and a nice dinner.

Matrimony
On last Thursday evening, at the residence of Mrs. MARY HARRISON, of this place, JOHN MILLER and Miss MARTHA HALL, both of Newport, were united in wedlock by Esq. JOHN W. HARTMAN.

Clinton
WILLIS HEDGES and MAY WHITCOMB, who are attending school at Greencastle, spent Thanksgiving at home.

W.G. MERRILL has sold his interest in the Brier Hill Coal Mine to a man in Chicago by the name of H.M. BENJAMIN. Mr. MERRILL is a good citizen, and we hope he will continue to reside at this place.

Died
At her home, near Gessie, IN, of consumption, at 7 o'clock in the morning, December 1, 1882, Mrs. SARAH ANGELINE CARRITHERS. Mrs. CARRITHERS was the esteemed wife of FRANK M. CARRITHERS, prominent farmer of Highland township. She was still young in years, being only little past 38 years of age. Mrs. CARRITHERS had been a patient and cheerful sufferer for nearly two years. During all that time, she had sat within the shadow of that cruel disease that ever bids to its victims hope yet even but deceives. She seemed resigned to it, and up to the last, her thoughts were on her dear children which she was going to leave behind. In her death the neighborhood has lost an ornament, and her family a patient mother and friend.

Home News
We understand that WILLIAM L. LITTLE is going to emigrate to Kansas next fall, and make that State his future home.

Retail liquor licenses were granted last week:

SAMUEL & JAMES HAIN – Perrysville
PATRICK FLYNN – Hillsdale
W.B. SIMPSON – Newport

DECATUR DOWNING, of Clinton, will not take his place as Commissioner until the December session of the Board, 1883.

OSCAR BETSON, a son of HAMILTON BETSON, left last week for Colorado, to buy a big stock farm, if he can find one that suits him.

BEN BLANCHARD has taken in a new partner. The little fellow arrived here on last Sunday night, and is the very image of his mother.

JOE C. DAVIS of Asbury University, and JOHN COLLETT Jr. of Wabash College, came home last week to eat Thanksgiving turkey with their folks. The boys are both in the enjoyment of good health.

SAM H. BRADLEY, of Hume, IL, an old member of Company C, 18th Regiment, IN Volunteers, was in town last week. He looks as natural as he did when he was carrying a musket and knapsack in the Army. Sam is now earning his living by physicking people.

Miss MATTIE KAUFMAN and Miss LILLIE CRANE, two good looking young ladies of Dana, spent Monday night in town and left on the train yesterday morning for Danville, where they intend to spend a few days visiting relatives and friends.

Mrs. C.S. DAVIS and Mrs. S.B. DAVIS went down to Dana yesterday to visit Miss EMMA FILLINGER who is down with the consumption and in a very critical condition.

We made a slight mistake in giving the number of acres purchased in Kansas, by WILLIAM L. LITTLE recently. He bought 548 acres, for which he paid $5,965.10.

WILLIAM L. LITTLE has sold his prairie farm, SW of town, consisting of 114 acres, to JAMES ASBURY. Consideration $5,100.

J.P. YORK, late of Dana, this county, is now a resident of Clyde, Cloud County, KS.

B.K. DICKEN left on last Monday for Alma, Wisconsin, where he intends to remain quite a spell.

L.C. ALLEN, a former citizen of this place, is now located in Oakland, OR.

WILLIAM CADY has been confined to his home for about 6 weeks with the sore eyes.

Wednesday, December 12, 1882

Home News
BILLY HAGENBAUGH, of Clinton, has failed, and made an assignment for the benefit of his creditors. He thinks he has enough assets to pay out in full.

Our esteemed young friend, Miss CLARA WHITCOMB, who is well known in society circles in this place, is now teaching a large class of deaf mutes the art of painting, at Staunton, VA, and is employed and paid by the State. Miss CLARA is among the best artists in the West, and officials of that State are to be congratulated upon their good fortune in securing the services of this estimable young lady.

Clinton Herald

Helt Township Items
For four long months, we have passed through much affliction and deep sorrow. Four of our family have been afflicted with typhoid fever. Two have passed away from the effects of that dreadful disease. We take this opportunity of extending our heartfelt gratitude to our neighbors and friends for their kindness during our afflictions. We will ever hold them in grateful remembrance.

J.B. FILLINGER and wife

Little MORTON, son of J.B. and K. FILLINGER, died November 27, aged nearly 5 years. He had just recovered from a very hard spell with typhoid fever, when dropsy and heart disease set in, which caused his death. Only about two weeks before, they lost their oldest daughter, Coral. They have the sympathy of the entire community.

Highland
Dr. J.C. HARRISON and family will start in a short time to Kansas where they expect to locate.

FRANK STRAIGHT and Miss FRANCES B. PEARMAN were united in wedlock on last Sunday by G.W. SAXTON.

Miss ELLA SMITH of New Goshen is visiting her sister, Mrs. SHOWALTERS, of this place.

HENRY LONG, who has not been expected to live for over a year, died on last Tuesday morning in his 64th year.

Mrs. COMPTON is lying at the point of death.

MIKE CLEMENS, a brother of WILLIAM CLEMENS of this place, who resides at Tuscola, was at Montezuma last week visiting his sister, and while there became a raving maniac. He was taken on Saturday last to the Illinois Insane Asylum.

Clinton
HARLOW WASHBURN aspires to be a granger. Saybrook, IL, is his prospective location.

Perrysville
JOHN WINTERS has gone to Greenwood, Dakota, where he has a situation at the Indian School.

Mr. CROCKETT and Mr. STINGLEY are now running the Wabash Hotel.

TOMMY JONES, who has been living with M.J. RUDY, was last reunited to his little family, a wife and daughter just arrived from Wales, whom he had not seen in 13 years.

JAMES CHISLER, and Mr. FOSTER, late of Stringtown, have leased a hotel in Covington and moved up there last Sunday, to take charge of the house.

Real Estate Transfers for month of November 1882

SOLOMON C. LEWIS to DAVID LARR
115 acres in Helt townshop - $2,500

JOHN H. BOGART and wife to SUSAN A. PERRIN
Part outlot 6, in Clinton - $650

JONAS S. SHANER and wife to OLIVER J. BERRY
Part lots 3 & 4, in S. addition to Perrysville - $350

WILSON ZURMELY and wife to SAMUEL K. TODD
Outlot adjoining Eugene - $1,050

JAMES A. BROWN and wife to JOHN F. DUGGER
1/6 of 80 acres in Helt township - $125

STEPHEN WRIGHT's estate to HARRIET WRIGHT
76.57 acres in Highland township - $3,012

THOMAS J. GROVES etal to JOHN HOUCHIN
40 acres in Helt township - $1,000

JOHN F. DUGGER and wife to WILEY JONES
80 acres in Helt township - $320

LORA JOHNSON and wife to EDWARD Y. STOKES
8 acres in Vermillion township - $80

OLIVER J. BERRY and wife to JONAS S. SHANER
Part lot 31, in Perrysville - $350

DAVID W. PEER and wife to HENRY A. NYE
9 acres in Helt township - $325

THOMAS PATRICK and wife to NATHAN WHITE
40 acres in Eugene township - $1,000

JOHN D. JOHNSON to JESSE HOUCHIN
Lots 1, 2, & 25, in Alta - $2.08

LEANNA WILTERMOOD and husband to Chicago N.C. & Cole Co.
$385

MARY A. SWAN to VIOLA V. BRUCE
Lots 2, 3, & 6, block 6, in Clinton - $1,000

WILLIAM C. EICHELBERGER and wife to GOTTFRIED D. KINDERMAN
Lot 52, in Eugene - $100

SOLOMON G. DUNBAR and wife to THOMAS J. MITCHELL Sr.
Lots 24 & 25, in G & S addition to Perrysville - $50

JOEL H. BENTON and wife to JOSEPH MILLER
Lots 2 & 3, M & H addition to Perrysville - $300

BENJAMIN F. MOREY etal to JANE C. LEE
Lot 1, block 14, in Clinton - $625

EDWARD Y. STOKES and wife to LORA JOHNSON
8 acres in Vermillion township - $80

EMMA MOORE etal to NELSON C. ANDERSON
Lots 1, 4, 5, 8, & 9, block 29, in Clinton - $1,200

EDWARD A. FLAUGHER and wife to HENRY O. PETERS
Lot 6, in Eugene - $200

DANIEL W. PERRY and wife to JOSEPH SANDERS
10 acres in Vermillion township - $250

LEWIS E. REED etal to BENJAMIN F. DEARDOFF Jr.
107 acres in Eugene - $2,000

SUSANNA M. SMITH etal to J.M. DOUGHERTY
80 acres in Eugene township - $280

SUSANNA M. SMITH etal to WESLEY MALONE
80 acres in Eugene township - $2,505

Notice of Non-Residence
PETER L. WRIGHT vs. HENRY C. HANSICKER
Case No. 2250
JUMP & WARD attorneys
HENRY C. HANSICKER is not a resident of Indiana
Must appear before first Monday of February 1883
December 9, 1882
JAMES ROBERTS, Clerk
By NORTH CRAIG, Deputy Clerk

Home News
CHARLEY VANNEST has bought FIN NEWHOUSE's popular restaurant in Clinton.

JOHN P. HENSON, of this place, and Miss MARY HOLTZ, of Eugene, will unite in bonds of wedlock tomorrow.

Mrs. MALINDA FRASIER, of Helt township, was granted a divorce from her husband last week, who ran off a few weeks ago, taking about $1,500 of her money with him.

F.M. BISHOP returned home last week from Kansas. He is well pleased with that State, but does not now talk much like he was going to move out there. We hope MARION will remain a citizen of old Vermillion County.

NORTH CRAIG has sold the building now occupied by JOE McCORMACK as a butcher shop, to JAMES ARRASMITH, consideration $260

JOHN BLUNK, residing North of town, has a new boy baby at his home.

S.V. ODEKIRK and lady, of Opedee, leave on a train this morning for Wisconsin, to visit his old mother, who is 80 years of age.

R.M. ETTER, of Whitestown, Boone County, IN, was down here last week and this visiting his brother JOHN ETTER. Mr. S.H. NEESE, of the same place, and a brother to JEROME NEESE, came along with him, and both enjoyed a very pleasant time while in our city.

Death
The wife of GEORGE W. ODELL, of Hutchinson, KS, died at about 3 o'clock on last Wednesday afternoon. The deceased was formerly a resident of this place, and had been an invalid for many years. She was a kind and warm hearted woman, a Christian lady and esteemed by everybody. Her many friends here were cast down with sorrow when the sad news of her death was flashed over the wires.

For Sale
Pedigree shorthorn cattle and Poland China hogs. Over 15 years as a breeder. Come and see.
L.H. AIKMAN – Dana, IN

Notice to Non-Residents
CLARA CAMPBELL vs. JOSEPH CAMPBELL
Complaint No. 22790
JUMP & WARD attorneys
JOSEPH CAMPBELL is not a resident of Indiana
Must appear before first Monday of February 1883
December 12, 1882
JAMES ROBERTS, Clerk
By NORTH CRAIG, Deputy Clerk

Wednesday, December 20, 1882

Burned to Death
An old lady by the name of DORCAS REED, aged 80 years, who resided 8 miles southeast of Danville, IL, was burned to death on Saturday last. She was living by herself, in a little log hut, and it is supposed she had laid down on a pallet, near the fireplace, and dropped off to sleep when her clothes caught fire and burned her to death before she could extinguish the flames. Some neighbors passing the house in a short time afterwards, noticed smoke coming out of the door and windows, and went to the house, opened the door and found the old lady lying near the fireplace, burned to a crisp. Her bed and everything in the room was then in flames. Her husband burned to death in the same fireplace about 12 years ago. He was old and helpless, and no one being in the room, it is supposed he fell in the fire and was not able to get out.

Death
On last Monday morning, EMMA FILLINGER departed this life, aged about 24 years. About 1 ½ years ago, she became a sufferer from the disease consumption, and it became evident to her friends that the ice band of death would soon chill the beating pulse of life. She herself gave up all hopes of recovery several weeks ago, and with meekness and Christian patience, resigned herself to the stern decree. Her cheerful disposition to the last, evidenced a sunshine of hope in something brighter than earth affords, and she met death without so much as a murmur of regret. Thus with the bloom of youth upon her brow, EMMA was called upon to lay aside her earthly mantle. The funeral of the deceased was preached at Salem Church on Tuesday morning.

J.M. SCHWIN, attorney at law, of this place, has been appointed Deputy Prosecuting Attorney, by Prosecuting Attorney H.H. CONLEY.
Covington People's Paper

Obituary
ODELL – ELVIRA MYERS ODELL was born near Newport, Vermillion County, IN, December 14, 1835, and was married to GEORGE W. ODELL at the same place, November 15, 1854. She professed religion at a revival held near Mattoon, Coles Co., IL, and joined the M.E. Church in January 1862. For several years, she had been in poor health and came to this place December 5, 1881, to receive benefit from change of climate, but her health gradually grew worse. While at the depot waiting for the train that was to take her back to her relatives, the friends and home of her childhood, she was taken with a fainting spell from which she never recovered. Her death occurred at 3 p.m., of the same day, December 6, 1882. She leaves a husband, 2 sons, and a daughter to mourn her death. She was afflicted with heart disease and asthma; and though at times she seemed quite well, during the last 3 months of her illness, she was a great sufferer. She bore all without complaint and was prepared to go whenever the Master should call. The bereaved family has the sympathy of all in their sorrow and also the sweet consolation that she is far happier now than ever before.

Hutchinson, KS

Died
At the family residence in Montezuma, on Tuesday, December 12, 1882, Mrs. MARY BURNS, wife of JOSEPH BURNS. Mrs. BURNS bore a high place in the esteem of all who knew her, and as a model wife and mother was idolized by her loving and bereaved family. The funeral services conducted by Rev. McMASTERS, took place from the house on Saturday afternoon, and were very largely attended by those who knew her best and will miss her most.

Montezuma
Mr. M.L. AIKMAN and wife, of Bono, Sundayed here, the guests of their aunt, Miss KATIE FORD.

JOHN RILEY, a former resident here, late of Hillsdale, having received an appointment as section foreman at Camargo, IL, has gone there to fill the place.

Our good old Christian friend, THOMAS GRIFFITH, has received the appointment as postmaster of Montezuma and will take charge about January 1st.

A Mr. TINSLEY, late of Veedersburg, has bought HENRY LANGFORD's saddle and harness shop here and will run it in the future.

ALBERT BEARD and Miss EMMA FUQUA, by Rev. McMASTERS; and JAMES HADLEY and Miss SADIE DAVIS, by Rev. GRIFFITH, had the connubial knot tied here last week, and henceforth will trod on life's journey in double harness.

Perrysville
GEORGE MOORE was made happy last week by the arrival of a little lady kid.

CHARLEY CHEZUM has bought a half interest in R.W. DICKENSON's confectionary.

Home News
OTHO CHAMBERS, a former resident of Helt township, this county, is now a resident of Ft. Calhoun, NB.

D.C. JOHNSON is now proprietor of the Central House at Clinton.

Mrs. MARY MILLER, of this township, is sister to Road Superintendent, A.J. DAVIS, who had been taken to the Insane Asylum last fall, has been returned, and is pronounced cured.

Miss MATTIE LAMB left yesterday morning for Nebraska, where she will shortly marry.

Death
Mrs. MARY BURNS, the wife of JOSEPH BURNS of Montezuma, died at 5 o'clock on last Thursday evening, after several weeks illness. The deceased was the daughter of the late STEPHEN MILLIKEN, who at one time resided on a large farm in Dana. She was well and favorably known by many of our citizens. She was kind to everyone, and leaves a host of friends who will deeply lament the loss of so noble a Christian lady.

Marriage
On last Thursday evening at the residence of the bride's parents in Eugene, JOHN P. HENSON, of this place, was united in wedlock to Miss MARY HOLTZ, Rev. J.H. HOLLINGSWORTH, pastor of the M.E. Church performing the ceremony. There were nearly 100 invited guests. Among the presents was a deed to 40 acres of Kansas land, that being donated by BEN BLANCHARD, of this place.

VOL FOOS, of Hillsdale, was in town yesterday.

Commissioners Court December 1882

Allowances	
H.C. SMITH, Poor, Highland township	267.20
A. FABLE, Poor, Eugene township	229.40
JAMES CHIPPS, Poor, Vermillion township	389.90
GEORGE W. FULTZ, Poor, Clinton township	204.50
JOSEPH CONRAD, Supt. Poor Asylum	875.22
DANIEL SEARS, poor by the board	30.00
R.E. NICHOLS, poor by the board	15.00
ERASTUS MACK, physician	25.00
JAMES WALLACE, physician	48.75
R.E. STEPHENS, poor by the board	.77
Criminals	
CHARLES VANNEST	10.00
EARNEST WEBER	7.00
W.C. MYERS	60.80
THOMAS BRINDLEY, janitor	50.00
School Superintendent	
H.H. CONLEY	194.00
A.J. JOHNSON	32.00
W.C. MYERS	8.65
Books and Stationery	
C.M. BROWN	30.50
W.B. BURFORD	18.00
Elections	
W.C. MYERS	16.10
Highways	
W.C. MYERS	2.90
JOHN RICHARDSON	2.00
ELIAS LAMB	1.50
County Printing	
S.B. DAVIS	28.50
County offices	
MAURICE HEGARTY	4.70
R.E. STEPHENS	10.20
Ditches	
W.C. MYERS	7.85
Board of Health	
M.L. HALL	29.00

Officers Fees and Salaried	
H.O. PETERS, Treasurer	200.00
ELIAS PRITCHARD, Auditor	657.01
Bridges	
M.L. CASEY	20.00
P.Z. ANDERSON	15.00
Public Buildings	
R.H. NIXON	47.90
County Bonds	
H.O. PETERS, bonds $500 each, gravel roads	1,000.00
Courts	
W.C. MYERS	34.30
JAMES A. ELDER	28.00
J.R. DUNLAP	31.50
J.L. THOMAS	31.50
Hazel Bluff Gravel Road	
H.O. PETERS, Coupon paid	35.00
Clinton & Paris Gravel Road	
DAVID P. ROSS, gravel	29.37
P.Z. ANDERSON, Surveyor	35.00
JOSEPH A. CLOVER, gravel	91.10
H.O. PETERS, coupons paid	35.00
Newport & Quaker Point Gravel Road	
E.B. DAVIS, Printing	12.50
JAMES HASTY, Stone	11.50
ELIZABETH J. McKANNON, damages	25.00
W.S. FRAZIER, damages	25.00
H.O. PETERS, Expense selling bonds	28.19
P.Z. ANDERSON, surveyor	309.00
SUSANA BECKETT, damages	15.00
JOHN W. PARRETT, gravel	76.80
Newport & Walnut Grove Road	
H.O. PETERS, coupons paid	248.73
Perrysville & Southwest Gravel Road	
S.B. DAVIS, printing	15.00
W.C. MYERS, sheriff	4.10
CHUNN's Gravel Road	
H.O. PETERS, expense selling bonds	11.81
P.Z. ANDERSON, engineer	118.00

Wednesday, December 27, 1882

Highland
JOHN BROWN, a student of Dayton Biblical Seminary, returned home last Saturday.

SAM AIKMAN, of Bono, now of Dayton, OH, is at home spending vacation.

Clinton
JOE WHITE and FRANK DAVIS arrived home from Indianapolis last Friday, where they had been attending medical college.

WILLIAM AIKMAN, of Kansas, formerly of this township, was in town last week. He came back after his boy who had been laboring under mental derangement and who is now in the poor asylum of this county.

Montezuma
Our marble men, Mr. GOFF and Mr. GOEBLER, move to Rockville soon. Sorry to lose them, as they are enterprising and useful citizens.

Dana
CALE JACKSON is home from college, looking the picture of health.

Mrs. HELM, of Murdock, IL, attended the funeral of EMMA FILLINGER last Tuesday.

Obituary
Mrs. MARGARET RAMSEY, who kept the boarding house in the first building south of this office, took down sick last August, and lingered until 5 o'clock last Sunday morning. She had a combination of diseases, being afflicted with heart, liver, and kidney complaints. Aunt MARTHA DICKEN, who was similarly affected, died one year before, today. Both were large women. Mrs. RAMSEY was born in Ohio, and her mother dying while she was quite small, she was taken in by ROBERT NIXON, now a resident of Oswego, KS, who kept her until she was 13 years of age. When she grew to womanhood, she was united in marriage to a Mr. RAMSEY, whom she lived happily with until his death, a few years ago. The deceased was 38 years of age, and had been an earnest and zealous Christian in the M.E. Church for the last 26 years. She had many warm friends and no enemies, and lived an honorable, upright life. Her funeral took place on last Monday afternoon, from her late residence, Rev. WILLIAM L. LITTLE performing the last rites, after which her remains were followed to the Thomas Cemetery and there interred beside her husband. The deceased leaves two bright little girls, aged about 8 and 10 years.

Home News
WILLIAM MOREHEAD is seriously ill.

C.W. WARD made his good wife a Christmas present of a fine, six octave, organ.

A Mr. DeHAVEN, of Arcola, IL, a brother of P.W. GRUBB's wife, is in here on a short visit.

W.P. HENSON and his wife were joined in wedlock 22 years ago last Monday.

E.Y. JACKSON Jr. will open out the RAMSEY boarding house in a few weeks, and conduct it on first-class principles.

Mrs. F.H. MUNSON, of Onarga, IL, daughter of Hon. O.P. DAVIS, and Miss MINA BROWN, of the same city, are here on a visit.

JOE McCORMICK has sold out his butchering outfit to L.J. PLACE, who will carry on the business hereafter. Mr. McCORMICK intends to move to Kansas.

WILLIAM O. WASHBURN, who has been in the west for sometime, has returned to Clinton.

JOHN C. JOHNSON is down bedfast, and is reported to be in critical condition. Old age is said to be the cause.

W.P. WRIGHT'S parents have moved to this place, and are now occupying the Dr. SHEPARD property. They moved from Parke County.

Miss MINNIE CAMPBELL, a bright and beautiful young lady of Crawfordsville, is in town visiting, the guest of her cousin, Mrs. J. JUMP. WILLIAM E. JUMP and his sister, Miss SUSA JUMP, of Redman, IL, nephew and niece of attorney J. JUMP, were also over here on a visit.

Wednesday, January 3, 1883

An old German beer swigger of Terre Haute, by the name of WILLIAM RENZENBRINK, took on too much on last Saturday evening, and collapsed and died. He ceased to breath at about 9:30 o'clock.

Died
Miss FLORA E. CARITHERS, died of consumption at her home in Gessie, IN, on Tuesday morning December 26, 1882. FLORA was the oldest daughter of FRANK M. CARITHERS and only survived her mother by 26 days, her mother having died of the same dread disease on the first day of the month. Her age was 25 years, and in the early dawn of her womanhood she was called on to enter the life beyond. She was a lovely girl in looks and in disposition, and left a host of friends to mourn her loss.

Summit Grove
B.F. MILES and Miss FRANCES M. STRAIN were married at the home of the bride's parents, December 31, 1882, by the pastor of the M.E. Church.

Helt township
CLATE and CLARENCE HOOKER have returned home from Kansas, looking hale and hearty.

Clinton
JOHN CAMPBELL, who has been employed as a clerk at Columbus, OH, returned home on a visit last week. He is just recovering from a spell of sickness.

Home News
R.H. NIXON has been appointed administrator of the Estate of MARGARET E. RAMSEY, deceased.

The infant child of Mrs. EMMA WILSON, aged 3 or 4 days, died on last Friday night.

On last Sunday, H.H. CONLEY was elected Superintendent of the M.E. Sabbath School at this place.

A Mr. JAMISON, of Ellettsville, a brother of Mrs. Z.T. GALLOWAY and Mrs. OL DAVIS, is here on a visit.

Dr. FRANK FONCANNON, a former resident of this county, is now practicing medicine at Edgar, IL, and is said to be doing a good business.

H.S. CADY, who is engaged at work at Freedom, Owen County, was at home last week, visiting his family.

JOHN A. WILTERMOOD has resigned his school and has taken a position in the County Treasurer's office as Deputy.

Sudden Death
HENRY CRABB, an old and respected farmer residing a short distance southwest of here, who has been ailing for some time, died very suddenly on Friday last.

S.R. WHITE, of Ridge Farm, IL, went down to Helt's Prairie last Saturday evening visiting his friends and relatives.

Administrator's Sale

Estate of MARGARET E. RAMSEY, deceased
Sale at late residence in Newport, between 10 and 4
Friday, January 26, 1883
Personal property
Hogs, corn, coal, an organ, library, provisions, household and kitchen furniture, etc.

ROBERT H. NIXON, Admr.

Sheriff's Sale on Execution

Saturday, January 13, 1883
At courthouse between 10 and 4
Real estate
Undivided 1/9 of N ½ NE ¼ Sec 18, T 15 N R 9 W
CUTHBERT F. KEYS, HIRAM SHEPARD vs. WILLIAM BOREN
$331
J.C. SAWYERS, attorney
December 20, 1883

WILLIAM C. MYERS, Sheriff

Wednesday, January 10, 1883

THOMAS H. ALLEN, of Clinton, is applying for an increase in pension. He is now getting $24 per month, and is justly entitled to $72. He had nearly entirely lost the use of both legs, and suffers intensely every hour of his life. In fact a man in his condition should have not less than $1,000 per month.

High School Items
B.M. McKNIGHT, principal of the Covington School, gave us an interesting talk Thursday afternoon.

Clinton
JOHN NOURSE and MINNIE HAGENBAUGH were united in marriage lat week in the State of Ohio. They will return to this place shortly and commence housekeeping. JOHN is a carpenter by trade and a first class workman.

Mrs. HARRY SHEPARD departed this life on last Thursday evening, after a painful and protracted illness of about 6 weeks. Her funeral was preached Saturday afternoon by Rev. M.L. GREEN, of Newport, after which her remains were interred in the cemetery at this place.

Highland
The following persons were on the sick list since our last report:
FRANCIS MIDDLEBROOK, LAURA AIKMAN, MERTIE SHOWALTERS, and Mrs. RANDALL

JAMES McDOWELL of this township received a pension of $2,000 back pay last week.

Mr. HAWORTH, of Watseka, is visiting his daughter, Mrs. AYE.

PERRY MERRIWETHER, is teaching a singing class in our town.

Old Mrs. LEATHERMAN, of this township, aged about 70 years, died December 25, 1882. She had been a member of the Christian Church for many years and lived a consistent Christian life. Her remains were interred in the Trowbridge Cemetery at this place, December 26, 1882.

Items from Hutchinson, KS
Mr. JOHN BATES and wife and Mr. JACOB REMLEY are expected to arrive soon from Newport, IN, to remain as citizens of Kansas.

ED ODELL came near getting badly burned last Saturday in the office of the Howard House. The cause was potash in his vest pocket igniting accidentally, burning his vest, right hand and overcoat badly.

Notice of Final Settlement of Estate

Estate of JAMES H. HUTSON, deceased
January 6, 1883

JAMES ROBERTS, Clerk
By NORTH CRAIG, Deputy Clerk

Notice of Final Settlement of Estate

Estate of MARY J. RUMSPIRT, deceased
January 3, 1883

JAMES ROBERTS, Clerk
By NORTH CRAIG, Deputy Clerk

Home News
L.F. GARRETT, of Hillsdale, is going to move to Precept, NB.

GEORGE R. GRIMES and Miss LIZZIE B. ALLEN, of Clinton, will be united in wedlock on the 16th of this month.

NORTH CRAIG will start for Kansas about the first of March, where he intends to locate and make his future home.

JOE McCORMICK will move to Kansas in about 2 weeks. He is going to locate in Wichita, and engage in stock raising.

L.A. MORGAN, trustee of Highland township, was in town on Monday last. Mr. SMITH has not yet turned over the papers, books, and money to him, but is getting ready to do so.

ED E. DAVIS, son of Hon. O.P. DAVIS of Opedee, caught on over to Indianapolis last week, and secured a clerkship under Secretary A.J. KELLY. He gets $35 per week.

D.C. JOHNSON, the accommodating and obliging landlord of the Central House at Clinton, is fast gaining a good reputation among the traveling public. He has the credit of keeping the best hotel in the county.

On Tuesday night of last week, Vermillion Lodge No. 594, I.O.O.F. installed its officers:

R.E. STEPHENS – N.G.
JAMES CHIPPS – V.G.
JOHN DARBY – Treasurer
THOMAS CUSHMAN – Secretary

Prosecutor H.H. CONLEY has a new boy baby at his house. The little fellow arrived sometime last week.

Real Estate Transfers for December 1882

FIELDING RABOURN's estate to MARY LEWIS
10 acres in Highland township - $180

WILLIAM H. STUTLER etal to JAMES J. LEWIS
Lots 13 & 14, in Gessie - $325

JOHN C. JOHNSON to CATHERINE JOHNSON
20 acres in Vermillion township – love and affection

AMEY E. BOGART etal to JOHN WARD
85 acres in Vermillion township - $2,425

HANNAH TATE to WILLIAM H. TATE
Lot 8, in G. & C.'s addition to Perrysville - $150

JOHN F. HULL and wife to PETER PEARMAN
10 acres in Helt township - $500

ELIZABETH J. SCONCE to SAMUEL NAYLOR
4 acres in Eugene township - $90

HENRY BETSON's estate to AMOS J. BETSON
40 acres in Vermillion township - $640

LEWIS SHEPARD to ROBERT WRIGHT
Outlot adjoining Newport - $1,650

JOSHUA JUMP and wife to JAMES CHIPPS
Lot 95 in Newport - $1,000

PHOEBE A. SKIDMORE etal to JOHN W. BLAKESLEY
119 acres in Helt township - $2,000

IRA SOUTHARD etal to ROBERT A. WILMAN
Lot 4 and part of lot 5, block 6, in Clinton - $300

PETER S. MOUDY and wife to LEWIS A. MORGAN
Part lot 5, in Perrysville - $26

Wednesday, January 17, 1883

We see by the Crawfordsville Journal, that JOHN E. HANNA, the wide awake editor of the Review of that city, was united in wedlock on Tuesday of last week to Miss MARY T. BROWN, a bright, beautiful, and accomplished young lady.

Mrs. CY THOMAS, of Graysville, Sullivan County, was thrown from a sleigh last Wednesday evening and instantly killed. She had just gotten into the sleigh to accompany her husband to a neighbor's house, and while standing up to adjust her wearing apparel, the horses gave a sudden start, throwing her out and breaking her neck.

Clinton
GEORGE GRIMES and LIBBIE ALLEN were united in marriage at the Presbyterian Church last night, Elder BUCKLES officiating. They could not have selected a more favorable season of the year.

Home News
S.S. COLLETT is now cashier of the bank.

JOHN A. WILTERMOOD is now Deputy Treasurer.

WILSON HASTY, of Streator, IL, is in here on a visit.

Attorney WILLIAM L. RABOURN, of West Lebanon, is down with the mumps.

Dr. E.B. CANNON, of Montezuma, is in poor health, and has gone to New York to be treated.

JAMES F. WELLER Sr., formerly a citizen of this place, is running a meat shop at Veedersburg.

JOE WELTER, of Veedersburg, was in town visiting, the guest of his brother-in-law, NORTH CRAIG.

NORTH CRAIG has sold his residence on Extension Street to JOHN W. PARRETT, consideration $750.

GEORGE NICHOLS and SICILY JONES, of this township, were united in marriage last week by Rev. J.H. HOLLINGSWORTH.

A number of Dr. J.C. HARRISON's warm friends at Hillsdale, are trying to persuade him out of the notion of moving to Arkansas. It looks to us like a wild goose chase.

J.W. GALLOWAY was called to Ellettsville on last Saturday by telegram, to attend the funeral of his little 6 year old niece, EVA PUETT. She is said to have been a bright and remarkably intelligent child.

W.E. MOFFATT is going to move to St. Joe, MO, where he intends to engage in the manufacture of flavoring extracts on an extensive scale. He says there is no establishment of that kind in the west, and he thinks there is big money in it. Mr. MOFFATT is one of the finest chemists in the country, and thoroughly understands the business which he is going to engage in. We wish him success.

Obituary
Mrs. MARY WRIGHT, died near Clinton, IN, December 18, 1882, at the residence of her son, aged 77 years. She was born November 13, 1805, in New York. She came to Indiana in the year 1817 and lived for a few years in Terre Haute. Fifty years ago she moved and settled on the farm where she died. This county was then a wilderness and in common with the early settlers, mother WRIGHT suffered many hardships, but she was of an iron constitution and well calculated to share with her friends and neighbors the privations of pioneer life. She was the subject of several severe accidents, such as having her limbs broken, but from all these she recovered, and until a few days before her death, she was quite active for a person of such an advanced age. Early in life she was married to her now deceased husband and became the mother of 5 children, 4 of whom are dead. Her only surviving child, Ex-Commissioner WILLIAM WRIGHT, of Clinton township, with whom she has lived for 30 years, and assisted in rearing his family of 6 children to whom she was very strongly attached. She united with the Missionary Baptist Church, September 1859, under the ministry of Rev. McMASTERS, and lived a quiet, faithful Christian life and died in the faith of the gospel. A large circle of friends mourn her loss.

Miss JOSIE MORRIS, of Perrysville, spent last Sunday in town visiting her sister, Mrs. GEORGE W. ZOOK.

B.F. MANTZ, a tailor who formerly worked here, is now located at Potomac, Vermilion County, IL.

We are sorry to learn that WILLIAM WOOSTER, of Montezuma, is seriously ill, but hope to hear of his speedy recovery.

Wednesday, January 24, 1883

FLYNN & JACKSON
Dry Goods, Groceries, Cigars
Hillsdale

ED VANSICKLE
Country Store
Hillsdale

BEN BLANCHARD, Proprietor
Vermillion Co. Abstracts
Newport

WILLIAM GIBSON
Dry Goods, Groceries, Boots
Newport

P.T. WILLIAMS
Harness Maker
Newport

Highland
JULIA NICHOLS, of Newport, is keeping house for ANDREW JACKSON.

One of WILLIAM UNDERWOOD's children died on last Monday.

Mrs. CATHERINE COMPTON, wife of HALL COMPTON, died on last Thursday evening, January 18, 1883, in the 53rd year of her age.

Home News
FRANK LANGSTON, of Summit Grove, will shortly unite in marriage to a young widow of that village.

JIMMY McDOWELL, of Helt township, says we were mistaken about him getting $2,000 in back pension. He only got $800.

D.C. JOHNSON, of Clinton, has been appointed postal clerk on the Wabash and Pacific Railway, between Lafayette and St. Louis.

CHARLEY JAMES, of Helt township, is now a dad.

Capt. R.B. SEARS left on last Monday morning for Washington, DC, to accept an appointment as clerk in the treasury department. His family will remain here until sometime in the spring.

After the first of next month, ADAM B. LITTLEPAGE, who has been reading with JUMP & WARD, is going to hang out his shingle as an attorney and do business on his own account. He is an honorable, upright young man, a hard student, and we predict for him a bright future.

FRANK WHITE, son of JACOB and CHARITY WHITE of Assaria, Salem County, KS, met with a sad accident one day last week while out hunting. The gun burst and destroyed one eye and not much hopes of saving the other, and a probable termination of his life.

JOHN W. GALLOWAY has sold out his half interest in the drug store, known by the firm name of RHOADS & GALLOWAY, to his partner, HARRY RHOADS, who is now sole proprietor. Mr. GALLOWAY is going to try his luck selling musical instruments.

Wednesday, January 31, 1883

SMITH and GEORGE JONES are the best fiddlers in this part of the country.

AD THOMPSON, of Dana, has sold out and is going to Hutchinson, KS.

Obituary
Once again the cold, icy hand of death has taken one of our most beloved and respected neighbors from among us. MALISSA PEARMAN was born in Vermillion County, IN, February 25, 1848, and died at her residence in Helt Township, Vermillion County, IN, January 23, 1883, and was interred in Helt's Prairie Cemetery on the day following. She leaves a husband, 4 children and a loving father to mourn her loss and many friends to grieve over her absence. Consumption has preyed upon her delicate constitution for several years, but at last her frail nature yielded to the relentless hand of death. She was a member of the U.B. Church, and had been a true Christian woman, a kind and loving wife and mother.

Home News
ED JACKSON has gone to Kansas to live with his uncle, NORTH CRAIG.

A Miss HINCKLE, of Hillsdale, and ANDREW BURK of Spring Hill, united with the M.E. Church on Sunday last.

Mr. JOSIAH BEECH and Miss AMANDA BENNETT were married on Thursday last by Rev. E.R. JOHNSON, of Helt's Prairie.

Z.T. & J.W. GALLOWAY have leased the Newport Hotel for one year, with the privilege of five.

DAVID MACK, who emigrated from Helt township to Kansas about 17 years ago, has got all he wants of that country and has come back to old Vermillion to live and die.

NORTH CRAIG left on last Saturday morning for Kansas, where he intends to make his future home. He will locate near Altamont, in Labette County, where he has purchased 170 acres of prairie land that has never yet been tilled.

Marriage
WILLIAM DARRINGTON, of Montezuma, aged 85 years, was united in wedlock at the hotel of this place, on last Wednesday evening, to Mrs. SARAH MOORE, of Eugene, aged about 50 years. Rev. S.C. ZOOK, of the U.B. Church, performed the ceremony. This makes about the eighth time Mr. DARRINGTON has been married since he was weaned. If he holds out faithful, he is good for 2 or 3 women yet.

Sudden Death
JOHN HEPBURN, of Eugene, died very suddenly on Sunday last. He was as well and hearty as usual on Saturday morning, and while out on the porch washing his face and preparing for breakfast, he suddenly fell over and became insensible, in which condition he laid until 10:30 o'clock Sunday morning. He was about 35 or 40 years of age, and a man who was generally respected and esteemed by his neighbors.

Matrimony
On last Monday evening, Mr. C.M. HAYS and Miss CHARLOTTE DEAN were united in bonds of wedlock, Esq. SAMUEL C. HOLLINGSWORTH performing the ceremony.

Matrimony
Last Wednesday Mr. HARRY McDOWELL and Miss A. RODMAN, of Dana, IN, passed through Chrisman on their way to Paris, IL. When they returned in the afternoon, they were Mr. and Mrs. McDOWELL.

On last Wednesday, JAMES ROBERTS installed ALFRED R. HOPKINS, as deputy during the remainder of his term. Mr. HOPKINS was elected Clerk at the fall election, and this appointment will give him the benefit of a 6 years term as County Clerk.

Death
RICHARD W. GREER, a resident of Eugene, who has been in poor health for a long time, died at the residence of his brother, JAMES A. GREER, of Highland township, on Thursday last. DICK, as he was familiarly known, was about 40 years of age, and when the tocsin of war was sounded in 1861, he shouldered his gun, and went down south to help defend the old flag of our country.

Mrs. JOHN WRIGHT met with a painful accident Thursday. As she went to step out of the door at Mr. DOWNING's residence, she fell and broke her arm. She is an aged lady and this will make the accident more painful.

JAMES T. MOORE and WILLIAM B. MOORE, three miles north of Dana, are going to sell off their personal property at public sale on February 13th, and in a short time afterwards will leave for Kansas.

There will be a change in the post office at this place in a few days. R.E. STEPHENS has resigned as postmaster and recommended JOHN RICHARDSON as his successor. Mr. RICHARDSON bought the stock of goods and notions, with the exception of the watches and jewelry. He also sold 73 acres of land, lying south of the Eugene and Newport gravel road to S.H. DALLAS, and took Mr. DALLAS' residence, in this place, at $1,400 as part pay. Mr. DALLAS is talking of moving to the country.

Wednesday, February 7, 1883

Mistake
Your informant was greatly mistaken when he said that DAVID MACK, after living nearly 17 years in Kansas, was returning to live in Vermillion County. Mr. MACK said Kansas is a much better country than this. He came back on a visit to see his old friends and dear relatives. He is having a good time, but plans on returning to Kansas about May or June. He and his brother, SPENCER MACK, have gone into a manufacturing business at Summit Grove, where they will make and sell Mack's Garden Hand Cultivator, and Mack's Check-row for corn planters.

Application for Liquor License

JEREMIAH CONLEY – Dana
JOHN F. PEELER – Dana

Real Estate Transfers for January 1883

M.M. DAVIDSON to JOHN WHITCOMB etal
75 acres in Clinton township - $106.98

CAROLINE GARRETT and husband to SARAH A. WHITSON
Lots 20 & 21, in Hillsdale - $225

ELIZABETH B. CLARK to GEORGE W. CLARK
80 acres in Vermillion township - $500

SAMUEL AIKMAN etal to DANIEL MILLER
Lot 8, in Dana - $50

JOSEPH RUHL and wife to SARAH A. STUTLER
Lot 3, in Perrysville - $300

THOMAS S. HOOD and wife to JAMES KNIGHT
80 acres, in Helt township - $4,600

THOMAS S. HOOD and wife to JAMES J. KNIGHT
80 acres in Helt township - $3,400

NORTH CRAIG and wife to JOHN W. PARRETT
Outlot adjoining Newport - $1,000

NORA A. WATT and husband to GEORGE E. HALL
Lot 16, in Perrysville - $30

LEWIS NICKELS and wife to JOHN NICKELS
5 acres in Vermillion township - $225

FRANK THRIFT and wife to D.W. GARDNER
Lot 1, in Clinton - $250

JOHN F. DUGGER to NANCY E. HOWARD
--- acres in Helt township - $90

ABNER C. HOWARD to JOHN F. DUGGER
--- acres in Helt township - $32.50

RICHARD MORRIS and wife to ROBERT M. SHARP
Lot 15, in Perrysville – $120

BERGHARD VONDERHIDE and wife to MARTHA J. LEE
Lot 8, and W ½ of lot 5, block 32, in Clinton - $500

GEORGE KINTZ and wife to HENRY J. KINTZ
3 acres near Jonestown - $1,000

NORTH CRAIG and wife to JAMES A. ARRASMITH
Part lot 46, in Newport - $275

JAMES A. ARRASMITH to HENRY HOLLINGSWORTH
Part lot 46, in Newport - $260

JOSEPH MILLIGAN and wife to GEORGE W. STULTZ
80 acres in Clinton township - $2,400

JOHN L. EGGLESTON and wife to WILLIAM H.H. DALLAS
20 acres in Vermillion township - $1,500

WILLIAM F. LYDAY and wife to ELIZABETH DONEY
60 acres in Clinton township - $1,100

FRANCIS N. AUSTIN and wife to SARAH E. ANDREWS
Outlot near Bono - $25

STEPHEN JENKS to FRANCIS N. AUSTIN
3 acres near Bono - $250

ASHEL B. DAVIS etal to NATHANIEL W. DAVIS
1/5 interest in 140 acres in Vermillion township - $265

SARAH E. ANDREWS to FRANCIS N. AUSTIN
Outlot near Bono - $25

CLINTON WATSON to DeWITT C. WATSON
Lot 18, in Dana - $500

Home News
JOHN FLOOD, of Missouri, a brother of Mrs. WILLIAM GIBSON, is in here on a visit.

A little child of HENRY JENKS, of Bono, was buried at the Helt's Prairie Cemetery yesterday.

HUGH H. CONLEY has been appointed administrator of the estate of EDGAR C. HAGENBAUGH, deceased.

MONROE M. MILFORD, of Attica, is down at the Arkansas Hot Springs for the benefit of his health.

W.B. SIMPSON's wife, of Opedee, slipped and fell on the ice last Saturday evening, dislocating her wrist.

JAMES BLANCHARD, who was stricken down with nervous prostration about three weeks since, don't seem to be improving any.

W.H. BISHOP, of Clinton, is going to quit the saloon business when his license expires. He has bought the FIN NEWHOUSE restaurant stock of CHARLEY VANNEST.

JAMES JORDAN, of this place, and Miss MARY BROWN, daughter of DAVID BROWN, residing a short distance southwest of town, were married one night last week, Esq. J.W. HARTMAN performing the ceremony.

ADAM B. LITTLEPAGE, a young attorney of this place, was admitted to the bar yesterday morning. He is a steady, sober, and industrious young man, a close student, and we predict he will some day be a fine lawyer.

Marriage
Mr. OBE AYERS of St. Bernice, and Miss SADIE MAHAN of Bono, were united in matrimony on last Tuesday evening by Rev. J.A. MAST, at his residence near Bono.

Wednesday, February 14, 1883

Perrysville
Dr. RUSSELL, of Terre Haute, and Dr. RICE of Rockville, performed a delicate and dangerous operation, last Wednesday upon the wife of our fellow townsman, JOE BURNETT. For several months past, Mrs. BURNETT has suffered from an ovarian tumor, which on being removed was found to contain an aqueous fluid. The tumor weighed 28 pounds. The patient is slowly convalescing and the doctors think she will soon be permanently cured.

Gessie
Our esteemed citizen, JAMES A. PRATHER, Esq., has spent the winter in the house sick. We are sorry to say he seems to get no better.

Mr. CHARLES CARITHERS has been installed as Principal of the Gessie School, Miss DUNLAP assistant.

Mr. LYLE and his accomplished wife from Tennessee have taken up their abode with us. He is a fine workman and does a thriving business in the shoe line.

Highland
JOHN MARVIN fell off the coal dump, at Alta, last Thursday, breaking his collarbone.

Eugene Items
ALFRED DEVER is talking of returning to Holton, Jackson Co., KS. Mr. DEVER says that it is a better place for a young man than it is here.

L.R. WHIPPLE has attained the high position of Zulu Chief of Zulu Indians, S.A.

Miss SARAH TUTT, of this place, is visiting her sister, Mrs. PENWELL, of Pana, IL.

Mr. and Mrs. JOE McCORMACK left for Kansas on Thursday last. They intend making that their home. Mr. McCORMACK is going to deal in stock.

List of Lands and Town Lots with Delinquent Taxes

Highland Township

NAME	SEC	TWP	RANGE	ACRES	TAX
GOODNER, JOSEPH P.	20	18	10	25	7.83
JAMES, NANCY J.	3	18	10	17	5.41
JAMES, NANCY J.	17	19	10	10	5.05
JAMES, NANCY J.	5	18	9	40	
JAMES, NANCY J.	32	19	9	3	8.21
TROSPER, MARIA E.	8	18	10	5	2.05
WELLS, ELLEN	9	18	10	160	
WELLS, ELLEN	16	18	10	20	68.67

Vermillion Township

NAME	SEC	TWP	RANGE	ACRES	TAX
BROWN, DAVID	34	17	9	2	33.20
COOK, JOSEPH C.	33	17	10	20	4.09
COLLUM, JOHN	30	17	10	2	
COLLUM, JOHN	30	17	10	1	6.50
COOK, ASA	30	17	10	2.31	.63
DAVIS, JACOB heirs	31	17	9	10	2.26
DAVIS, MARY J.	31	17	9	10	3.07
KENDAL, JACOB M.	30	17	10	10	2.91
McMILLIN, JOHN heirs	2	16	9	15	12.42
SHRYER, SAMUEL	6	16	9	20	6.87
WILTERMOOD, ELIZABETH	34	17	9	15	7.22

Helt Township

NAME	SEC	TWP	RANGE	ACRES	TAX
CLARK, GEORGE W.	20	16	9	80	
CLARK, GEORGE W.	20	16	9	30	76.18
JAMES, LUCINDA	10	15	9	7	7.61
PAYTON, JOHN estate	20	15	10		2.87

Clinton Township

NAME	SEC	TWP	RANGE	ACRES	TAX
COTTRELL, ISAAC	34	14	9	80	
COTTRELL, ISAAC	34	14	9	40	35.70
CLARK, SARAH	28	14	9	25	
CLARK, SARAH	28	14	9	40	24.62
DOWDY, A.J. heirs	12	14	10	20	

DOWDY, A.M. heirs	12	14	10	55	33.42
FINKHOUSER, ISAAC	30	14	10	40	16.38
GOSNELL, ALONZO	33	14	9	20	7.69
HECKLIN, EMMA	8	14	9	4	1.75
HUFF, JOHN H.	27	14	10	40	
HUFF, JOHN H.	27	14	10	40	
HUFF, JOHN H.	27	14	10	40	36.19
HEDGES, LINCOLN etal	12	14	10	28	13.53
GARRETT, JOEL	28	14	10	40	13.38

Town Lots in Perrysville

BOLLS, DANIEL	Collett's addition (Gessie), lot 20	.71
ABDILL, GEORGE W.	Inlot 22	5.83
JAMES, BARBARA	Inlot 6 & 7, G & C. addition	3.78
LAWLYERS, ELVIRA	Inlot 18, M. & H. addition	.86
PERRIN, AMOS heirs	Inlot 23, G. & C. addition	8.08
STOCKWELL, NANCY	Inlot 7 & 8, M. & H. addition	5.04
SEAL, HENRY I. Heirs	Inlot 26, G. and C. addition	2.08

Town Lots in Newport

HANNAH heirs	Lot 8, Sexton's addition	5.61
HAWORTH, WILLIAM	Lot 37, Zener's addition	.71
LEAVITT, CLARK	Lot 29, Zener's addition	1.27
RICHARDS, PHOEBE E.	Lot 12, L. & A. addition	3.40
SEARS, IVA	Lot 59	8.61
VANDUYN, ELLA	Lot 37 & 38	1.19
GRIFFIN, ELIZABETH	Lot 53 & 54	5.63

Town Lots in Dana

CASTLE, M.J. & ZERAH	Lot 1, block 8	2.94

Town Lots in Clinton

BAILEY, R.B.	Part of outlot 12	56.80
BENSON, MIRIAM	Lot 8, block 1, Morey's addition	11.88
CASEY, MONT L.	Lot 6, block 27	33.06
CAMPBELL, JOHN G.	Lot 6 & 7, block 1	33.06
COFFEEN, HENRY A.	Outlot 6	14.25
FECHHEIMER, MARCUS	Lot 1, 2, 3, 4. 5., block 20	.99
HAMILTON, ALEXANDER	Lot 1, block , Knowles addition	15.59
JAMES, COLLIN	Lot 3, block 10	1.19
MORGAN, O.P.	Lot 10, block 1	31.15
PAYTON, SARAH	Lot 4 & 5, block 5	6.91
PATTON, RACHEL J.	Lot 2 & 3, block 31	111.21
THOMPSON, W.P.	Lot 8 & 9, block 1	15.66
WALKER, DOLLY	Lot 9 & 12, Livengood's addition	5.55

Home News
Mrs. SOLON JOHNSON of Dana, is dangerously ill with heart disease.

JOE HOLTZ of Eugene, was down last week visiting his daughter, Mrs. JOHN HENSON.

WILLIAM GIBSON has a new girl at his house. She arrived on last Thursday afternoon, and is as spry as a kitten.

Mrs. L.C. GARWOOD, of Champaign, IL, spent last Sunday in town, the guest of her sister, Mrs. TOM McKNIGHT.

P.T. WILLIAMS, our harness maker, is down with a lung complaint.

Landlord GIVENS will retire from the Newport Hotel on the first of March.

Mrs. MARGARET ARRASMITH is down at Dana attending the bedside of her sick sister, Mrs. SOLON JOHNSON.

A.J. ADAMS, ex-Editor of the Hoosier State, and WILLIAM E. LIVENGOOD, ex-Clerk of this county, both residents of Danville, IL, were in our city yesterday on business.

Mrs. SERENA J. WASHBURN gave a party at her residence Monday night in honor of the 5th anniversary of the marriage of her daughter, LELIA, to Prof. J.B. DeMOTTE. Enough woodware was accumulated to supply all households of the future generations of DeMOTTEs. Mrs. WASHBURN is the widow of the late Col. H.D. WASHBURN.

Greencastle Banner

CHARLEY TARRENCE, of Terre Haute, was in town on Monday and yesterday, visiting. He is compelled to go around on crutches, from the effects of a hurt received in CLIFT & WILLIAMS' planing mill some weeks ago. His foot was pretty badly crushed, and it will probably be quite a while before he will be able for duty.

Obituary

Postmaster R.E. STEPHENS received a telegram yesterday afternoon announcing the startling intelligence that B.K. DICKEN Sr., who left here late last fall to spend the winter in Wisconsin with one of his relatives, had died at 6 o'clock the evening before, and that his remains would be brought here for interment. Mr. DICKEN had many warm friends in this county who will regret to hear of his sudden and unexpected death. His disease was lung fever, and he only lingered a few days. He was born in this county in 1818, and at the time of his death was 65 years of age. The deceased was an honorable and upright citizen, generally respected and esteemed by our citizens, and if he had any enemies, we never heard of them. He had a genial disposition and won friends wherever he went. For a long time, he was Deputy Postmaster under R.E. STEPHENS, and not being of a vigorous constitution, concluded a change of climate would be beneficial to his health, and so on December 4th of last year, he started for Alma, Wisconsin, where he intended to remain until spring, and then return to Newport. His wife, who was as noble a hearted woman as ever lived, died and was buried one year ago last Christmas. His remains will arrive here on the southbound train tomorrow afternoon, and will be met at the depot by some of his old friends who will convey them to the residence of Mr. PICK DICKEN, where they will remain until 10 o'clock Friday morning, when they will be followed to the Thomas Cemetery for burial.

Keeled Over

Mr. JOHN HASTY, residing on East Extension Street, had an attack of heart disease on last Saturday morning, and it was thought by his family for a while that he was dead. He had just put some wood in the stove and gone to the water bucket to take a drink, and while in the act of drinking, he keeled over and fell upon the floor like a dead person. He was insensible for quite a spell, but finally rallied, and is now in about his usual health, which is not very good at best.

Circuit Court blew in again yesterday morning, and a very important case will be called today. JOHN STRAIN, of Helt's Prairie, who sold his farm about one year ago or more, to his two sons, D.E. Jr. and J.A. STRAIN, now brings suit to recover the farm back. He alleges that he was of unsound mind at the time he made the deed. After selling the farm he married a Terre Haute prostitute and squandered the money in riotous living. The old gentleman is dead broke and wants to raise another stake.

Miss EVA ADAMS, daughter of A.J. ADAMS, of Danville, IL, has been attending school at St. Marys. Her brother GEORGE ADAMS is attending school at Emporia, KS.

Administrator's Sale of Land

Estate of WALTER B. MOFFATT, deceased
Sale to be held at E.T. SPOTSWOOD & Son store
Saturday, March 17, 1883

Lot 51, & 8 feet off N side of lot 52, in Perrysville
& E fraction of NW ¼ Sec 34 T 19 N R 9 W – 83.94 acres in Fountain County

CALVIN HUGHES, Admr.

Wednesday, February 21, 1883

Eugene Items
CHARLEY DERBY was in town last week. He is better known as Crazy CHARLEY.

H.O. PETERS swapped his drug store at this place to a Mr. McFARLAND, of Ridge Farm, for a dry goods store. Mr. McFARLAND had an elephant on his hands as he is a druggist, and H.O. PETERS was in the same fix, so it was a good trade for both parties.

Perrysville
WILLIAM WINTERS, a farmer living three miles below town, is very low with brain fever. Dr. SPOTSWOOD is the attending physician.

JAMES HEMPHILL, a former citizen of this place, but now of Mattoon, IL, is visiting friends and relatives here.

Home News
PETER COOPER is 93 years old.

JOHN W. GALLOWAY and Miss FLORA EGGLESTON will be united in wedlock about the first of April.

GEORGE W. ENGLISH, of Danville, IL, claims the credit of giving the Hoosier State its present name.

CHARLES ODEKIRK, of Aurora, IL, who has been visiting his brother, S.V. ODEKIRK of Opedee for two or three weeks, left for home on Monday last.

JAMES BLANCHARD, who took down sick five weeks ago, is still confined to his bed, and with but little prospect of being out short of two weeks yet.

Funeral of B.K. DICKEN
The remains of B.K. DICKEN Sr. arrived here on last Thursday evening, accompanied by his niece, Mrs. MARGARET BAILEY and her husband, of Alma, Wisconsin. The remains were met at the depot here by some of his old friends and conveyed to the residence of PICK DICKEN, where they were kept until 10 o'clock Friday morning, when they were taken to the M.E. Church. Rev. J.W. PARRETT delivered a short and appropriate eulogy on the deceased. Friends and relatives were then invited to pass around and take their last view of the deceased, who looked as natural as he did the day he left here for Wisconsin last December 4th. The remains were then placed in the hearse and followed by relatives and sorrowing friends to the Thomas Cemetery and kindly laid to rest.

Drowned
The Diamond coal mine at Braidwood, IL, was flooded on last Friday afternoon, and 74 men and boys in the mine were drowned before help could be rendered them.

Will

Mr. B.K. DICKEN Sr. made a Will some time ago in which he requested that WILLIAM L. LITTLE act as executor. He left all his property to his two sisters at Georgetown, IL, and Peoria, IL, and his niece, Mrs. MARGARET BAILEY of Alma, Wisconsin. His estate will probably not amount to over $500 or $600 after paying his funeral expenses.

A Strange Accident

Rather a strange and uncommon accident happened to JOHN C. JOHNSON, of this place, on last Saturday. While turning in his bed, he broke his thighbone close to the hip joint. Mr. JOHNSON is 70 years of age, and has been confined to his bed with poor health since early last fall, and being so old and not using his limbs, the bone had become brittle. He says he cannot stand the operation of having it reset, and the doctor thinks it rather doubtful whether it would knit if set. The old gentleman's sands have about run out, and he cannot live but a few weeks at most. Before he deeded his property away to his children, he was the wealthiest farmer in the county, all of which he accumulated by hard work and close economy.

Compromised

The case of JOHN STRAIN, of Helt's Prairie, against his two sons, D.E. Jr. and J.A., was compromised on Friday last, the boys agreeing to give him $200 per year during his life. He brought suit against the boys to recover possession of his farm which contains 600 to 700 acres of land, which he sold to them more than a year ago. He alleged that he was of unsound mind at the time, and therefore was not accountable for his actions.

Married

Mr. WILLIAM H. GOUTY, of Perrysville, IN, and Miss FLORA A. ROGERS were married at the residence of Mr. SAMUEL ROGERS, father of the bride, three miles southeast of Danville, IL, February 15, 1883, by Rev. W.N. COFFMAN officiating. About 100 invited guests attended.

Circuit Court Proceedings

State of Indiana vs. DANIEL MAYSE
Larceny – continued

PEYTON F. DOUGLASS, LOLA M. CHURCH vs. LUCY E. DICKEN
Petition – continued for report of sale

CORA E. IKE vs. MORGAN IKE
Divorce – dismissed

IRENA HAWORTH, SARAH HAWORTH, vs. MARTHA J. HAWORTH, ANNA LULU HAWORTH
Partition – granted, deed ordered

ALVA WATSON vs. CHRISTIAN HOLD
Appeal from survey – continued

THOMAS BASINGER vs. JOHN LANDSAW
Damages – dismissed

PETER L. WRIGHT vs. HENRY C. HANSICKER
Note & mortgage – dismissed, costs paid

JOHN COLLETT vs. C. & E.I. RR Co.
Damages – dismissed

EMMA STULTZ vs. ALFRED STULTZ
Divorce – granted

SARAH KEIGER vs. JOHN BOSER, JEREMIAH HINSON
Change of venue – continued

WILLIAM P. SWAINE vs. WINFORD M. TAYLOR, admr. CHARLES TAYLOR estate
Claim – judgment for $6 for defendant

E.A. FLAUGHER vs. SAMUEL REED, MOSES REED, exec JAMES REED estate
Claim – stricken from docket

CLARA CAMPBELL vs. JOSEPH W. CAMPBELL
Divorce – granted
Plaintiff granted custody of child, EDITH CAMPBELL

JAMES COSSEY, exec of PETER COSSEY's Will vs. GEORGE SPARKS
Rents & accounts – judgment for defendant

WILLIAM J. HENDRIX vs. I.B. & W. RR Co.
Appeal – judgment for plaintiff for $45

Champion Machine Co. vs. WILLIAM HAGENBAUGH
Notes – judgment for plaintiff for $462.01

JOHN STRAINE vs. DANIEL E. STRAINE Jr., JOHN A. STRAINE
Damages – judgment for defendants

HUGH H. CONLEY vs. THOMAS KIBBY, ISAAC KIBBY, LOUISA BURTON
Notes – dismissed at defendants costs

WILLIAM DOWNING vs. WILLIAM HAGENBAUGH, AMOS CURTIS
Notes – judgment for plaintiff for $171.18

JAMES A. ELDER, guardian of CLARA A. ELDER vs. CEPHUS MACK, ZERELD MACK
Note and mortgage – judgment for plaintiff for $228.45

ROBERT H. NIXON vs. JOHN S. JAMES, WILLIAM H. JAMES, WILLIAM F. FORD
Note – dismissed

Mechanicsburg Machine Co. to AMOS CURTIS
Replevin – judgment for defendant

Hapgood Plow Co. vs. AMOS CURTIS
Replevin and damages – dismissed by plaintiff

LESLIE D. THOMAS vs. WINFIELD P. THOMAS
Account – judgment for plaintiff for $200

Rude Bros. Manufacturing Co. vs. WILLIAM HAGENBAUGH
Notes – judgment for plaintiff for $300

Halls Safe & Lock Co. vs. WILLIAM HAGENBAUGH, AMOS CURTIS
Replevin and damages – dismissed

JOHN WHITCOMB vs. WILLIAM HAGENBAUGH
Note – judgment for plaintiff for $560

State of Indiana ex rel HARRY O. PERKINS vs. JOSEPH B. CHEADLE, JOSEPH COLLETT etal
Suit on bond – continued

JOHN C. JOHNSON vs. JOSEPH B. CHEADLE, JOSEPHUS COLLETT
Note – judgment for plaintiff

NANCY B. CHEZUM vs. ALBERT CHEZUM
Divorce – granted

Attachment Notice
STEPHEN MILLER vs. Chicago and Newport Coal and Coke Co.
February 17, 1883
JOHN W. HARTMAN, J.P.

Sheriff's Sale on Decree
JOHN COLLETT, STEPHEN S. COLLETT, JOSHUA JUMP, MINNIE CAMPBELL, JENNIE C. TURNER vs. WALLACE MOORE, ELIZABETH MOORE
$2,263.68
Sale to be Saturday, March 17, 1883
Sale at courthouse between 10 and 4
SE fraction ¼ Sec 21 T 18 N R 10 W – 82.61 acres
N ½ NE ¼ SE ¼ Sec 18 T 18 N R 9 W – 20 acres
Total 102.61 acres
JUMP & WARD attorneys
February 21, 1883
WILLIAM C. MYERS, Sheriff

Wednesday, February 28, 1883

Home News
HENRY OSBORN, formerly a citizen of this county, has lately moved from Walsenburg, CO, to Empire City, same State.

Landlord GIVENS will step down and out of the Newport Hotel tomorrow and Z.T. and J.W. GALLOWAY will take charge of the house.

WILLIAM L. LITTLE has been appointed by the Judge of the Vermillion Circuit Court, the executor of the Estate of the late B.K. DICKEN Sr., deceased.

R.H. NIXON is the proud father of another girl baby. The little ootsy tootsy arrived here last Monday.

Prosecutor CONLEY's mother, who resides in Helt township, slipped and fell on the ice a few days since, sustaining severe injuries. She is now 84 years of age, and was in fair health up to the time of the accident.

PETER AIKMAN, of Helt township, is certainly the happiest man we have seen for a long time. It is all account of a bouncing big boy at his house. He now has 3 girls and 1 boy.

Perrysville
GEORGE R. HICKS is visiting relatives in Colorado.

Obituary
Died at the residence of his daughter, CATHERINE JOHNSON, in Newport, IN, on Thursday, February 22, 1883, after a lingering illness, JOHN C. JOHNSON, aged 75 years, 9 months, and 6 days. JOHN C. JOHNSON was born May 16, 1807 in Belmont County, OH, of respectable parents, and was raised like all western farmer's boys of that period, to hard work and with few advantages of school or society. He lived with his father until he arrived at majority, when he went out into the wide world with nothing but his hands, a brave, energetic heart and an honest purpose, to make his way. He learned the ship carpenter's trade at one of the boat yards on the Ohio River and followed that calling for some years. On February 24, 1833, he was married to ELIZABETH SHAVER, his first and only wife, who had greater advantages in youth than he. One year after his marriage Mr. JOHNSON and his noble wife removed to this county, laboriously pushing the boat loaded with all their earthly possessions up the Wabash, and landing near the mouth of the Little Vermillion on April 8, 1834, entered a small tract of land, built a cabin, and began a life in what is known as the "first bottom" which continued until 1854. The first person who visited them after they had built their cabin was Mrs. ELIZABETH HOPKINS, now the widow of JOHN HOPKINS, deceased, since which time a close friendship has existed between the two families and especially between those who so met in that lonely pioneer cabin. Mrs. HOPKINS, almost the sole survivor of Mr. JOHNSON's early friends, was present at his death and with her gentle, motherly and kind hands closed the eyes of her old friend. If Mr. JOHNSON could have chosen the person to perform this sad but gentle office, none other (since his good and loving wife had gone before him) would have been selected. In 1854, Mr. JOHNSON built the house where he lived until 1880, when he and his daughters CATHERINE and FLORA removed to the house in Newport where he died. Of the children born to Mr. and Mrs. JOHNSON, 7 survive, every one of whom is worthy of the honest and upright parents from whom they sprung. No child of theirs ever caused them any gloomy fears or an unhappy hour, and they are all now in the enjoyment of a competence accumulated by the patient industry and careful, yet reasonable, economy of their father and mother. Most of the bountiful fortune accumulated by Mr. JOHNSON he distributed in his lifetime among his children, all of whom loved and cared for him and watched over him with boundless affection during the many weary days and nights of his long sickness. Mr. JOHNSON was of the class that makes countries grand and rich. He was used to overcoming obstacles; he overcame the wildness of nature and turned hundreds of acres of trackless and malaria breeding river bottom forests into smiling, fruitful fields.

Death
Our Clinton correspondent gives the particulars of Dr. I.B. HEDGES' death, which occurred at his home, in that city on last Saturday evening. The doctor was a prominent and influential citizen, and was favorably known by many of our people. The deceased was born in New York in 1819, and had been a resident of this county since 1824. He leaves a large estate to his wife and 2 children.

Eugene Items
Report says that Mr. and Mrs. STROUD, of Terre Haute, formerly of this place, have dissolved partnership. Cause unknown.

GEORGE PINEGAR has retuned from visiting relatives near Ft. Scott, MO.

It is rumored that ALBERT McNEILL and Miss LIZZIE BELL were united in matrimony at Chicago last Thursday.

Married
SYLVESTOR GARLINGHOUSE and Miss LIZZIE CASEBEER, both of Hillsdale, were united in wedlock on last Wednesday evening, the ceremony being performed by Rev. E.R. JOHNSON, pastor of the M.E. Church. The bride is a daughter of Mr. AL CASEBEER.

Wednesday, March 7, 1883

Gessie
Mrs. RABOURN, wife of a prominent lawyer in Williamsport, together with her handsome children, is visiting her father, Mr. JONATHAN CARITHERS.

The neighborhood has lost two good citizens, ALEX STEWART and Mr. MENDENHALL. They chartered a car, loaded up their families and their goods and started for Dakota one day last week.

Clinton
Mrs. TAYLOR and ALICE CRANE, of Dana, who recently resided at this place, were back last week and removed the remainder of their goods to Dana.

Eugene
DAVID MEADE's school at Porter town closed on Saturday.

MARION WATSON's school closes on next Friday.

G.L. WATSON has gone into the sewing machine business.

DAN SOLLARS went with a carload of hogs to Chicago for HENRY RANDOLPH, one day last week.

JAMES REEVES' child died on Friday evening and was buried at this place on Sunday. Aged about 9 months.

Highland
Since our last writing, CHARLES PEARMAN and DAVID DOUGLASS have been made happy – two baby boys the cause.

JOHN HEAVY's school at this place will close in a short time when he will take charge of the school two miles west of here. Mr. HEAVY is a successful teacher.

HATTIE AIKMAN's school closed last Monday. She expects to attend the State Normal this summer.

Home News
Mrs. THOMAS BLUNK and Miss IDA FORTNER are on the sick list.

Capt. JOHN T. CAMPBELL, Chief Assistant in the Bureau of Statistics, has moved back to Rockville, his old home.

STRATT HOLLINGSWORTH, of Fontanet, Vigo County, IN, and his two little daughters, came up last Saturday on a short visit.

F.M. DAVIS, of Clinton, and E.A. FLAUGHER, of Eugene, graduated in the medical college at Indianapolis, last week.

Retail liquor licenses granted:
JERRE CONLEY – Dana
JOHN F. PEELER – Dana
OWEN MOFFATT – Clinton

Miss IDA ROBINSON, editress of the Fairmount Local, has changed the name of her paper to the Fairmount Veto. We think it a very appropriate name for a paper edited by a woman. They like to wear the breeches, or veto what a man does if it does not meet their approbation.

SAM SANDERS, of this township, is in luck. He received his pension certificate last week, which grants him a pension of $4 per month from June 13, 1865. The arrears will amount to $845. He filled out his voucher last Monday morning and will get his money sometime next week.

Married
At 6:30 o'clock on last Sunday evening ROBERT JAGGERS and Miss BELLE TATMAN were united in matrimony at the residence of the bride's parents, Rev. S.C. ZOOK, officiating.

Bastardy
ENNIS JACKSON, of Clinton township, did not love wisely, but too well. He is now spending the lonely hours in the county jail. He was arrested last week on the charge of bastardy, and bound over to the next term of Circuit Court.

Real Estate Transfers for February 1883

SARAH R. TALBERT to WILLIAM D. TALBERT
1/3 of 230 acres in Highland township - $1,916

DAVID S. UNDERWOOD and wife to SARAH H. COMPTON
11 acres in Helt township - $175

JOHN W. PARRETT and wife to DAVID R. GRAY
Outlot adjoining Newport - $750

JOHN PAYTON to NELSON C. ANDERSON
Part lot 1, in Clinton - $775

JOHN R. RALSTON and wife to JOHN E. HOOKER
67 ½ acres in Helt township - $3,210

COLUMBUS C. HEDGES and wife to BENJAMIN H. HARRISON
41 acres in Clinton township - $885.95

FRANCIS M. BISHOP to REBECCA F. STOKES
Lot 70 in Newport - $1,000

JAMES M. HOLLINGSWORTH and wife to WILLIAM L. PORTER
40 acres in Clinton township - $1,000

JOSEPH BURNS to SAMUEL KAUFMAN
41 acres in Helt township - $500

ELIZA J. LITTLE to RUFUS P. LITTLE
56 acres in Vermillion township - $900

MARY PAINE to JACOB A. BROWN
58 acres in Highland township - $400

SPENCER H. DALLAS and wife to JOHN RICHARDSON
Lots 43 & 44, in Newport - $1,400

JOHN RICHARDSON and wife to SPENCER H. DALLAS
75 acres in Vermillion township - $3,000

JOHN F. DUGGER and wife to ELSON J. SIMS
4/9 of 79 acres in Helt township - $600

JAMES A. CLEARWATERS and wife to ALLEN CLEARWATERS
15 acres in Vermillion township - $500

JAMES A. CLEARWATERS and wife to MARY CLEARWATERS
12 acres in Vermillion township - $138

ADIEUS B. HAYS and wife to JOHN F. WILSON
36 acres in Helt township - $545

MORGAN J. TUCKER and wife to ANNIE SLATER
Lot 10, in Clinton - $1,000

LILLIE J. THOMPSON and husband to JOHN O. ROGERS
Lot 16, in Dana - $530

JOHN R. RALSTON and wife to RICHARD B. DICKEN
21 acres in Helt township - $1,020

IRENA HAWORTH to JAMES F. CARMACK
9.84 acres in Vermillion township - $252.75

SAMUEL MOREHEAD to M.H. LEWIS
½ lots 9 & 10, in Newport - $300

WILLIAM E. LIVENGOOD etal to JAMES M. SAVAGE
110 acres in Vermillion township - $1,750

WILLIAM P. ANDREWS to WILLIAM TOOPS
Part lots 5, 8, & 9, in Clinton - $325

JAMES JORDAN and wife to SAMUEL W. JORDAN
320 acres in Helt township - $2,000

CLARK LEAVITT and wife to JOSHUA N. DAVIS
Lot 29, in Zener's addition to Newport - $50

HENRY C. HANSICKER to ALICE G. JONES
4 acres in Highland township - $300

WILLIAM J. LAKE and wife to C.A. GARLINGHOUSE
Lots 27 & 28, in Alta - $45

JOHN A. STRAIN and wife to SAMUEL FRIST
160 acres in Helt township - $3,500

ANNIE SLATER etal to MORGAN J. TUCKER
Part lot 16, in Clinton - $1,000

PHILO CURTIS and wife to M.J. RUBY
17 acres in Clinton township - $340

DAVID J. WOLFE and wife to MARION HOLLINGSWORTH
Outlot near Jonestown - $100

Notice of Final Settlement of Estate
Estate of ALEXANDER WHITE, deceased
January 23, 1883

JAMES ROBERTS, Clerk
By NORTH CRAIG, Deputy Clerk

Wednesday, March 14, 1883

Montezuma
O.P. BROWN's daughter EMMA BROWN was married last Wednesday to a Rockville man by the name of ADAMS. Rev. W.P. CUMMIMGS tied the knot.

FRANK and SARAH STRAIT left for California on Sunday night to join a brother who has been there for several years.

Report has it that AQUILLA LAVERTY Sr. is about to build a hominy mill in Armiesburg.

Married
By Rev. McMASTERS on March 5, 1883, MILES DAVIS and Mrs. LONG, late of Vermillion County.

Clinton
NING EDMONSTON and wife have split the blanket. NING now whiles away the long evenings in talking about the happy days gone by.

We understand that W.S. MERRILL, our former coal operator at this place, has secured a large tract of land in Dakota and will remove his family to that place soon.

JAMES KAUFMAN, of Dana, spent last Sunday in our burg. He was the guest of his sister, Mrs. CHIPPS.

EVAN DAVIS and LIZZIE KNIGHT slipped their heads into the matrimonial noose last week. Brother GRIFFITH, of Montezuma, adjusted the cords.

JOEL DYER, a man who was well advanced in years, departed this life last week. Mr. DYER had accumulated considerable of this world's goods, but some time ago he deeded all his property to his children, and was boarding around among them at the time of his death.

Items from Hutchinson, KS
Old Uncle BILLY MOORE and his two sons, JAMES and JOHN, with all three of their families, are now residents of our county. It they had more house room, they would be better satisfied. This they will have soon.

W.L. LITTLE and MANUEL SIKES, of Newport, IN, and a Mr. McMEEN, of Eugene, IN, are with us now. SIKES and McMEEN will remain with us. Mr. LITTLE will return to Newport soon, but will move his family to our city in the fall. We will gladly welcome them in our midst.

Perrysville
DICK MORRIS is very low with pulmonary consumption, and cannot survive many days.

Miss FLORA EGGLESTON, one of the many Newport belles, is unable to teach her school on account of sickness. Matrimonial fever is contagious as we speak from sad experience.

HOLMES GIBSON, of Peoria, IL, was in town last Monday.

Home News
JOHN ETTER has gone up to Perrysville to clerk in T.W. STEPHENS' saloon.

URE A. JOHNSON has been appointed administrator of his father's estate.

ROBERT A. PARRETT has been appointed administrator of the estate of ETTA A. ASBURY.

Mrs. ALMA COLE, of Helt township, united with the M.E. Church on Thursday last.

Prosecutor H.H. CONLEY, who has been seriously ill for several days, was worse yesterday.

STEPHEN A.D. THOMAS, of Eugene, left on last Monday for Terre Haute to attend Commercial College.

BRENTON CRAIG and Miss SAMANTHA WHITE, of this township, are making arrangements to work in double harness.

At the close of services in Hillsdale, on Sunday evening, ALVIN B. CASEBEER and MARY B. WOLFE united with the M.E. Church.

JOHN D. COLLETT, of this place, has been admitted as one of the students of the Rose Polytechnic Institute, at Terre Haute.

Mrs. LIZZIE SWITZER, of Eugene, was in town visiting on Thursday last. She was accompanied home by her mother, Mrs. ORPHA WIGLEY.

Prof. JOHN COLLETT, State Geologist, left Indianapolis, left on Wednesday last for the Arkansas Hot Springs to see if he could not recuperate his failing health. He has been in poor health for some time, and it is reported that he has nearly lost the sight of one eye.

JOSEPH JACKSON and Miss LAURA WALTERS, both of Dana, are making preparations to form a co-partnership during the remainder of their natural lives.

For his close attention and care during the late illness of JOHN C. JOHNSON, URE A. JOHNSON, and his sisters, Miss FLORA and Miss CATHERINE JOHNSON, presented WILLIAM P. WRIGHT with a magnificent gold-headed cane.

FIELDING SHEPARD, of Fayette township, Vigo County, a former citizen of Clinton, and well known by many of the people in the south end of this county, died on March 4, 1883, aged 72 years. He had been an invalid for the last 30 years. In 1835 he married a sister of Dr. HEDGES, of Clinton.

Divorce Wanted
AMELIA STROUD has brought suit in the Circuit Court for a divorce from CALVIN W. STROUD, to whom she was married in Vermillion County, IN, in September 1881. He abandoned her in January 1883, and on this ground she seeks a divorce. She charges him with being idle and lazy, refusing to work, and provide for herself, and her 5 children by her first husband. C.F. and J.G. McNUTT are her attorneys.

Terre Haute Sunday Express

Married
On last Tuesday, at the residence of the bride's father, MOSES THOMPSON, of Helt township, Mr. JAY COLE was united in wedlock to Miss ALVINA N. THOMPSON, Rev. E.R. JOHNSON, M.E. pastor of the Helt's Prairie circuit, performing the marriage. After the usual congratulations a sumptuous supper was served, all partaking of the bountiful feast to their hearts' content.

Obituary

SHEPARD HOLLINGSWORTH, a son of WRIGHT HOLLINGSWORTH, deceased, who resided three miles west of town, died shortly after 12 o'clock on Wednesday last, after an illness of 10 weeks. The deceased was a young man 23 years of age, and very highly respected by his neighbors and acquaintances. He was strictly temperate in his habits, honest, and industrious, and lead an exemplary life. His funeral took place on Thursday last and was respectable attended by his young associates and friends. His remains were interred in the Thomas Cemetery.

To all those who desire bibles and testaments at very low prices, contact one of the following:

R.H. NIXON – Newport
HAYS & CONLEY – Clinton
F.N. AUSTIN – Bono
O.M. KEYES – Dana
Mrs. LUCINDA BROWN – Eugene
J.F. LANGSTON – Summit Grove
W.D. McFALL – Jonestown
J.E. ROBINSON – Perrysville

The friends of Mrs. MARTHA WHITE, formerly of this city but now of Augusta, KS, will be sorry to learn that she is, at this writing, lying at the point of death. We hope to soon hear of her recovery.

Clinton Herald

Commissioner's Court

H.H. CONLEY etal – petition for appointment of constable for Vermillion township - RICHARD T. MITCHELL appointed

Liquor license granted:

JEREMIAH CONLEY – Dana
JOHN PEELER – Dana
OWEN MOFFATT – Clinton

Allowances

JACOB WIMSETT, road viewer	3.50
JOHN HIGHFILL, road viewer	3.50
W.Y. RICE, road viewer	3.50
GEORGE W. CAMPBELL, road viewer	3.25
F.E. COMBS, road viewer	1.50
MANFORD STEWART, road viewer	1.50
JAMES CHIPPS, Newport, Quaker Point Gravel Road	34.29
R.T. MITCHELL, Newport, Quaker Point Gravel Road	33.70
JOHN R. BIRELY, Newport, Quaker Point Gravel Road	31.50
H.T. SHEPARD, Inquest	25.00
D.S. HOPKINS, County offices	3.80
HENRY VOLKEL, ditch assessment	276.00
W.B. BUFORD, stationery	14.25
A.J. JOHNSON, County Superintendent	237.00
S.B. DAVIS, printing	136.20
H.O. PETERS, Hazel Bluff Gravel Road	87.93
HEDGES & WRIGHT, Hazel Bluff Gravel Road	25.00
JOHN O. WRIGHT, C. & P. Gravel Road, interest	100.00
H.O. PETERS, C. & P. Gravel Road, bond	1,000.00
H.O. PETERS, C. & P. Gravel Road interest	319.00
M.G. RHOADS, attorney fees	160.00
W.L. LITTLE, Criminals	3.96
H.O. PETERS, Salary as Treasurer	200.00

M. HEGARTY, public buildings	4.35
L.A. MORGAN, Trustee poor, Highland township	354.45
ANTHONY FABLE, Trustee poor, Eugene township	391.05
JAMES CHIPPS, Trustee poor, Vermillion township	286.95
JAMES OSBORN, Trustee poor, Helt township	196.72
GEORGE W. STUTZ, Trustee poor, Clinton township	261.85
JAMES WALLACE, Physician, poor	45.75
ERASTUS MACK, Physician, poor	25.00
R.E. NICHOLS, Physician, poor	12.50
JOSEPH CONARD, Poor asylum	365.54
M.L. HALL, Board of Health	35.00
D. AGGRAY, Janitor	50.00

Notice of Final Settlement of Estate
Estate of GEORGE SWITZER, deceased
March 8, 1883
JAMES ROBERTS, Admr.

Notice of Final Settlement of Estate
Estate of JESSE SMITH, deceased
March 6, 1883
JAMES ROBERTS, Admr.

Notice of Non-Residence
GEORGE R. HOPKINS vs. ENOS MITCHELL, CHARITY MITCHELL, Unknown heirs of CYRUS BOWEN
Complaint No. 2299
Residence of defendants is unknown
Must appear before fourth Monday of April 1883
March 13, 1883
JAMES ROBERTS, Clerk
By A.R. HOPKINS, Deputy Clerk

Eugene Items
ALEXANDER KINDERMAN has returned from the Medical College of Chicago, having completed the course. We understand that he will practice at this place.

E.A. FLAUGHER returned from Indianapolis last week where he completed his course of lectures and received his diploma.

Mr. TOPPING's daughter from Chicago, is visiting her father at this place, who she has not seen for 8 years. She went from here to Peoria, IL, to see her brothers.

Mr. WATSON's school closed on last Friday.

Mr. LEONARD LADD died on last Sunday morning, about 9 o'clock. Cause of his death was brain fever. In the death of Mr. LADD, we lose one of our best citizens, his family loses a kind and loving father.

Letter List

DILLEY, ALBERT L.	JEWELL, WILLIAM S.
BULGER, FRANK	HODGES, MILTON
SMITH, S.H.	SPANDAN, F.
THOMAS, JOHN H.	KING, Miss ELLEN
JONES, Mrs. MATTIE	

Wednesday, March 21, 1883

Attempted Suicide

About 10 o'clock yesterday morning, our citizens were startled by the sudden announcement that GEORGE DOUGLAS, a farmer residing ¼ of a mile south of town, on ABEL SEXTON's farm, had committed suicide by cutting his throat from ear to ear with a pocket knife. Dr. M.L. HALL, Dr. LEWIS SHEPARD, and Dr. LEWIS WALLACE were sent for, and on their arrival they found their patient in a rather critical condition. Sometime last fall, he sold out all his personal effects and moved to Kansas. He was not pleased with the country and in a few weeks moved back, dead broke. Not having means to support his family he became melancholy and this is the reason he attempted to end his career here on earth. He has a wife and 5 children. His wife is now in a delicate situation, and will be confined again in a few weeks. Mr. DOUGLAS is 39 years of age, and has been a resident of this vicinity since 1857. He was a sober, quiet, inoffensive citizen, and the last person anyone would have suspected of attempting to take his own life. The family is in destitute circumstances.

Clinton

WILLIS HEDGES is attending the Rose Polytechnic Institute.

GEORGE CRABB has bought HARRY WHITCOMB's stock of groceries and will sell them out at the old stand.

R.E. STEPHENS left yesterday on a trip to the west for the benefit of his health.

They had a regular jubilee out at ED KNOWLES last Thursday evening. FRANK LANGSTON and SARAH SHANNON, SAM HUP and AMANDA WICKS, were united in the holy bonds of matrimony, Brother WOOD officiating. It was a very enjoyable affair.

Home News

Miss KITTIE KAUFMAN and Miss LILLIE CRANE, of Dana, are making their wedding clothes.

BUCK FORTNER has a brand new baby girl baby at his house. It arrived on last Thursday morning.

Dr. O.C. BRICKER, a former resident of this place, is Superintendent of the Sunday School at Annapolis.

JEROME NEESE, like the pelican of the Clinton Herald, has taken a trip out west for benefit of his health.

Miss ANNA MILLER, of this place, and a young man by the name of MYERS, of Helt township, will be married sometime next month.

ALBERT ROBINSON, the young man who committed suicide or was murdered at Veedersburg, Fountain County, a couple of weeks since, was a nephew of PICK DICKEN's wife, residing on the hill, just southwest of town.

FRANK LANGSTON and SARAH SHANNON, of Summit Grove, were united in wedlock, at Clinton, on last Thursday evening, the ceremony being performed at the residence of ED KNOWLES. Rev. A.W. WOOD, pastor of the M.E. Church at that place, tied the knot.

ERNEST HIBERLY, of this township, left on last Monday to attend Normal School at Terre Haute.

JOHN A. WILTERMOOD, of this place, and Miss JESSIE WELLS, who is teaching at the London School House, this township, will be united in wedlock sometime in April.

WILLIAM L. LITTLE returned home last Saturday evening from a two weeks trip to Kansas. He is highly elated with the country and says that he is going to move out there next October.

Mrs. MARY M. HELT, wife of DANIEL HELT, deceased, is now probably the oldest person living in this county. She was among the early settlers of this county, and has resided where she now lives since 1818. At that time the county was very sparsely settled. Indians and wild game were plenty. The farm she lives on was entered from the government by her late husband.

Matrimony
OMER NICHOLS, of this township, and REBECCA SPANGLER, of Bono, were united in marriage on Thursday last, Rev. CHARLES EATON, of the U.B. Church, performing the ceremony. The young couple has the best wishes of their many friends.

Short Honeymoon
JAMES JORDAN, of this place, who was united in marriage to Miss MARY BROWN, aged 16, some 4 or 5 weeks ago, separated last week. JORDAN was jealous of his young wife and says she was untrue to him, while she claims that he was traveling in the same boat and gave her a loathsome disease. She has returned to her father, DAVID BROWN, and is now undergoing medical treatment.

Obituary
ELSIE E. EFAW, wife of BENNET EFAW, of Larchland, Warren County, IL, died of heart disease March 10, 1883. Sister EFAW was born in Vermillion County, IN, January 11, 1858, and was the daughter of Rev. JOSEPH and SARAH JONES of Hillsdale, IN. Sister EFAW, while living under the paternal roof, was endeared to her friends by her amiable disposition, and ever retained the same characteristics in her life.

Bono
On last Thursday evening, REBECCA SPANGLER and OMER NICHOLS, near Newport, were united in holy wedlock, Rev. EATON officiating.

ORRIE HENNICE has been given up to die by the physicians attending him. Vitality of his lower limbs has given way to paralysis, so death is approaching him inch by inch.

ALBERT SHARP, a former clerk of JESSIE PEERs, has purchased the AD THOMPSON grocery store and is doing good business. The latter has moved to Kansas City, MO.

Miss BELLE MOBRY and DICK VANGILDER, while out horsebacking on last Thursday, chanced to stop with Esq. LEG and were tied together in one matrimonial knot. May they never sever the ties.

Montezuma
The family of SOLOMON WRIGHT, who moved to the State of Oregon, some 10 years ago, are now on their return to Indiana and will probably locate in Montezuma. Mr. WRIGHT who is in poor health will remain some months in California in order to close up some unsettled business in that State.

Eugene
Mr. GEORGE STRUBLE, of Lafayette, and Miss SUSIE SOLLARS, of this place, were united in wedlock on March 14, 1883.

Miss LACIE MORRIS, who has been teaching in Fountain County, closed her school on last Friday and has returned to our little village.

WILLIAM LADD, from Neosho, KS, arrived here on last Tuesday, March 13, 1883, to attend his brother's funeral. He started for home on Monday last. He says Kansas is the best State of all.

JAKE PETERS, who has charge of his brother's store at Ridgefarm, IL, was in the city Sunday.

JOHN BRILES, of Clinton, has opened out a blacksmith shop at this place.

Notice of Final Settlement of Estate
Estate of SAMUEL JONES, deceased
March 13, 1883
JAMES ROBERTS, Clerk
By A.R. HOPKINS, Deputy Clerk

Wednesday, March 28, 1883

Clinton
S.P. McCREA was in town last week and succeeded in obtaining the principalship of our school for next winter. Mr. McCREA is a graduate of the Terre Haute Normal School, is highly recommended as a teacher, and we presume will be able to superintend the school successfully.

Miss MAGGIE DUFFY, the teacher at Pleasant Hill Schoolhouse, was buried last week. MAGGIE was a talented young lady and had by her own industry and economy prepared herself for the profession of teaching. She is deserving of great credit for her noble behavior and clever attainments, and has given us an example worthy of emulation. Had her life been spared she would no doubt have become one of the shining lights in her chosen profession. But now that she is gone we can but strew her grave with flowers and remember her kindly for the good she has done.

Montezuma
Miss SARAH MOTTE, of Bloomingdale, who has been the teacher in the primary school here, has resigned her position and expects soon to go to California. Her sister MARY MOTTE, it is understood, will take the vacated position.

By a letter lately received from Dr. E.B. CANNON, now under treatment in New York City, it is learned he is fast improving in health, but will not return home for some time.

A Mrs. FORBES, who has been sick with consumption for several months in the south part of town, was sent to her relatives in Tippecanoe County, by our township Trustee on Saturday last.

Perrysville
CYRUS WRIGHT and wife have severed in twain the sacred ties that once made their young hearts to rejoice, and intend trying single blessedness again.

At the commencement exercise of Bennett Medical College of Chicago last Wednesday, Dr. B.I. POLAND received the highest honors of the graduating class, and now his shingle is dangling in the breeze, kissing every zephyr that comes in contact with its polished surface. We congratulate the doctor on his success.

Mr. WOODYs school will close next Friday evening with an exhibition for the benefit of Mound Chapel, after which Mr. WOODY will leave for Danville, IL, where he intends to spend the summer in school. He may take an instructor with him.

WILLIAM TATE has left for Iowa.

Mrs. L.F. SCONCE's baby has been very ill, but is some better at the present writing.

CHARLEY CLARK has a very sick child.

Highland
Dr. SMITH, of Newman, IL, has located at this place to engage in the practice of medicine.

LEONARD RANDALL, aged about 17 years, died on Tuesday night, March 13, 1883, of quick consumption.

Dr. J.C. HARRISON, who is now a resident of Southern Arkansas, writes that he likes the country and is having a good practice.

MILTON SHOWALTERS will move to Chrisman, IL, in a few weeks. A Mr. HENDRIX has rented the farm that he occupied.

JOHN HEAVY's school closes on Wednesday of this week.

Eugene
The HATTON JAMES' school closed on last Thursday.

BOB HOLTZ is learning the carpenter trade.

Bono
JASPER SKIDMORE has secured the agency of this county and Edgar County, in selling the champion washer.

ED TIFFANY, a former resident of this county, has come among us again, locating on the KERNs property, near Bono. ED is a good neighbor and has many friends.

Home News
Call on D.R. GRAY for Plasters hair, Lath, and Shingles.

J. JUMP has been appointed administrator of the estate of Dr. I.B. HEDGES.

H.E. RHOADS of Waveland spent last Sunday with his brother, MARTIN G. RHOADS of this place.

Mr. HARRY RUGAN, who has been visiting his sister, Miss RENA RUGAN, for a few days, returned home on last Saturday morning.

G.B. OTT, who moved from the south part of this county to Viola, Wisconsin, has moved back again, and was in town on Monday last. He says his wife was dissatisfied with the country.

F.M. BISHOP will move on his claim 2 ½ miles east of town in a few days to indulge in the peaceful pursuit of agriculture this season, in consequence of which onions promise to rule lower this fall.

Garden City, Kansas, Irrigator

MANUEL SYKES, who went out to Kansas some 5 or 6 week ago, has returned and does not bring back a very favorable report. He says there are too many sand and wind storms out there for him. He prefers Indiana to Kansas.

JIM HAINS, of Perrysville, is up at Baraboo, Wisconsin. We received a gallon jug of "maple molasses" from him on Monday last.

GEORGE DOUGLAS, residing just south of town, who attempted suicide last week by cutting his throat with a common pocket knife, is now improving and the doctors have hopes that he will get well. The fearful wound he made in his neck is healing nicely.

Auditor PRITCHARD and wife left on Monday last with their daughter, Miss ELLA PRITCHARD, who has been in delicate health for some time. Their point of destination is Oswego, KS, where Mrs. PRITCHARD and daughter will remain sufficient time to test the climate and see if it will benefit her failing health. Miss ELLA is a bright and intelligent young lady, and her many young friends will be glad to hear of her speedy recovery. Dr. C.F. KEYS, of Helt township, was up here on Friday, and suggested they make the trip.

Matrimony
On last Thursday evening, at the residence of the bride's father, JAMES KAUFMAN, of Dana, Mr. CARTER and Miss MATTIE KAUFMAN were united in holy bonds of wedlock, Rev. E.R. JOHNSON, M.E. pastor of Helt's Prairie circuit performing the solemn ceremony.

Death
Mrs. RICHARD POTTS, widow of the late RICHARD POTTS, who resided 2 ½ miles south of town, died at 3 o'clock on last Sunday morning. The deceased was born in Ohio in 1812, and when only 15 years of age, moved with her parents to this county, where she remained up to the day of her death. Her husband, RICHARD POTTS, who died some 8 years ago, was a prominent citizen of this county, and held the office of Sheriff for two terms, filling it with honor to himself and to the entire satisfaction of the people. The deceased has two brothers still living – GEORGE W. and E.Y. JACKSON, Sr. Her funeral, which was very largely attended, took place on last Monday morning at Vermillion Chapel, Rev. J.H. HOLLINGSWORTH, of the M.E. Church, preaching the discourse. Mrs. POTTS was a kind and good hearted woman and very highly respected by all of her acquaintances. One child, CHARLES P. POTTS, survives her, and now lives at the old homestead, where he and his wife kindly cared for her during her late illness. She was never blessed with but 2 children. The other one, THOMAS POTTS, died several years ago.

Obituary
Mrs. EMMA KITCHEN, daughter of WILLIAM GIBSON, of this place, died at Danville, IL, on Friday last, and her remains were brought down to Perrysville on the day following for interment. The deceased was 22 years, 3 months, and 22 days old. She had been afflicted with consumption, caused by exposure, since the first of last January. She was a good hearted woman and had many warm friends in this place. She leaves a husband and 2 or 3 little children.

Obituary
SUSAN HOWARD, who was the wife of the late JOSEPH HOWARD, of Highland township, this county, died in Nebraska on Thursday last, aged about 66 years. The deceased has a brother and sister still living, ROBERT DAVIS, of Helt's Prairie, and Miss ELIZABETH DAVIS, of Blacksburg, VA. Mrs. HOWARD was born in Virginia, and with her brother ROBERT and his family moved to this State in an early day, locating near Annapolis, Parke County. They afterwards moved to Waveland, where she was married to JOSEPH HOWARD, who died several years ago. Mrs. HOWARD had been a member of the M.E. Church since her youth, and was a true Christian lady. She had many personal friends in the north part of this county who will regret to hear of her death.

Clinton
Miss LEOTA MOREHEAD, of Newport, was the guest of her sister, Mrs. JENNIE BISHOP, a few days this week.

Wednesday, April 4, 1883

Perrysville
WILLIAM NEEL, who has been attending school at Ladoga, is spending his vacation at home.

Death
Miss ELLA PRITCHARD, only daughter of Auditor PRITCHARD, died at Oswego, KS, at 4 o'clock on last Friday afternoon, aged 16 years, 5 months, and 28 days. Auditor PRITCHARD and wife left here one week ago last Monday for Oswego, where they had been recommended to take their daughter by their physician, to see if the change of climate would not restore her fast failing health. She had been in feeble condition for some time, and when they left here with her, she was not able to walk without being supported by someone. They arrived at their destination on Wednesday, and she did not seem to be fatigued any from the long trip. On Thursday, the day after their arrival, she sat up quite a while, but in the evening took a chill, which caused a nervous prostration, but the next morning she rallied and was able to sit up an hour. In the afternoon she felt worse and informed her parents that she was going to die, that everything looked dark and she could not see them. A short time before she died, she regained her sight, and said everything was bright. She bade them all good-bye, and in a few moments her spirit took its flight. Miss ELLA was a modest, unassuming young lady, and the idol of her parents. Everybody was her friend, and when the sad news reached here upon the wire that she was dead, there were many sorrowful faces among her numerous friends. She was kind and generous hearted, and no one could help but admire and respect her. She was a member of the M.E. Church, and tried to live a Christian life. Her remains arrived here on last Monday evening, and were met at the depot by at least 100 of her friends and associates. Short funeral services will be held at the residence of the parents today at 10 a.m., when her remains will be conveyed to the Thomas Cemetery, 2 miles northwest of town, and there quietly laid to rest.

Perrysville
JOSEPH RUHL and family are preparing to move to Dakota in May.

Our school closed last Friday under the management of Prof. DEALAND as principal.

Home News
W.S. McCONNELL's wife is quite ill from a severe sore throat.

JOE C. DAVIS, who is attending school at Greencastle, spent last Sunday at home.

ISAAC RUSSELL is lying very sick at his mother's in Clinton, with pneumonia and pleurisy.

Miss MAY HOLMES, of Delphi, is here visiting her sister, Miss MATILDA HOLMES, who is one of the teachers in our public schools.

Mrs. WILKINSON, of Oswego, KS, an aunt of Mrs. PRITCHARD and Mrs. WELCH, of Terre Haute, a cousin, accompanied her home.

Uncle ANDY WIMSETT, the great revival preacher of Streater, IL, is in here on a visit to his brother, JACOB WIMSETT, and many old friends.

WILLIAM GIBSON is talking of visiting Scotland, his native home, some time this month. We wish him a safe trip across the briny deep.

Bono
MARCUS HASKELL, of Kansas, is back to old Hoosier once more, visiting friends. He looks as hale and robust as can be.

FRANK DAVIS is the champion musician of Jonestown.

Married
At the residence of Mrs. S.E. VANKIRK, 2 ½ miles west of Gessie, by Rev. W.N. COFFIN, Mr. JAMES A. JONES and Miss IDA VANKIRK, both of Vermillion County, IL.

Married
Yesterday, at the residence of Rev. JOHN W. PARRETT, Newport, IN, JAMES WARD Esq. of Ridge Farm, IL, and Miss EMILY K. TENBROOK, of this city, the ceremony being performed by Rev. PARRETT in usual happy style.

Married
On last Thursday evening, Mr. JAMES F. CARMACK and Miss ADDA NEWLIN, daughter of ALFRED NEWLIN, residing two miles southwest of town, were united in wedlock, Rev. J.H. HOLLINGSWORTH performing the marriage ceremony. Only a few invited guests of the bride and groom were present.

Death
Mrs. MARY HOOD, of Eugene, better known by the name of Aunt POLLY HOOD, died on Saturday last, aged 82 years. She was the mother of POLK HOOD. She is said to have been a noble and good woman, a kind and affectionate mother and very highly respected by her neighbors. Her funeral took place at 2 o'clock on last Sunday afternoon, and was respectably attended by her friends and acquaintances.

Montezuma
EDWIN MOORE, a young workman in CASE's planning mill, met with a terrible accident here on last Saturday. While working with the player, he got his right hand caught, and his hand was so badly lacerated that amputation was necessary of all his fingers. MOORE was an industrious boy, and a great help to his aged parents.

WALTER CANNON, son of Dr. CANNON of this place, has received an appointment as Railway mail route agent on the I.C.RR and will take his place April 4th.

Eugene Items
WILLIAM PULLIFORD and Miss ALDWIN were united in wedlock on Wednesday last.

Administrator's Sale of Personal Property

Estate of ETTA A. ASBURY, deceased
Sale at residence of Dr. JOHN GILMORE in Vermillion township
Sale Saturday April 14, 1883
Personal property

Bradbury piano, stool and cover, gold watch and chain, one cow, one sewing machine, Brussels carpet, mirrors, clock, books, beds and bedding, silver and tableware, chinaware, glassware, etc.

March 26, 1883

ROBERT A. PARRETT, Admr.

Newspapers for dates April 11, 1883 through April 1, 1885 are unavailable.

Wednesday, April 8, 1885

Highland Items
BILL JACKSON and wife started for Nebraska last Monday.

From Opedee
The other day while BILL HAT was burning brush, his little boy got too near the fire, burning the little fellow severely.

Home News
Mrs. JOHN N. JONES, of Perrysville, is down with erysipelas.

JOHN HUMRINGHOUSE, of Humrie, Illinois, was in town on Saturday.

A Mrs. BLUNK, of Danville, Illinois, is here visiting her cousin, Mrs. MARY SHARP.

JOHN F. STEWART, the old color bearer of the 18th Indiana Regiment, was in the city on Saturday last.

Mrs. SOLON JOHNSON and her son PEARL, of Dana, were in town a couple of days last week visiting.

JAMES KAUFMAN, EV. THOMPSON, LOS. GOODWIN, and JOHN PATTON, of Helt township, were in Newport on Saturday.

REESE MITCHELL and Miss CARRIE DUNLAP, both of this township, will be united in wedlock on the 16th of this month.

Judge JOSEPH M. RABB, of Williamsport, was in the city on business on Thursday last and made the Hoosier a pleasant call.

Miss HATTIE MILLIKEN, of Eugene township, has been taken to the Insane Asylum at Indianapolis.

Rev. J.S. BROWN and his daughter, ZULA, of Perrysville, were in Newport Thursday and Friday of last week.

Mrs. Z.T. GALLOWAY and Mrs. OL. DAVIS returned from Ellettsville on Friday last where they had been for two weeks attending the bedside of a sick sister.

Miss MINA BROWN, of this place, is working in the Insane Asylum of Illinois, at $15 a month and board. She gets a ten day furlough each year to come home and see her friends.

Death of a Deaf Mute
Miss FANNY MILLER, daughter of JOHN MILLER, who resides in the west part of this township, died at 9 o'clock on last Wednesday morning, after an illness of twelve weeks of typhoid fever. FANNY was 21 years of age, and was a bright and cheerful lady. She had received a fair education at the deaf and dumb institute, Indianapolis. She knew she was going to die, and told her parents, the clothes she wanted to be buried in. She was an estimable young lady, and had a host of friends.

Obituary
Miss BELL DAVIDSON, an estimable young lady residing 3 miles West of Clinton, died of consumption on Sunday last. She was about 18 years of age, and leaves a large circle of warm friends to lament her untimely death.

Obituary
Esq. JAMES A. PRATHER, an old and estimable citizen of Gessie, died on Monday, March 30, 1885, after a two weeks illness of lung fever, aged 70 years. His funeral took place on the day following, and was respectably attended by his relatives and numerous friends.

Insane
An inquest was held on JOHN SHUTE, residing 2 miles north of Gessie, on Wednesday last, who is pronounced to be insane, caused by lung fever. Application has been made to have him taken to the asylum. Sheriff DARBY will probably get the order and take him over some time this week. Mr. SHUTE is 50 years old, has a wife but no children.

Matrimony
On Thursday last, April 2, 1885, Mr. JOHN CADE, deputy postmaster at Gessie, was united in wedlock to Miss MALISSA J. HAINS, daughter of JOHN HAINS of Highland township. Both have the best wishes of their many young friends. We acknowledge the receipt of a box of nice cake. May they live long and prosper.

Death
GEORGE McDONALD, of Montezuma, aged 65 years, died on Monday last after a two months illness. He has been traveling salesman for Bement, Rea and Co., of Terre Haute for over 20 years. No man on the road had more friends than Mr. McDONALD.

Notice of Insolvency

Estate of ALBERT COX, deceased
WILLIAM COX, administrator
March 23, 1885
A.R. HOPKINS, Clerk

Estate of JOHN SMITH, deceased
JAMES CHIPPS, administrator
March 23, 1885
A.R. HOPKINS, Clerk

Real Estate Transfers for March 1885

NELSON C. ANDERSON etal to MORGAN J. TUCKER
190 acres of land in Clinton township - $6,000

ELIZA J. SMITH to MORGAN J. TUCKER
45 acres in Clinton township - $800

WILLIAM WOOD and wife to ELIZABETH M. MARTIN
39 acres in Clinton township - $1,365

SARAH M. PAYTON to ALICE BROWN
Lots 4 & 5, block 5 – love and affection

MARY A. MARTIN to MILDRED MARTIN etal
45.83 acres in Clinton township - $350

SUSAN SHANNON to MARTHA J. DAVIS
2 acres in Clinton township - $25

JOHN GRONDYKE to CHARLES E. CROCKETT
Lot 30, Eugene junction - $75

ELIAS PRITCHARD and wife to REBECCA TILLOTSON
6 acres in Bono - $1,500

FRANCIS M. SALYER to LEVI WRIGHT
37 acres in Clinton township - $1,000

DAVID W. GARDNER and wife to REBECCA GREEN
One lot adjoining Clinton - $100

DANIEL MILLER and wife to ISAAC M. WATSON
Lot 8, block 8, Dana - $125

HENRY BROCK to WILLIAM T. SOUTHARD
5 acres in Helt township - $100

JOSIAH C. JACKSON and wife to THOMAS MONAGHAN
Lots 10, 11, & 12, Bricker's addition, Hillsdale - $165

SYLVIA V. NICHOLS to CATHARINE NICHOLS
50 acres in Vermillion township - $1,610

ROSA A. BREWER heirs to ALBERT E. VILLARS
31.92 acres in Highland township - $500

SPENCER H. DALLAS and wife to WILLIAM RICHARDSON
40 acres in Vermillion township - $35

ANNA SLATER and heirs to MARGARET MARTIN
Lot 5, block 14, Clinton - $500

AMANDA J. HOLLINGSWORTH to JAMES P. BOATMAN
30 acres in Clinton township - $600

B. HOWARD WHITCOMB to ELIJAH JACKSON etal
1/12 OF 40 acres in Clinton township - $95

THOMAS S. HOOD and wife to CATHARINE R. FILLINGER
40 acres in Helt township - $1,600

WINFIELD S. CRABB and wife to PERMELIA GREEN
Part of lots 1 & 4, block 28, Clinton - $400

JAMES WALLACE etal to NANCY J. PORTER
77 acres in Vermillion township - $1,540

WILLIAM J. ANDREWS and wife to WILLIAM D. McFALL
10 acres in Helt township - $300

JOHN GRONDYKE to JAMES FARTHING
Lots 20 & 21, Eugene junction - $175

E. WHITE JAMES etal to LEWIS D. STUTSMAN
40 acres in Helt township - $2,400

DARWIN O. CRAIG to DEREXA CRAIG
E ½ of lot 10, block 5, Clinton - $300

JAMES WATSON and wife to SARAH P. HEDGES
12 acres in Clinton township - $250

NANCY J. FENNIMORE and heirs to LEVI JACKSON
21 acres in Clinton - $50

CATHARINE NICKELS to JOSEPH LEVACK
5 acres in Vermillion township - $35

Notice of Final Settlement of Estate
Estate of JOHN RICHARDS, deceased
April 7, 1885
A.R. HOPKINS, Clerk

Notice of Non-Residence
MARIA MASON vs. WILLIAM MASON
SAWYER & GIBSON attorneys for plaintiff
WILLIAM MASON is not a resident of Indiana
Must appear before first Monday in June 1885
April 6, 1885
A.R. HOPKINS, Clerk

Notice to Non-Residence
State of Indiana ex rel ALICE HELT vs. JAMES RALSTON
WARD & DAVIS attorneys for plaintiff
JAMES RALSTON is not a resident of Indiana
Must appear before first Monday in June 1885
March 30, 1885
A.R. HOPKINS, Clerk

Assignee's Notice
Appointed assignee for WILLIAM COLLETT, of Eugene, IN
For benefit of creditors
LESLIE D. THOMAS

Assignee's Notice
Appointed assignee for McCORMICK & REEVES, of Clinton, IN
Composed of JOSEPH S. McCORMICK and JAMES W. REEVES
Owners of a Livery, Feed, & Stable
For benefit of creditors
HENRY O. PETERS

Notice of Non-Residence
MARY J. COFFEY vs. THOMAS J. COFFEY
SAWYER & GIBSON attorneys for plaintiff
THOMAS J. COFFEY is not a resident of Indiana
Must appear before first Monday in June 1885
March 10, 1885
A.R. HOPKINS, Clerk

J.M. STUDEBAKER
Windmills
Summit Grove

RILEY WHITNEY
Dry Goods, shoes
Newport

O.B. LOWRY
G.H. FISHER
Farming implements
Dana

ADAM B. LITTLEPAGE
JOHN WILTERMOOD
Attorneys at Law
Newport

HUGH H. CONLEY
Attorney at law
Newport

MARTIN G. RHOADS
Attorney at law
Newport

BEN BLANCHARD
Attorney at law
Newport

M.B. DAVIS
Attorney at law
Clinton

C. SAWYER
O.B. GIBSON
Attorneys at law
Newport

J. JUMP
C.W. WARD
Attorneys at law
Newport

Wednesday, April 15, 1885

Gravel Road
SOLON MITCHELL and family, of this place, have moved to Perrysville.

Country Dudes
Rev. BROWN, of Perrysville, was visiting a brother here Tuesday.

Highland Items
JAMES STUTLER, of Gessie, is dangerously ill at present with pneumonia.

Mrs. LIB GROVES, of Springfield, Illinois, is visiting friends of this place.

Miss CONNOR, of Montezuma, was visiting her brother of Perrysville last week.

Miss NETTIE MOORE commenced school at Butternut last Monday.

The dwelling house of DAVID GOUTY was burned last Wednesday. But few of the household goods were saved.

Home News
URE A. JOHNSON, of Vigo Co., was in town on Wednesday last.

SIMON HIRSCH and ELMER HENSON of Terre Haute, were in the city on Monday.

QUILL MOREHEAD, one mile west of town, is dangerously ill with consumption.

Mrs. M.G. RHOADS was up at Perrysville, last week, visiting her parents and friends.

H.C. HANA, of Rockville, has moved to Danville, Illinois, where he intends to permanently reside.

Uncle CEPHUS MACK, of Helt's Prairie, is quite seriously ill with hemorrhage of the kidneys.

Mrs. ANNA TARRENCE and her sons, EDDIE and WILLIE, of Terre Haute, are here on a visit to their numerous friends.

Mrs. MARIA SMALLWOOD, an old and estimable lady of Perrysville, was in town over Sunday, visiting Mrs. M.G. RHOADS.

WILLIAM SNIDER, of Washington County, an acquaintance of JAMES SYKES, has come out here to remain during the summer.

The Clinton Argus states that Attorney M.B. DAVIS is talking of pulling up stakes at that place and locating at some point in Nebraska.

Rev. JOHN HARRISON and lady leave for Homer, IL, in the morning, to attend the wedding of their cousin, Miss FLORA EWIN to Mr. H.J. BENNETT, of the same town. The ceremony will take place at 8 o'clock in the evening, and be performed by Rev. HARRISON. On Friday evening, they will come back to Danville.

Rockville Republican
Hon. JAMES T. JOHNSTON was called to Greencastle on Monday, by a dispatch stating that his brother, CHARLEY, had met with a terrible accident and was not expected to live.

Matrimony
Married at the residence of THOMAS MITCHELL, Perrysville, Vermillion Co., Indiana, by Rev. J.S. BROWN, Wednesday, April 8, 1885, at 8 o'clock P.M., HERSCHEL N. CADE to Miss MARY WRIGHT.

Notice of Settlement of Estate
Estate of JOHN RICHARDS, deceased
June 1, 1885
A.R. HOPKINS, Clerk

Notice of Non-Residence
WILLIAM GIBSON vs. JOSEPH C. McKIBBEN
WARD & DAVIS – attorneys for plaintiff
JOSEPH C. McKIBBEN is not a resident of Indiana
Must appear before first Monday of June 1885
April 7, 1885
A.R. HOPKINS, Clerk

Wednesday, April 22, 1885

Home News
JOHN F. LEITON, of Clinton, has struck something richer than a post office. He has just been granted a pension, dating back to 1862, from which date he gets $6 per month, until some time in 1870, and from that date he is to receive $12 per month. His first draw will amount to about $1700.

HARRY JAMES, son of WILLIAM A. JAMES, of Helt township, who has been jerking lightning on the Missouri Pacific railroad at some point in Nebraska for the last 18 months, is at home on a visit, but will return the latter part of the week. He is highly pleased with the country, and said although they had a severe winter out there, it was not so changeable as here.

United in Wedlock
On last Thursday evening, at the U.B. parsonage, Mr. REESE D. MITCHELL and CARRIE E. DUNLAP were joined in holy bonds of wedlock, Rev. W.N. COFFMAN performing the pleasant task of knot tying.

An Incendiary

He Burns a Barn in Highland Township and is Arrested

Highland township has been visited by another fire. This time fire was set to the building. Mr. HENRY VOLKEL, a farmer residing two miles south of Gessie, some time since employed a tramp to work for him by the name of AUGUST ELDER. After he had been there a while, Mr. VOLKEL concluded that he was not the kind of a hand he wanted and on the morning of the 13th instant, he paid him off and discharged him. The tramp made the remark at the time that he would get even with him before 48 hours. He went to Gessie and started off up the track. Just before night he was again seen near the residence of Mr. VOLKEL. That night after all honest people had retired to their peaceful rest, the cowardly scoundrel sneaked up to the barn and applied the torch, destroying the barn and consuming all the contents it contained, amounting to several hundred dollars. Mr. VOLKEL had an insurance of $200 on the building. The scoundrel was tracked to Danville, Illinois, where he was arrested, and brought down here last week by Sheriff DARBY and lodged in jail. He was taken before Esq. EGGLESTON on Saturday and plead guilty to the charge of arson, and was bound over to court. Not being able to give bond, he was sent to jail.

Sad Accident

WILSON HARSHAW Drowned in the Little Vermillion

One of the saddest accidents that has befallen this place for a long time, occurred late last Sunday evening. The victim was WILSON HARSHAW, son-in-law of JOE MOREHEAD, who resided about one mile northeast of town, and in 200 yards of the bank of the Little Vermillion River. After dinner Mr. HARSHAW went up to see QUILL MOREHEAD, residing one mile west of town, who has been dangerously ill for several days. He returned late in the evening arriving home shortly after 5 o'clock. Just opposite his house, in the Vermillion, was a large raft of sycamore logs, which Mr. HARSHAW had been helping some Summit Grove parties get out to raft to Terre Haute. MARION LEE, of Summit Grove, who was in charge of the raft noticed that the creek at that point was falling and for fear it might be too low in the morning to float their raft down the river, he got MORT CHURCH and Mr. HARSHAW to assist in starting the raft. When near the raft they suddenly noticed their boat had sprung a leak, and water pouring in by the bucket full. The craft began to sink, and Mr. HARSHAW told Mr. CHURCH to jump on the raft, but he fell in the water, and if it had not been for a long pole projecting out from the raft, which he caught, he too would have met a watery grave. At this point the creek is from 10 to 15 feet deep and has a very rapid current. The boat sank with Mr. HARSHAW, and the only chance left him was to swim to shore, a distance of 40 or 50 feet. He started to swim but went down and drowned in a few feet of the shore. His wife who had come down to the creek to see them start the raft, witnessed the struggles of her drowning husband but was unable to render him any assistance. The news was soon brought to town, and nearly 200 of our citizens turned out to assist in recovering the body. Search was immediately instituted. At 8:20, less than 2 hours after the accident, WILSON HASTY succeeded in bringing the body to the surface with a pair of ice tongs. He was found sixty feet from where he was seen sink the last time. The gold watch on his person stopped nine minutes before 6 o'clock P.M. The remains were conveyed to his residence, and on Monday morning Coroner BRINDLEY held an inquest, rendering a verdict in accordance with the facts above stated. The deceased was 30 years of age, and had been a resident of this locality about two years. Three years ago last March he and Miss MAGGIE MOREHEAD were united in marriage. The result of their union is one child, 7 months old. His father, aged 76, and his mother 61, reside at Clarinda, Iowa. He has one brother living in Chicago. The sad news was telegraphed them on Sunday night. The deceased was a man whom everybody liked. He was friendly and kind to all, and his death is deeply regretted by everyone who knew him. In his death the people lose a great citizen, and the wife an affectionate husband.

Home News

DAN SOLLARS, of Eugene, is Dad of a girl baby.

MARSH HARRISON is Dad. It is a girl and takes its catnip straight.

LEVI ARRASMITH has a little ootsy tootsy at his house. It is a boy.

Miss MARY B. LANE, of Lodi, Parke County, was in town Saturday.

URE ASTON is the father of another boy baby, born on last Friday morning.

Professor J.W. PERRIN, late of Catlin, Illinois, schools, is in town visiting his old friends.

Mrs. CAD HARVEY, of Mattoon, Illinois, is here visiting her mother, Mrs. JAMES A. BELL.

We forgot to mention in our last issue that WILLIAM JONES, who resided near the depot, has a new boy baby at his house.

Misses MATTIE and EMMA DAVIS and their sister, Mrs. BARBARA WALKER of Clinton, were in town over Sunday visiting their parents.

ALBERT FORD, PAT FLYNN, JAMES LEWIS, HENRY JORDAN, J.H. FONCANNON, and WILLIAM HOUGHLAND, of Helt township, were in the city on Monday.

Hon. JAMES OSBORN, CALE BALES, ABE WISHARD, N.T. LEITON, J.M. HARPER, Surveyor FRED RUSH and several others of Helt township, were in town on Friday last.

JOE COLLETT, of Terre Haute, was up here on Saturday last. He recently returned from California, where he had gone to recuperate his health. He is now looking hearty and well.

Miss MATTIE and Miss EMMA DAVIS have removed their stock of dry goods, notions, etc., from Rushville, this state, to Gibson City, Illinois, where they will again open out in business this week. We wish them success.

Home News

HENRY VOLKEL, of Highland township, seems to have bad luck in caring for tramps. Last winter he took in a hungry tramp who was penniless, and kept a few days, when the fellow suddenly died on his hands. Last week another tramp who had been working for him a short time, got mad because he turned him off, and set fire to his barn that night and burned it to the ground.

In Trouble

A Perrysville Man Taken Into Camp

On Thursday evening of last week, the Sheriff of Benton County, this state, visited Perrysville and arrested MIKE CROCKETT, and spirited him away. No one could learn what the charge is against him. It must be something of rather a serious nature or they would not have sent down here after him. Mr. CROCKETT has always borne a fair reputation since he resided in our county, so far as we know.

Notice of Insolvency

Estate of BARSHEBA JAMES, deceased

OSCAR B. GIBSON, administrator

April 20, 1885

A.R. HOPKINS, Clerk

Notice of Insolvency

Estate of JOHN HAWORTH, deceased

JOSEPH HANN, executor

April 20, 1885

A.R. HOPKINS, Clerk

Wednesday, April 29, 1885

A Card
Letter expressing thanks for the help in recovering the body of WILSON J. HARSHAW.
WILLIAM and CATHERINE HARSHAW, parents

Retirement of Professor COLLETT
Prof. JOHN COLLETT will retire from his position of State Geologist on Saturday, and will be succeeded by Mr. J. MAURICE THOMPSON,of Crawfordsville. Prof. COLLETT will take up his residence at his old home, Newport, Vermillion County, but will also have local habitation in this city for several months at least.
Indianapolis News

Obituary
GERTIE WEBB, daughter of Dr. WEBB and wife, of Perrysville, Indiana, died Wednesday evening April 22, 1885, aged 7 years, 4 months, and 27 days. The funeral services were conducted by Rev. J.S. BROWN. GERTIE was always a good and obedient child, and was loved and admired by all who knew her. She bore her afflictions very patiently, and often expressed a desire to depart from this world of sickness, sorrow and death. During her illness she selected a hymn to be sung, and the XXIII Psalm to be read at her funeral. GERTIE has paid the debt we all must pay sooner or later. While her relatives and friends mourn over her departure, she is resting sweetly in the arms of the one who said suffer little children to come unto me, and forbid them not, for of such is the kingdom of heaven.

Obituary
Death of a Former Citizen of Newport
We made mention in last week's issue of the death on Tuesday, March 31st, of E.M. GROVES, a highly respected citizen of Union township. We have learned since, the following facts with reference to this life. Mr. GROVES was born in Tennessee. When he was 8 years of age, his parents moved to Indiana. Mr. GROVES moved from Indiana to this county 14 years ago. He was in his 62nd year. The 23rd of the present month would have been his 35th marriage anniversary. His wife and two sons and one daughter survive him. Mr. GROVES joined the Methodist church in 1853 and was a devoted Christian. The funeral services were held at the family residence on the 1st instant, conducted by Rev. H.C. BOLEN. The mortal remains were laid to rest in Oak Hill Cemetery on April 1, with Masonic honors, J.W. HARMAN, W.M., of Pickering Lodge No. 472 A.F. and A.M. officiating.
Nodaway (MO) Democrat of April 9th

Highland Township News
Rev. HALL, of Warren County, was visiting his son, Dr. W.I. HALL, of Gessie, last week.

Mrs. CORDREY started for Ohio on the 19th to witness the interment of her aged mother.

Miss MARY BRODERICK, a charming young lady of Montezuma, is visiting her cousin, Mrs. HARRY HUGHES.

Home News
ROBERT J. HOLTZ, of Waterman, Indiana, was in town on Saturday last.

W.H. HASKELL of Clinton, was in town on Friday and Saturday last.

JOSEPH NORTON, of Waterman, Parke County, was in town on Thursday last.

Miss ALMA BLANCHARD, of Terre Haute, came up last Saturday, and spent Sunday with her mother and brother.

Obituary
Mrs. J.H. ARRASMITH, residing near Quaker Point, this township, died on Friday last, from dropsy, and was buried on Sunday.

In this week's issue, will be found the announcement of FRANK P. HASTY, as a candidate for City Marshall. He is a good, clever, young man, and in every way qualified for the office.

Mr. and Mrs. HARSHAW, of Clarinda, Iowa, parents of WILSON HARSHAW, who was drowned in the Little Vermillion last Sunday evening one week ago, left for home on last Monday morning.

ERNEST HIBERLY and his brother FRED were competitors in the examination held at Terre Haute last week for appointment to West Point and the Naval Academy. The result of the examination will not be known till the latter part of this or the first part of next week.

EDDIE STEPHENS, of this place, a student of Depauw University, has just been elected Second Sergeant of the Military Co. there, and also Vice President of the Literary Society.

Wednesday, May 6, 1885

A Happy Surprise
At the residence of Mr. FRANK M. RILEY, a few miles east of the city at Riley's station on the C. & E.I. railroad, was the scene of the grand surprise, which was conceived and successfully carried out by Mrs. RILEY and friends, the occasion being in honor of the 41st birthday of her husband, which event came on Tuesday of last week, which proved an absolute surprise to him. A large number of his friends from the city and country had been invited by his good wife, all of whom were received and entertained in a most hospitable manner. Mr. and Mrs. ELISHA ROGERS, parents of Mr. and Mrs. RILEY also attended. It was also honored, as he reached his 71st birthday on that day.

Danville (Illinois) Commercial

Home News
HENRY HOLLINGSWORTH is still on the sick list.

Mrs. JENNIE BISHOP, of Clinton, is in poor health.

JAMES STOOTSMAN, of Helt township, left last Thursday morning for Kansas on a visit to relatives. He will be gone all summer.

Mr. H.S. CADY and wife returned home on last Wednesday evening from three weeks visit to relatives in the southern part of this state.

TOBITHA YORK, of Dana, who was sent to the Insane Asylum last fall for treatment, was brought home sound and well on last Saturday by Sheriff DARBY.

MART SEELY received a telegram on Wednesday last stating that his brother, who resided at Indianapolis, died that morning of consumption. He had been in poor health for a long time.

Mrs. FRANK COMBS, of Helt township, has gone to Washington territory on a years visit to her parents, who she has not seen for 25 years. She is a relative of the late Gen. STEELE of Rockville.

Miss MAY QUICK, of Clinton, returned home on Monday last from an extended visit to Michigan.

MIKE CASEY was re-elected Marshall of Clinton on last Monday by a large majority.

The fine residence of D.B. OTT, of Rockville, caught fire from a defective flue on Wednesday last and burned down. The loss is estimated at $3,000, on which was an insurance of $1400.

Obituary
Uncle CEPHUS MACK, an old and respected citizen of Helt's Prairie, who has been ailing with a serious affection of the kidneys for a long time, died at 8 o'clock on last Wednesday morning. The deceased was born in Massachusetts in 1815, and was therefore 70 years of age. He emigrated to this county in 1836, and had been a resident of this county ever since. At one time in life he was in fair circumstances, but had been unfortunate in business transactions, and did not own much of this world's possessions at the time of his death. He was an honest citizen and had the respect and esteem of all his neighbors and acquaintances. We don't suppose he had an enemy in the county. His funeral took place on the day following his death and was very largely attended by his relatives and neighbors. The funeral discourse was preached by Rev. E.R. JOHNSON, after which his remains were taken to Helt's Prairie Cemetery and laid away to rest.

Application for liquor license
HENRY C. HAY – Jones
WILLIAM MALONE – Eugene
CHRIS HALD – Eugene
THOMAS DICKERSON – Eugene
MORGAN J. TUCKER – Clinton
EDMOND EDMONDS – Eugene
GEORGE W. EDMONDS - Newport

Notice of Non-Residence
EMMA WILSON vs. THOMAS WILSON
No. 2636
WARD & DAVIS attorneys
THOMAS WILSON is not a resident of Indiana
Must appear before first Monday in June 1885
May 5, 1885
A.R. HOPKINS, Clerk

Notice of Non-Residence
ALMIRA BAMFORD vs. EHUD BAMFORD
WARD & DAVIS attorneys
EHUD DAVIS is not a resident of Indiana
Must appear before first Monday in June 1885
April 21, 1885
A.R. HOPKINS, Clerk

Notice of Non-Residence
HENRY JORDAN vs. Unknown heirs of WILLIAM DATY, Deceased; Unknown heirs of ADAM G. MAPPA, deceased; Unknown heirs of JOHN STORRS, deceased; Unknown heirs of BENJAMIN BRAYTON, deceased; Unknown heirs of WILLIAM AYERS, deceased; Unknown heirs of JOHN HAMILTON, deceased; and WILLIAM BOGART
M.B. DAVIS attorney for plaintiff
All defendants are not known to reside in Indiana
Must appear before June 15, 1885
April 20, 1885
A.R. HOPKINS, Clerk

Assignee's Sale

Creditors for the firm of McCORMICK & REEVES
Sale on Saturday, May 23, 1885
Sale at livery stable in Clinton at 10 a.m.

6 head of horses, one double carriage, 3 buggies, 1 buckboard, 3 sets of light double harness, 1 set of heavy double harness, 3 sets of light single harness, with robes, blankets, whips, etc.

HENRY O. PETERS, Assignee

Sheriff's Sale on Decree

Aetna Life Insurance vs. ISAAC COTTRELL, CYNTHIA ANN COTTRELL, MARY HADLEY, State of Indiana ex rel ANDREW GRIMES, Auditor of Vigo County, IN, and the Board of Commissioners of Vigo County, IN, JAMES DAILY, WILLIAM W. WATKINS, JAMES L. ROSS, GEORGE C. DENY
$2,543.20
Sale Saturday, May 9, 1885
Sale at courthouse 10 to 4

E ½ NE ¼ NW ¼ of NE ¼ Sec 34 T 14 N R 9 W – 120 acres
Vermillion County, IN

A.M. BLACK, attorney for plaintiff
April 15, 1885

JOHN A. DARBY, Sheriff

Wednesday, May 13, 1885

Montezuma Reporter
Mrs. SIMPSON, of Newport, was a guest of her daughter, Mrs. SOLLARS, the forepart of the week.

BAYLESS W. HANNA, the next minister of Persia, accompanied by his wife and three daughters, has left for their new home.

J.M. HAMMOND, of Hamburg, Iowa, a former citizen of this county, says a 14 year absence has not lessened the great interest he feels in his many friends of this county, and believes the Hoosier is the best source through which he can obtain information regarding them.

Another subscriber, by the name of WILLIAM BOGART, a former citizen of this county, but now a resident of Clinton County, Missouri, encloses us $1.00 for a six month subscription and says: "We cannot do without it. We are much obliged to you for past favors. You have been so punctual in sending us the paper. We expect to take the Hoosier as long as we live. When we get the Hoosier, we hear all the news of the county."

Highland Township
Mrs. ANN BEAUCHAMP and daughter, of Missouri, are visiting relatives of this township.

AMOS FLESHMAN returned home from Kansas, where he has been on business.

Home News
Mrs. ALICE ODEKIRK, of Opedee, left yesterday for New Hampshire, to be gone all summer.

OLIVER KNIGHT, a former citizen of this place, is chief clerk of the land office at Garden City, KS.

Clinton Siftings
Mrs. PETER LAMB is dangerously ill at her home in the north part of the city.

Miss MATILDA HOLMES, one of our teachers in the Newport Schools, left for her home at Delphi, this state, on Monday last.

Miss MOLLIE DE LA BARR, one of the teachers in the public schools of Clinton, is up here visiting her cousin, Mrs. JOHN A. WILTERMOOD.

Miss VINA ALEXANDER, teacher in the grammar department, left for her home in Bruceville, Knox County, on Tuesday last.

Mrs. PATIENCE YEARGIN, mother of the editor of the Oakland, Illinois, Ledger, died at her home, near Vermilion, Illinois, on Friday, May 1st, aged 91 years.

Yesterday was the fifth wedding anniversary of Mr. and Mrs. ED AIKMAN, of Highland. Quite a number of their relatives and friends gave them a happy surprise. Several went from this place. Long may they live.

Miss MAY DALLAS, of St. Paul, Minnesota, was down here visiting last week, the guest of her cousin, Miss ELLA PARRETT. She left for home yesterday, and was accompanied by Miss ELLA, who intends to make her a short visit.

Dr. J.H. BOGART, of Clinton, was in town yesterday.

STRATT HOLLINGSWORTH of Fontanet, Vigo County, was up here yesterday.

The world renowned Dr. W.J. CADLE, of Dana, was in town yesterday.

Real Estate Transfers for April 1885

SAMUEL HARRIS and wife to MATTHEW W. STEWART
15 acres in Highland township - $450

JOHN F. DUGGER and wife to SUSAN M. GOODWIN
12 acres in Helt township - $240

SALLIE CARROL etal to MILTON BRODOCK
Lot 3, block 4, Knowles addition to Clinton - $80

MARY E. WARD etal to THOMAS WILLIAMS
5 acres in Vermillion township - $200

JOHN FLETCHER and wife to FRED HIBERLY
13 acres in Vermillion township - $150

JOHN S. GRONDYKE to EMMA DICKERSON
Lot 12, in Eugene Junction - $75

JOHN RILEY and wife to A.B. CASEBEER
Lot 7, in Alta - $20

MARY A. CONLEY etal to JAMES CONLEY
10 acres in Helt township - $200

LUCY E. PEER and husband to LEVI H. AIKMAN
Lot 1, block 8, in Dana - $250

ALBERT E. VILLARS to ROSA A. BREWER
18 ½ acres in Highland township - $500

JAMES WARD and wife to ALEXANDER COLLIER
7 acres in Eugene township - $100

WILLIAM F. PANLEY and wife to JOHN W. DARBY etal
20 acres in Clinton township - $550

ROBERT WELCH to PATRICK WELCH
40 acres in Helt township - $1,000

THOMAS S. HOOD and wife to WILLIAM B. HOOD
80 acres in Helt township - $3,200

MICHAEL CONAWAY and wife to ALEXANDER CINDERMAN
Part lot 21, in Eugene - $600

A.B. HAYS and wife to W.L. HAYS etal
Lot 18, block 6, in Dana - $350

WILLIAM L. HAYES etal to ADAHNE AIKMAN
Lot 18, block 6, in Dana - $300

WILLIAM W. WISHARD etal to ANNA B. HUEY
90 acres in Helt township - $4,500

JOHN R. SPURGEON to ISABEL CARTER
7.35 acres in Helt township - $200

SAMUEL W. JORDAN and wife to ELIAS PRITCHARD
178 acres in Helt township - $7,300

PETER AIKMAN and wife to JOSEPH BURNS
74 ½ acres in Helt township - $1,200

HENRY HOLLINGSWORTH and wife to JOHN L. EGGLESTON and son
40 acres in Vermillion township - $625

GEORGE W. LEGG and wife to JOHN F. HUNT
80 acres in Vermillion township - $800

Notice of Non-Residence
CHARLES M. WHITE vs. WINFIELD S. CRABB
M.B. DAVIS, Attorney for plaintiff
WINFIELD S. CRABB is not a resident of Indiana
Must appear before first Monday in June 1885
May 5, 1885
A.R. HOPKINS, Clerk

Notice of Final Settlement of Estate
Estate of JOHN HAWORTH, deceased
May 4, 1885
A.R. HOPKINS, Clerk

Notice of Final Settlement of Estate
Estate of BARSHEBA JAMES, deceased
May 4, 1885
A.R. HOPKINS, Clerk

Wednesday, May 20, 1885

Dana Items
A.B. HAYS, has moved to Waveland, Parke County, Indiana.

A Mr. HUTCHINSON of Paris, Illinois, has moved to this town.

Home News
COON SOLLARS, of Montezuma, was in town yesterday.

ALLEN HALL, of St. Louis, is here visiting his mother and sisters.

CHARLEY TARRENCE, of Terre Haute, is the proud father of another baby.

WATSON PARRETT has returned from Kansas, and is looking remarkably well.

ERNEST L. HIBERLY is reading law with LESLIE D. THOMAS, of Terre Haute.

A girl baby was born to Mr. and Mrs. F.M. DAVIS, of this place, on last Monday morning.

Mrs. MARIA PATRICK, who lives with Auditor PRITCHARD, is down visiting friends in Helt township this week.

Mrs. N.T. LEITON, of Summit Grove, was out West of here about 8 miles on Sunday last visiting her brother, Mr. S.R. WHITE.

HENRY DENNIS and Miss EMMA WILSON are making arrangements to get married as soon as she gets a divorce.

CALE BALES, of Helt township, who has a national reputation as the loudest snorer in the West, was in town yesterday. He had his nose with him.

S.P. McCOWN and wife, of Clinton township, were up here visiting over Sunday, the guests of his brother-in-law, Treasurer WILLIAM L. PORTER.

Attorney M.B. DAVIS has postponed his departure for Lincoln, Nebraska, until after the June term of Circuit Court.

Clinton Argus

EVAN W. WILLIAMS, of Hutchinson, Kansas, returned on a visit last Monday. Mr. WILLIAMS is superintendent of BEN BLANCHARD's farm and stock ranch south of Helt.

Married
On last Wednesday evening at 7 o'clock, at the residence of Mr. RILEY WHITNEY, of Newport, Mr. GEORGE HEAP and Miss IDA CRARY, both of Farmersburg, Indiana, were united in marriage, Rev. JOHN HARRISON, pastor of the M.E. church, officiating. The young couple left for their home at Farmersburg on Thursday morning, and were accompanied by Mr. WHITNEY and family. May peace and happiness accompany them through life.

Sudden Death
An infant child of LEVI ARRASMITH, of this place, aged about 5 weeks, died very suddenly at an early hour on last Friday morning. It took down with spasms during the night which continued until the little innocent thing breathed its last. The funeral took place Saturday.

Birthday
Mrs. BETSY JAMES, of Helt's Prairie, will celebrate her 80th birthday today. We have received a kind invitation to be present, but are sorry circumstances are such that we cannot accept. The good old lady has our best wishes, hoping she may live to be 100 years old, and always enjoy good health.

A Beautiful Piece of Work
E.C. HODGES, of Terre Haute, has just completed a beautiful monument for the SHAW family that far excels anything in the Thomas Cemetery. It is a most magnificent piece of workmanship, and shows the artistic skill of the mechanic. The monument was ordered by Mrs. WILSON NAYLOR, of Terre Haute, who is paying all of the expenses out of her own pocket. It is twelve feet high, with a beautiful urn on top. The base is 4 feet square. The monument is $650 and the fence $150, making a total of $750.

Wednesday, May 27, 1885

Opedee Items
Mrs. PHOEBE FOULK is dangerously ill with consumption.

DICK WIMSETT is in Clay Center, Kansas, working in the water works.

Gleanings from Jonathan Creek
JIM BRAZIL is the happiest daddy we know of; it's a boy.

Highland
WILLIAM UNDERWOOD has a new baby at his house. It made its appearance one day last week.

W.A. ROEBACK, who received a handsome pension, some few weeks ago, has bought the HENRY OSBORN farm.

Miss JULIA MIDDLEBROOK had a birthday party last Friday evening. All present had a good time, and went away feeling that long would be remembered the happy occasion.

Miss IDA SWINDELL's birthday social of last Saturday evening will not be forgotten for many years by those who attended. Good music and a good time were had by all. She received many nice and valuable presents.

Our Dead Comrades
The following is a list of the brave boys who defended their country, and are quietly sleeping in the several cemeteries of this township. If there are any omitted from the list we hope their friends will notify us of the fact immediately.

Thomas Cemetery

JAMES A. BELL - 18th IN REG
ELI W. THOMAS - 18th IN REG
WARREN THOMAS - 43rd IN REG
SIMEON SHAW - 97th IN REG
JEROME B. DICKEN - 14th IN REG
MARION McDONALD - 14th IN REG
GEORGE WILFON - 97th IN REG
WESLEY CORDOR - 18th IN REG
SAMUEL TRUITT - 97th IN REG
MICAJAH HARRISON - 149th IN REG
MOSE J. EMLEY - 18th IN REG
JOSEPH WALLACE - 18th IN REG
JACOB BROWN - REG unknown

JACOB REMLEY - 97th IN REG
E.A. JONES - 22nd WISCONSIN
JAMES PETTY
DAL DOWNING

Johnson Cemetery
JOSEPH WEBB - 14th IN REG

Wimsett Cemetery
JOHN GIBBENS - 14th IN REG
JOHN HALL - 18th IN REG
HENRY AXTON - 43rd IN REG
ELI DILL - 79th IN REG
S.V. ODEKIRK - 24th NY

Cemetery Unknown
THOMAS PIERCE - 8th REG IL CAV
VINCE DOUGLAS
THOMAS J. BLUNK - 123rd IN REG
DAVID BRUNER - 153rd IN REG
I.B. LAMB
PERRY JONES
J.W. ARRASMITH - 6th IN CAV
JASON NOYES - 18th IN REG
CHARLES DAWSON
PRESSLEY JOHNSON - 6th IN CAV
STEVE BIGANY - 123rd IN REG

Miscellaneous
JOHN FLOYD - 123rd IN REG - Manley Cemetery
WILLIAM F. FLOYD - 123rd IN REG - Chattanooga, TN
HERROD FRINGER - 123rd IN REG – Indianapolis

Helt Cemetery
Maj. JOHN C. JENKS
JOHN CASTLE
DYER CASTLE
ELIJAH AIKMAN
WILLIAM AIKMAN
DANIEL HARPER
ASA SKIDMORE
REUBEN MACK
SAMUEL JAMES
BEN PEARMAN
HENRY FORD
SAUL HUNTER
JAMES HARBISON

Highland
Mr. ABRAHAM STRAWSER, of Gessie, will move to Danville soon, where he will engage in the butcher business with DAVID HUGHES.

Home News
S.E. KAUFMAN, GRANT DAVIS, and HARLEY HUTCHINSON, of Dana, were in Newport, on Saturday last.

It is currently reported that BILL WIGLEY, of this place, will wed a fair damsel of Jonathan Creek before many moons.

Mrs. EMMA GRAY, of Chicago, arrived here on last Saturday afternoon, and will remain about two months visiting her relatives and numerous friends.

BRENTON CRAIG, of Remington, this state, is here on a visit.

Mrs. S.S. COLLETT will leave the first of next month for Charleston, West Virginia, to visit her daughter, EVA.

Final Settlement of Estate

Estate of JOHN NICKELS, deceased
June 15, 1885

A.R. HOPKINS, Clerk

Wednesday, June 3, 1885

Home News

BOB GIBSON, who has been at work in the South part of the state, was in town one day last week.

Mr. A.R. HARPER and wife, of Chesterton, this state, relatives of Mrs. Rev. JOHN HARRISON, were in town visiting several days last week.

WILLIAM L. LITTLE, of Hutchinson, Kansas, is back here on business. He will remain about one week. He is highly pleased with his western home.

Attorney M.G. RHOADS' mother, who is here visiting him, is 88 years of age. She is in very feeble health, and has to go on crutches, owing to a hurt she received five years ago.

JOSIAH CAMPBELL, of Eugene township, is now the happy father of several children. The last addition arrived about two weeks ago, and is a sweet little daughter.

Mrs. S.S. COLLETT left last Monday morning for Charleston, West Virginia, to visit her daughter, Mrs. ADAM B. LITTLEPAGE. She will be absent about one month.

Mrs. ROBERT LANDON, who has been afflicted with a rose cancer in one of her eyes for the last 18 or 20 years, is now in a precarious condition, and will probably not linger long. In the last two weeks it has developed very rapidly, now being as large as a man's fist, and occasionally bleeds profusely. She suffers intensely and grows very weak.

ROBERT E. SHAW and his two sisters, Mrs. WILSON NAYLOR and Mrs. ELLEN GROEN-DYKE, of Terre Haute, came up here last Saturday and decorated their parents' graves with a lot of beautiful flowers.

Mrs. SOPHRONIA MALONE, of Eugene, was in town Monday and Tuesday visiting her mother, Mrs. B.W. SIMPSON. She went down to Montezuma yesterday evening to pay her sister, Mrs. COON SOLLARS, a visit.

Obituary

On last Saturday night, Mrs. SPENCER NORRIS died at the ripe age of nearly 80 years. She had only been ill a few days until the messenger of death called her from earth to that better world. She was one among the early settlers of this county, and was one of the noble women of our county. Her remains were buried in the Manly Cemetery on Sunday last.

Committed Suicide
WILLIAM DICKEN, who resided about 4 miles North of Scotland, Illinois, became deeply involved in debt, and could not stand the pressure, so on Tuesday morning of last week he put an end to his troubles here below by going to the barn and hanging himself by a strap from one of the beams. He had been dead about three hours when discovered. He was a man who was considered to be worth not less than $60,000 a few months ago. And it is now thought that the estate will be able to pay out and have $18,000 left for the widow and children. His total indebtedness amounts to $42,000. There are now on the farm 400 cattle that are estimated to be worth $25,000 to $30,000. His wife has a handsome residence and 200 acres of land in her own right. The deceased had a number of relatives residing at this place, and had rather an extensive acquaintance in this county.

Wednesday, June 10, 1885

Death
OLLIE OSBORN, of West Lebanon, Warren County, aged 22 years, loved a young maiden of Covington, who seemingly looked upon his suit with favor, but a few days ago she went to church with another young man and this was too much for his little heart. He bought poison, bid fare-well to all things earthly, and his spirit wafted hence.

WALTER D. JONES, of Crawfordsville, who was studying for the ministry, has gone astray. On January 4th he married a young lady of that county by the name of Miss JENNIE HORNER. In a couple of months after their marriage he went down to Terre Haute Normal to complete his edu-cation, and while there wrote his dear wife some very affectionate letters. About two weeks ago, he wrote her a farewell letter, telling her she would see him no more, that ere his letter would reach her he would be far away, in another land, with one he loved far better than he loved her. The name of his new victim is Miss ADDIE McLAUGHLIN, a fair damsel of Terre Haute. He is said to be a regular heart smasher, and it would not surprise us to hear, in a short time, of his having abandoned his last catch for some other pretty and gay woman.

Death of an Old 18th Boy
Died, at his residence, No. 733 South First Street, MICHAEL WHELAN, after a long and painful illness. He leaves a wife, an aged mother, several brothers and sisters, and a large circle of friends to mourn his loss. Mr. WHELAN was 53 years of age and has been a resident of Terre Haute eight years. He was a good citizen and a devoted husband; esteemed by all for his un-varying kindness to those by whom he was surrounded, and his uprightness and honesty. That he died as he had lived, at peace with his fellowmen was fully attested to by his fellow workmen and friends to whom the relatives wish to return thanks for their manifold kindness during the period of his illness and their bereavement. The remains were taken today to the family burying ground near Paris for interment.

Terre Haute Gazette of Saturday last

Gravel Road Items
Miss JENNIE CRAIG is seriously ill at this writing.

Mrs. FREE DOGGETT is visiting her parents Mr. and Mrs. JOHN RUSSELL.

MARY ELLEN LAKE, who has been seriously ill, is convalescent.

Highland
DUDLEY STRAUGHN, the best looking widower of Opedee, spent a Sunday with us recently.

The following parties are long madam rumor says, will trot no longer in single gears:
Mr. GEORGE RUSSELL & Miss DELLA SMITH
Mr. MARION INGRAM & Miss ALICE RUSSELL

Mr. JOHN TAYLOR & a belle of Montezuma
Mr. JAMES INGRAM & GEORGIA McLAUGHLIN

The above are all intelligent and highly respected young persons. They have our best wishes for a pleasant voyage down life's pathway.

Home News

AMOS BETSON, of this township, has a new piano thumper at his house. The little ootsy arrived last Friday.

L.R. WHIPPLE, of Eugene, was in town on Monday.

Prof. JOHN COLLETT is now at Arkansas Hot Springs. He fell the other day and hurt himself, but is now getting along nicely.

Mrs. ELLEN JONES left on last Thursday for Washington, to visit her daughter, Mrs. REITA HUNTER, who is working in the pension department.

The estate of the late JOSIAH CHURCH, in Helt township, is to be divided among the heirs. The petition for that purpose was acted on favorably by Judge JUMP last week.

Prof. A.A. PARKER and his estimable lady left on Monday afternoon for Unionville, Ohio, to pay their parents an extended visit. They will be absent until August 1st.

MART ADAMS returned from Florida on last Saturday morning, where he has been working in the timber several months getting our railroad ties for JEFF STARK. He says JEFF talks of moving to Kansas before long.

Miss SALLIE ASTON left for Frankfort, Clinton County, on Thursday last to visit Mrs. JOE B. CHEADLE, who is in delicate health.

J.F. SMITH and wife, of Perrysville, leave this morning for Garden City, Kansas, to visit their sons who are in business at that place.

Accident

A Mrs. ELLIS of Terre Haute, aged about 32 years and the mother of 2 or 3 children, met with a sad accident last week. She and her husband and several others of her neighbors had gone on a pleasure excursion up the Wabash river, and on their return home in the evening she had occasion to pass through the engine room, and her dress accidentally caught on the large shaft, drawing her in and horribly mangling both legs before assistance arrived or the engine could be stopped. Both of her legs had to be amputated above the knees. At last accounts she was getting along very finely and it is now thought she will get well.

Elopement

A Man Runs Off With His Pretended Wife

A few years ago a man in Helt township who had been paying his distresses to a young lady in Summit Grove went out to Kansas to locate and make that State his home. After he had been out there a short time he wrote to his sweetheart and requested her to come out and they would get spliced. She went, and after two or three years both returned to Helt's Prairie, and as a result of their labors in the great west they brought back with them a couple of little kids. At first they did not live together. The lady, Miss MOLLIE MILLER, claimed that she had left him on account of cruel treatment. But they soon made up again and were living together as happy as two king bees. Her relatives were always suspicious that they were not married, and so on last Monday week demanded that they produce their marriage certificate if they were legally united. They could not furnish the necessary evidence to show that they were man and wife, and that same day eloped for a more congenial clime and have not been heard of since.

On Friday evening of this week, C.E. VANDEVER, chief of the Terre Haute Police Force, will be united in wedlock to Miss MINNIE COLGROVE, of that city.

Real Estate Transfers for May 1885

CRAWFORD FAIRBANKS etal to WILLIAM I. HALL
Lot 23, Collett's addition to Gessie - $35

SILAS HUGHES to WILLIAM I. HALL
Lot 22, Collett's addition to Gessie - $20

DANIEL BOLLS by Auditor to WILLIAM I. HALL
Lot 20, Collett's addition to Gessie - $.71

HENRY N. SCHUYLER and wife to MARY E. SHORTRIDGE
--- interest in Helt township - $2,700

JAMES M. MOORE and wife to WASHINGTON KING
Lot 10, block 2, in Clinton - $1,500

MARTHA J. NAYLOR to ELIZABETH J. LASHLY
Lot 2, Groendyke addition to Eugene - $400

ISABELL CARTER and heirs to JOHN R. SURGEON
S ½ block 6, in Hillsdale - $200

HENRY HOLLINGSWORTH and wife to CHARLES P. POTTS
Lot 4, in Newport - $330

JOHN S. GRONDYKE to JOHN G. CARSMAN
Lot 16, in Eugene Junction - $100

WILLIAM HAINS and wife to JAMES BLUNT
6 acres in Highland township - $300

RUHAMA UNDERWOOD and heirs to EDGAR VANSICKLE etal
Lot 19, Bricker's addition to Hillsdale - $55

ISAAC L. LEWIS to JOHN H. PRATHER
20 acres in Highland township - $350

LUCIEN R. WHIPPLE and wife to CLARA B. FULTZ
--- acres in Eugene township - $2,000

HENRY O. PETERS to WILLIAM W. FULTZ and wife
Lot 49, in Eugene - $400

NANCY FORTNER and heirs to J.M. CLARK
22 acres in Eugene township - $1,000

NATHAN WHITE and wife to GEORGE W. ELLIS
40 acres in Eugene township - $600

GEORGE PENN to EDGAR VANSICKLE and wife
Lots 24, 25, 26, Bricker's addition to Hillsdale - $50

BRIDGET LAMB and heirs to SARAH A. NATION
Part outlot 6, adjoining Clinton - $600

SARAH A. NATION and heirs to LYDIA A. DUNLAP
¼ of 70 acres in Clinton township - $500

SUSANNA SHAW and heirs to ALBERT R. FLEMING
--- acres in Eugene township - $3,000

HENRY T. WATKINS and wife to JAMES AMMERMAN
Lots 4 & 5, block 1, in Jones - $1,083

JAMES HARLAN etal to WILLIAM C. GROVES
Interest in 60 acres in Vermillion township - $300

JOHN W. ROUSE to DEBORAH ROUSE
1/9 of 10 acres in Highland township - $1,000

HENRY STURM and wife to OSCAR B. LOWRY
40 acres in Helt township - $1,000

GEORGE W. ODELL by Sheriff to HIRAM S. CADY
Lots 9 & 10, in Parrett's addition to Newport - $168.22

JAMES M. AMMERMAN and wife to HENRY T. WATKINS
72 acres in Clinton township - $2,376

Wednesday, June 17, 1885

Sudden Death in Rockville
At about 7 o'clock on last Sunday morning, JAMES CLARK, of Rockville, aged about 50, died very suddenly of apoplexy. We have known Mr. CLARK since early boyhood, having been a schoolmate of his when we attended school in an old log house way back in the 50's. JIM was a clever, genial fellow, and a few years ago was in fair circumstances, but had met with reverses of late and lost nearly all his property. He had been a resident of Rockville for 18 to 20 years.

Dana Items
Mrs. PALMER, the better half of our new druggist and grocer, has returned from a two weeks visit among relatives in Parke County, where she has been for her health, which seems to be considerable better.

Home News
WILLIAM HOUGHLAND, of Helt township, was in town Monday.

Mrs. ROBERT LANDON, who is sorely afflicted with cancer, is slowly growing worse.

PARIS P. THOMAS, of this township, graduated at Wabash College last week.

Miss NORA COOK, of Helt township, is up here visiting her sister, Mrs. EMMA HASTY.

Mr. L.C. GARWOOD and lady, of Champaign, Illinois, were here last week visiting TOM McKNIGHT and family.

Grandma BELL, of Eugene township, aged 79 years, is in town visiting, the guest of the editor and his family.

WILLIAM HAMMAN, of Harveysburg, Fountain County, passed through on Friday last and gave the Hoosier a call.

Prof. JOSIAH CAMPBELL, of Eugene township, has been employed to teach the Camargo, Illinois, schools the coming year at $75 month.

Mrs. CAD HARVEY, of Mattoon, Illinois, who has been visiting her mother here for the last 2 or 3 months, gave birth about 12 o'clock on last Monday to a fine looking boy.

Mother RHOADS, who is living with her son, MARTIN G. RHOADS, took down suddenly ill on last Saturday evening, and it was thought for awhile she was going to die, but she finally rallied, and is now in her usual health.

SAMMY COLLETT, who has been attending a military school at Charleston, West Virginia, during the last year, arrived home last week on a visit. He has improved in size and appearance wonderfully since he left here.

Obituary
Death of Postmaster LEITON at Clinton
On last Saturday evening postmaster JOHN F. LEITON, of Clinton, died of congestion of the stomach and bowels, after an illness of about ten days, aged 45 years. The writer has known Mr. LEITON since a boy and when he says he was an honest and upright citizen he means just what he says. There were no better hearted men than the deceased. When the war broke out he enlisted in the service and fought gallantly for the old stars and stripes. He had been postmaster of Clinton since 1877. He leaves a wife and 2 or 3 children, and a host of friends to mourn his death. His funeral took place on last Sunday evening. He held a $4,000 policy.

Capt. R.B. SEARS will leave tomorrow for Maxinkuckee to spend several days on the lake fishing with an old bachelor friend of his who was a member of the late defunct legislature. His mother, Mrs. HARRIET TURPENING, will accompany him as far as Kewanee, where she will stop to visit a couple of sisters whom she has not seen for 20 years.

Rural Items
From the Montezuma Reporter
A relapse of the measles caused the death of ex-commissioner JOHN D. COLLINS, last Monday evening.

Mrs. IDA NEBEKER, of Clinton, has been visiting her parents, Mr. and Mrs. E.G. WILSON, during the week.

The Boss Daddy of the County
TOM THOMAS, of Opedee, has 8 children of school age -- between 6 and 21 years. He is the only man in the county who has that many school children. He is deserving of a gold medal for his enthusiasm in trying to sustain our common schools, the hope of our country.

Summit Grove
Yesterday morning at 9 1/2 A.M. Mr. R.D. SMITH, of Gessie, and Miss SABRINA E. STRAIN were married at the home of her father, DANIEL E. STRAIN. The pastor of the M.E. church performed the marriage ceremony.

Commissioner's Court for June term 1885
Roads

GEORGE VANDEVENDER	1.50
S.H. DALLAS	1.50
HARRISON JAGGERS	1.50

Gravel Roads

W.P. THOMAS, Perrysville SW	18.80
WILLIAM JONES, Dana & Stumptown	5.00
W.L. PORTER, Feather Creek	8.46
W.L. PORTER, Hillsdale & Highland	7.60
W.L. PORTER, Dana & Stumptown	4.97
W.L. PORTER, Newport & Quaker Point	5.80
W.L. PORTER, Toronto	34.20
W.L. PORTER, Perrysville & SW	109.37
W.L. PORTER, Clinton & Paris	7.07
W.L. PORTER, Dana	2.03
W.L. PORTER, Chunn's Foard	6.66
W.L. PORTER, Newport, W.G.E.	8.30
W.L. PORTER, Hazel Bluff	5.02
W.L. PORTER, Gravel Road Bonds	250.00
J.C. GROVES, Dana & Stumptown	105.00
P.Z. ANDERSON, Dana & Stumptown	6.00
P.Z. ANDERSON, Perrysville	8.00
P.Z. ANDERSON, Center Church	32.00
Books and Stationery	
O.H. HASELMAN	108.60
WILLIAM B. BURFORD	243.15
A.R. HOPKINS	4.40
JOHN RICHARDSON	1.25
S.B. DAVIS	2.00
A.J. JOHNSON	.75
BAKER & THORNTON	1.50
Public Buildings	
M. HEGARTY	17.90
JOHN A. DARBY	77.15
Poor	
JOSEPH CONRAD, Superintendent, Poor Asylum	425.09
ERASTUS MACK	25.00
C.M. WHITE	20.00
A. KINDERMAN	27.50
JAMES WALLACE	62.50
JAMES MALONE, Trustee Eugene township	185.05
JAMES CHIPPS, Trustee Vermillion township	287.30
L.A. MORGAN, Trustee Highland township	196.60
GEORGE W. STULTZ, Trustee Clinton township	209.43
WHITE JAMES, Trustee Helt township	180.66
HAMMON JONES	37.00
JOSEPH HANN	1.00
Assessing	
JAMES B. RICHARDSON	120.00
LEWIS H. JOHNSON	18.00
JOSEPH H. NICHOLAS	240.00
JOHN RICHARDS	135.00
JOHN W. WILTERWOOD	130.00
JOHN R. STAHL	220.00
R.M. RUCKER	220.00
R.H. NIXON	75.00
WILLIAM CHENOWETH	75.00
JAMES KAUFMAN	75.00
CLAUDE MATTHEWS	75.00
Miscellaneous	
WILLIAM L. PORTER, fees & salary	204.00

M.L. HALL, County Board of Health	65.00
S.B. DAVIS, printing	8.00
C.S. DAVIS, copying records	176.00
A.J. JOHNSON, County Superintendent	235.75
WILLIAM FONCANNON, Criminals	10.00
M.B. RHOADS, Attorney	109.00
E.F. DAVIS, Criminals	10.95
DAVID AGGRAY, Janitor	50.00
E. PRITCHARD, fees & salaries	500.01
JOHN A. DARBY, courts	14.00
FRED RUSH, on account bridges	27.00
P.Z. ANDERSON, on account bridges	60.00
JAMES CHIPPS, on account bridges	35.50
D. DOWNING, courts	35.50
FRANK RILEY, courts	49.00
JOHN B. WRIGHT, courts	28.00

Wednesday, June 24, 1885

BAYLESS W. HANNA is happy. The President has changed his sentence. He will now be sent as minister to the Argentine Republic instead of Persia.

Murder
Another murder was committed in Parke County last week. Two neighbors by the names of URIAL DELPH and WILLIAM JARVIS, of Sugar township, had gone to Jackville together in the same vehicle. On their return home they got into a dispute about something, when JARVIS ordered DELPH out of his wagon, and struck him with his fist while climbing out. JARVIS then jumped out and followed him up with his seat board into a fence corner, and while trying to strike him, DELPH shot him dead. This is DELPH's story of the sad tragedy. No one saw the shooting and of course it will be pretty hard to make a case against him. Both were under the influence of liquor. DELPH is an old farmer about 55 years of age, and has been a resident of that township for many years. JARVIS was about 40 years of age, and worked on a farm in that vicinity. He came there from the south a few years ago. The murderer is now in the Rockville jail awaiting trial.

Highland Township
Miss BELL, of Iowa, is visiting friends here.

HAM WOODWARD, of Illinois, was visiting relatives in this vicinity last week.

Eugene Items
J.L. NELSON and wife are the proud parents of a bouncing boy, named JOHN A. LOGAN NELSON. He was born Monday June 8th.

FRANK RICHARDSON is the happiest father of a girl baby. 8 pounds is its weight.

JOHN BISHOP and wife have a fine boy at their house. JOHN is getting along nicely.

CHARLES NEWLIN will go to Kansas, JOHN C. JOHNSON, more generally known as EUCHEE JOHNSON, will go with him.

BILLY SNYDER, an old soldier of the 71st Regiment band, is visiting L.R. WHIPPLE.

Home News
ED STEPHENS returned home from Depauw University on Thursday last.

BILLY AGGRAY, of Marshall, Illinois, is back here on a visit, and looking remarkably healthy.

JAMES CRANE and lady spent Sunday in town visiting, the guests of S.H. DALLAS and family.

Mrs. JOHN FORD, of Helt township, was in town last week visiting, the guests of S.H. DALLAS and family.

Mrs. FANNIE CHURCH and her son JOHN were in town last Saturday and Sunday visiting friends and relatives.

CHARLES SHIEL, of Danville, Illinois, came down here last week to visit his brother-in-law, JOHN W. CROSS.

It is reported that Trustee E.W. JAMES, of Helt township, will shortly lead Miss EMMA INGRAM to the hymeneal altar.

DAVID TEAGARDEN, of Snoddy's Mills, Fountain County, was in town last Friday, the guest of her cousin, JOHN H. WIGLEY.

JOE MURPHY, an attorney of Paris, Illinois, was in town on Thursday last, and admitted to the Newport Bar on motion of C.W. WARD.

JAMES and JOHN HARLAN returned from the French Lick Springs on Friday last, where they had gone for the benefit of their health. Both came back improved.

A divorce was granted in the case of RICHARD VANGILDER vs. ISABEL VANGILDER on Thursday last; incompatibility of temper seems to have caused their trouble.

Mrs. SAMUEL MALONE, of Eugene, and Mrs. JOHNSON, of Missouri, relatives of Lieutenant LEWIS COIL, were in town visiting his family on Saturday last. Mrs. JOHNSON left for Missouri the first of this week.

Rural News
Miss GERTIE BENSON, left on Tuesday morning on an extended visit to friends in Iowa..

Obituary
Mrs. PERTHA JONES, of Sylvania, Parke County, who has been suffering with cancer of the breast three or four years, died at the residence of her son, in Danville, Illinois, on last Monday night, where she was undergoing treatment by a physician of that city. She was 57 years of age, and the mother of WILLIAM JONES of this city. Her remains were brought down here on the train yesterday morning, and conveyed to Parke County for interment.

Drowned
Two weeks ago last Sunday CHARLEY JAMES, a former citizen of Helt's Prairie, was drowned while bathing in Brouillett's Creek, a few miles west of Jonestown. He was about 22 or 23 years of age. His remains were recovered and buried in Helt's Prairie Cemetery.

Death of JAMES YOST
JAMES YOST, a farmer residing 2 1/2 miles northwest of Clinton, died on Saturday last of epileptic fits. Mr. YOST had been subject to them for many years, but had not had an attack of them for over 3 years until a couple of weeks ago, and had about come to the conclusion that he was rid of them. During the war he enlisted in the 123rd IN VOL INF, and served his country near 3 years. He was a good soldier, a kind neighbor and respected by everybody. He was about 45 years of age. The deceased leaves a wife and two little children. His funeral took place on Sunday last, and was largely attended.

From the Montezuma Reporter
Grandma BROCK died in her 89th year, at Hillsdale, one day last week.

What a Weed Can Do
A Singular Death in Eugene Township
There was rather a singular death occurred in Eugene township on last Friday. Two weeks ago last Sunday a 13 year old son of MORGAN HAY ran a weed in his leg, about half way between the ankle and knee joints. The weed was nearly as large as a lead pencil. His father removed all of the weed he could find in the wound, and as the boy did not complain much, he thought he would be all right in a day or two. The boy worked in a field, following after a harrow and uncovering corn. The first of last week his wound began to grow very painful. A physician was sent for, and after probing the wound, he extracted a piece of weed nearly four inches long. Blood poisoning had then already set in, and the little fellow suffered severely until Friday, when death came to his relief. He was a bright and intelligent boy for one of his age, and was very highly respected and esteemed by his associates. The funeral took place on Saturday last, Rev. W.N. COFFMAN, pastor of the U.B. Church, preaching the discourse.

State Prison
Sheriff DARBY, before leaving for Jeffersonille, made inquiries as to what the men that have been sentenced from here to do time, have been doing. Some are as follows:

JOE ATCHINSON and JOHN SANDERS, who were sent up for 3 years during the April term of court in 1884, for burglarizing GEORGE H. McNEILL's store at Perrysville, are both hearty and well. Both are working in the machine shop.

GEORGE WHITTED, sentenced at April term, 1882, for 20 years for the murder of EVAN THOMAS, of Helt township, is in the best of health. He is engaged in the making of saddle trees.

SAMUEL McINTOSH, sentenced at April term, 1884, for 3 years from Clinton township for forgery, is as hearty as a buck, and is working in the foundry. He is inclined to be a little devilish, and needs to change his ways.

AUGUST ELDER, a tramp, sentenced at the present term of court for 5 years for burning down the barn of HENRY VOLKEL of Highland township, is doing polishing in the machine shop.

JOHN GIBSON, sentenced from Vincennes, Knox County, last spring, for burglarizing a saloon, is fat and saucy, and is working in the machine shop.

ANDY DICKEN, of this place, sentenced at April term, 1884, for 4 years on the charge of theft, is hearty and well, and in good spirits. He is working at the carpenter business, and is frequently given work outside the prison walls. He has won the confidence of the prison officials, and is given more liberty than many others.

WILLIAM S. McCONNELL, sentenced at the present term of court for 5 years, as an accomplice in the burglary of ADAMS' saloon, has been given a job in the paint shop.

CHARLEY BLUNK, sentenced at this term of court for 2 years, for burglarizing BOB ADAMS' salon, is cracking rock on a stone pile.

Wednesday, July 1, 1885

Going West
Today our brother MEL DAVIS, of Clinton, will leave for Lincoln, Nebraska, where he expects to cast his lot and engage in the practice of law for a livelihood. He is a bright and intelligent young man, notwithstanding the relationship existing between us, a graduate of Asbury University, and we presume will be able to carve his name on the roll of fame at sometime in the distant future. We have always found him to be honest, and don't believe the citizens of Lincoln need have any fears in trusting him with the collection of notes and accounts.

Attorney C.W. WARD received a telegram yesterday morning, from his old home in New Hampshire, conveying the sad news that his mother was dying and to come immediately.
Hill, New Hampshire, June 30, 1885

Feathered His Nest

Another Helt Township Elopement

On last Sunday, RICHARD VANGILDER and Miss JENNIE SHAW, both residents of Helt township, planned and carried out a successful elopement. Miss SHAW is a daughter of the late CHARLEY SHAW, and the ward of JACOB MILLER who has been looking after her affairs since her father's death. Mr. MILLER was opposed to the match and did all he could to break it off. The young lady went out buggy riding that day with some young friends, and after driving some distance from WILLIAM BOGART's, her brother-in-law's, where she was temporarily staying, Mr. VANGILDER hove in view with a team and buggy. She exchanged buggies and got in with the man. She expected to be joined in wedlock as soon as they could drive over the line into the State of Illinois. They went to Esq. JOE HUTSON's, who performed the ceremony, after which they drove to Clinton, where they took lodging for the night. On Monday morning they came up here and spent the day, returning home on the afternoon train. Mr. VANGILDER was divorced from his first wife one week ago last Thursday, with whom he had only lived about one year. In his last marriage he has feathered his nest well, his wife being worth nearly $20,000.

Eugene Items

The infant son of Mr. and Mrs. JOHN BISHOP died last Thursday.

MARION WATSON is teaching a band of 22 members at Hutchinson, Kansas.

Miss MAUDE PERRIN, of Danville, came down last week on a visit to her mother and sisters.

Home News

GEORGE W. EDWARDS has been appointed Postmaster at Clinton.

VICTOR NIXON is home from Depauw University.

The wife of JOE B. CHEADLE, of the Frankfort Banner, is lying very low with consumption.

Prosecutor H.H. CONLEY is not as mad at the democracy as he was. It is a sweet little girl, and arrived here on last Sunday morning.

FRANK BURROUGHS, residing just south of town, has a new dishwasher at his home, last Friday.

SAM SHARP, of Bellmore, Parke County, was in town over Sunday visiting his brother, WILLIAM SHARP.

Miss CORA HARPER, of Helt's Prairie, was up here visiting Miss BERTHA HALL on last Friday and Saturday. She was accompanied home by Miss HALL.

FRED RUSH has been employed as Principal of the Dana Schools, with Miss SALLIE KEYES and Miss ALLIE THOMPSON. They are all splendid teachers.

The infant child of HORACE PERRIN, of Clinton, died very suddenly on last Thursday night. The funeral took place on Friday afternoon.

VOL FOOS, of Hillsdale, was caught on the river Saturday afternoon by the hardest wind storm that ever struck Montezuma. His boat was overturned and he was nearly drowned before being rescued.

Miss ALICE MITCHELL, of Piqua, Ohio, arrived here on last Saturday night to visit the bedside of her dying mother, Mrs. ROBERT LANDON, who cannot possibly live but a few days.

Mrs. RAIRDON, wife of JIMMY RAIRDON, of Montezuma, died on Friday last and was interred in the Catholic Cemetery at Armiesburg on Saturday. The deceased was a devout Catholic, and a most estimable lady. She was very charitable, and had a host of friends who will long remember their kind and noble hearted friend. She leaves a husband and two little girls, aged 2 and 10 years.

Wednesday, July 8, 1885

Circuit Court for June term

State of Indiana vs. JOSEPH NORTON
Murder – continued

State of Indiana vs. ED WHIPPLE
Selling liquor to a minor – acquitted

State of Indiana vs. PETER MITCHELL, CHARLES REEDER etal
Riot – continued

State of Indiana vs. PETER STUTLER
Keeping house for gaming purposes - $10

State of Indiana vs. CHARLES BLUNK
Burlary – sent to Jeffersonville for 2 years

State of Indiana vs. AUGUST ELDER
Arson – sent to Jeffersonville for 5 years

State of Indiana vs. WILLIAM FORTNER
Larceny – sent to county jail for 90 days

State of Indiana vs. WILLIAM S. McCONNELL
Burglary – sent to Jeffersonville for 5 years

State of Indiana vs. THOMAS J. HENDERSON
Continued

State of Indiana vs. JOHN TAYLOR
Acquitted

ALMIRA BAMFORD vs. EHUD BAMFORD
Divorce – granted

JOHN W. PARRETT vs. WILLIAM HARPER etal
Default - $172.02

B. HOWARD WHITCOMB vs. ELIJAH JACKSON etal
Partition – dismissed

GEORGE A. CRABB etal vs. WINFIELD S. CRABB etal
Partition and sale – continued

ROBERT H. NIXON vs. JOHN W. SKIDMORE etal
Note – default for $441.60

HENRY C. SMITH vs. ABRAM STRAWSER etal
Continued

MARY E. LOPP vs. GEORGE W. LOPP
Divorce – dismissed

State of Indiana ex rel ALICE HELT vs. JAMES RALSTON
Bastardy – judgment for plaintiff for $100

THOMAS W. STEPHENS vs. WINFIELD P. THOMAS etal
Suit on contractors bond – change of venue to Parke County

MARY J. COFFEY vs. THOMAS J. COFFEY
Divorce – not granted

GEORGE W. LAMBERT vs. JOSEPH H. LAMBERT etal
Partition – order of sale and continued

JOHN G. BARKER etal vs. WINFIELD P. THOMAS etal
Suit on contractors bond – change of venue to Parke County

AMANDA KERDOLFF vs. JOSEPH S. McCORMACK etal
Note – default judgment for $243.46

Aetna Life Insurance Co. vs. WILLIAM COLLETT etal
Foreclosure – judgment for $23,134.40

MAHALA JONES vs. JOHN H. FRAZIER etal
Note and foreclosure – default judgment for $121.48 and foreclosure

JOHN HESS vs. AQUILLA LAVERTY
Change of venue from Parke County – judgment for one cent and costs

M. ESTELLA NEWLIN vs. WILLIAM RHEUBY
Note – default judgment for $82.44

ALANSON CHURCH, admr. of JOSIAH CHURCH's estate vs. DAVID A. RANGER
Foreclosure – judgment for $199.50

MAURICE HEGARTY vs. JOSEPH S. McCORMACK etal
Note – default judgment for $366.03

MARIA MASON vs. WILLIAM MASON
Divorce – decree granted

M. ESTELLA NEWLIN vs. HENRY N. TRIECE
Note – default judgment for $169.31

WILLIAM GIBSON vs. JOSEPH McKIBBEN
Note and attachment – dismissed

EMMA WILSON vs. THOMAS WILSON
Divorce – decree granted

ALANSON CHURCH etal vs. SUSAN PERRIN etal
Partition – made and approved

Eagle Machine Works vs. JACOB L. THOMAS
Note – default judgment for $277.55

SAMUEL W. STRONG vs. JOHN CAMPBELL
Complaint on contract – dismissed

WILLIAM B. HOOD vs. JOHN A. AYERS etal
Foreclosure – default judgment for $242.36

HENRY JORDAN vs. Unknown heirs of WILLIAM DOTY, deceased etal
Quiet title – defendants default – decree for plaintiff

WINFIELD P. THOMAS vs. WILLIAM T. BENNETT
Account – dismissed

THOMAS J. NICHOLS vs. JACOB L. THOMAS
Complaint – judgment for an award – judgment for $404.71

WILLIAM B. HOOD vs. ERASTUS M. BENSON etal
Complaint to enforce vendors lien – dismissed

ELIZABETH S. LASHLEY vs. WILLIAM COLLETT etal
Default – judgment for $621.53

GEORGE R. HICKS vs. LOUIS L. HICKS etal
Partition – continued

LAURA TAYLOR vs. JAMES TAYLOR
Divorce – decree granted

Singer Manufacturing Co. vs. SAMUEL R. KAUFMAN
Note – default judgment for $72.10

GEORGE R. FINLEY vs. JESSE DONEY etal
Note – default judgment for $111.45

DAVID C. SMITH vs. HARRISON H. JONES
Note – default judgment for $111.45

CHARLES M. WHITE vs. WINFIELD S. CRABB
Account – default judgment for $54.50

ANDREW JACKSON vs. I.B. & W. RR Co.
Damages – appeal from Justice of Peace court
Affidavit for change of venue filed by defendants

ROBERT J. GESSIE vs. RACHEL MACK etal
Foreclosure – judgment and foreclosure

ROBERT H. NIXON vs. JOHN W. SKIDMORE etal
Note – default judgment for $441.75

CHRIST GLENDNIER vs. GOTTLIEB D. HEIDBREDER
Appeal from Justice of Court – judgment for plaintiff and possession

WINFIELD P. THOMAS vs. HENRY HOLLINGSWORTH
Complaint to show suretyship and have benefit of judgment – dismissed

AMANDA A. WHEELER, admr. vs. I.B. & W. RR Co. etal
Change of venue from Parke Co. – judgment for plaintiff for costs

GEORGE W. McCUNE vs. I.B. & W. RR Co.
Change of venue from Parke Co. – continued

SALEM P. HANCOCK etal vs AQUILLA LAVERTY
Change of venue from Parke County – judgment for plaintiff for costs

JOHN B. COX vs. THOMAS L. NEVINS
Change of venue from Parke County – judgment for defendant for $320 and costs

State of Indiana for use of SAMUEL D. HILL, drainage commissioner vs. AQUILLA LAVERTY
Change of venue from Parke County – judgment for defendant for $1,1718.11

JEREMIAH GOFF vs. PHILANDER GOFF
Damages – dismissed

M. ESTELLA NEWLIN vs. JOSEPH HOLTZ
Note – dismissed

WILLIAM K. McNEILL, guardian SKINNER and heirs vs. RACHEL MACK
Partition – made

MELVIN B. DAVIS vs. THOMAS VICTOR, AMOS CURTIS etal
Note – judgment for $134.74

ANDREW TROGDEN vs. HIRAM P. DEWY, MARTHA A. DEWY
Appeal from Justice of Peace court – dismissed

CORA S. RUSSELL vs. NORMAN L. JONES
$5,000 damages – change of venue from Parke County – changed to Fountain County

WILLIAM T. BENNETT vs. WINFIELD P. THOMAS
Appeal from Justice of Peace court – dismissed

WILLIAM DEERING vs. MICHAEL RUSSELL etal
Note – dismissed

WILSON BETZER vs. HENRY N. TRIECE
Note – dismissed

CHARLES H. GIDDINGS vs. MORGAN HAY
Note – judgment for $57.28

JOHN OSBORN vs. WILLIAM HOUGHLAND
Note – judgment for $283.50

VANGILDER vs. VANGILDER
Divorce – decree granted

GEORGE R. HICKS vs. McCLELLAN
Note – judgment for $93.25

Obituary
Death of Rev. W.N. COFFMAN's Mother
Mrs. MARGARET COFFMAN, the mother of Pastor COFFMAN, died at her home, near Scottland, Illinois, on last Friday, July 3rd, 1885, and was buried in the cemetery near that place on the day following. She was aged 76 years, 2 months, and 10 days. One year ago the 17th of last month, she was stricken down with paralysis, but had partially recovered. Nearly one year from the first stroke, she had a second stroke which proved fatal on the day above mentioned. She had resided in the neighborhood of Scottland since 1837, and had been a member of the U.B. Church since 1852. She was the mother of 7 children, 5 of whom are still living -- 3 daughters and 2 sons. Both of her sons are ministers of the U.B. Church. One is the worthy pastor of the church here, and the other one belongs to an Illinois conference. Her husband died 4 years ago last October, aged 77 years. Peace to the good woman's ashes.

Home News
WILLIAM O. WASHBURN, formerly of Clinton, is now residing in Kansas.

A Sufferer for 18 Years
Death of Mrs. ROBERT LANDON on Saturday Last
At 6:30 o'clock on last Saturday evening, July 4th, 1885, the spirit of Mrs. CELINA LANDON, wife of the late ROBERT LANDON, took its flight for that better world. The deceased had been afflicted with a rose cancer for the last 18 years, which grew in one of her eyes, soon causing her to lose the sight of that organ. Of late years it had been very painful, and she was compelled to keep under the influence of morphine day and night. No one knows the terrible suffering she has endured during the time she was afflicted. The deceased was born at Springfield, Ohio, on July 31st, 1823, and had been a resident of Newport about 9 years. Her husband died on February 27th, 1884, aged 79 years, 11 months, and 14 days. Mrs. LANDON had been a member of the M.E. Church for many years, but was unable to attend on account of her affliction. She leaves 3 daughters and 3 grandchildren. Her funeral took place at 3 o'clock on last Sunday from her late residence, Rev. JOHN HARRISON, pastor of the M.E. Church, performing the last sad rites, after which her remains were followed to the Thomas Cemetery by her children and a goodly number of friends, where they were consigned to the silent tomb to await the morning of the resurrection.

Home News
Miss EMMA PORTER, of Clinton township, is here visiting her brother, Treasurer WILLIAM L. PORTER.

The infant child of F.M. DAVIS, of this place, died on Monday last, July 6th, 1885, of cholera infantum, after an illness of only a few days. This makes the sixth infant child Mr. DAVIS has lost by death. The funeral took place yesterday at 11 o'clock A.M.

Sudden Death
SAMUEL FERGUSON, of Danville, Illinois, a former citizen of Perrysville and a brother of WILLIAM T. FERGUSON, died very suddenly at his home on Monday last. He leaves an estate worth $20,000.

Col. GRAFTON COOKERY, of Terre Haute, who was stricken down with paralysis a few weeks ago, is now lying at the point of death, and cannot possibly survive but a few days. He has served as Mayor, Councilman, and Justice of Peace, and for a number of years was editor of the Terre Haute Daily Journal. Later – the spirit of Col. COOKERY has taken its flight for the world beyond. He died at 9:30 on last Sunday night.

Wednesday, July 15, 1885

Dana Items
Miss MINNIE PALMER, of this place, spent the 4th with relatives at Marshall, Indiana.

A brother of WILLIAM DARNELL, of this vicinity, arrived here from California last week. Mr. DARNELL had not seen his brother for 30 years and talked with him quite a while before he recognized him.

THERA, the son of TAYLOR PALMER, of this place, has had quite a serious attack of St. Vitus Dance, but is better at this writing.

Opedee Items
BILL THOMAS and ED MACK started to Kansas on Monday last.

TOM THOMAS is the happiest man alive for he has 5 of the best looking girls in this place.

HENRY HOLLINGSWORTH is the tallest man in Opedee.

Home News
Mrs. LIZA GILBERT, of Illinois, is here visiting her sick father, HENRY HOLLINGSWORTH.

Miss BESSIE RHOADS of Waveland, is here visiting her brothers HARRY and CHARLEY.

A.O. SEXTON and wife of Columbus, Wisconsin, are here visiting his brother, ABEL SEXTON.

GEORGE WELSHANSE and wife of Streater, Illinois, are here visiting his father-in-law, Mr. JOHN HASTY.

A letter from JAMES A. JONES, of Arkansas, a former resident of Eugene township, says the crops in that state are good.

Week before last we had an item stating that Attorney C.W. WARD had received a telegram from home, stating that his mother was dying. He started on the next train, but she died before he got there. He reached there in time to attend the funeral.

Reaper Accident
The sad news reached our town last Monday morning, that LEWIS MORGAN, Jr., son of LEWIS MORGAN, Sr., Trustee of Highland township, Vermillion County, while driving a binder last Friday, on a sidling place, upset the machine, falling on him and breaking his back and otherwise fatally wounding him. He was a young man universally respected, and his sad fate is lamented by the entire community wherein he resides.

Covington's People Paper

Obituary
Miss JENNIE CRAIG, of this township, died on Wednesday last, aged about 25 years, of consumption. Her parents died when she was quite small. She had always made her home with Mother CLEARWATERS. She was an estimable young lady, and had a host of warm personal friends. Her funeral took place on Thursday last, Rev. J.H. HOLLINGSWORTH, pastor of the M.E. Church at Frankfort, preaching the discourse.

Eugene Items
Married -- Mr. JOHN GILLIS and Miss MARY BANNAM were married at the residence of WILLIAM MALONE, Tuesday evening, July 7th, 1885.

Real Estate Transfers for June 1885

LESLIE D. THOMAS, assignee to JAMES C. TUTT
--- acres in Eugene township - $1

BARSHEBA JAMES to SALLIE NICHOLS
Lots 6 & 7, in Gessie and Cushman's addition to Perrysville - $90

JONATHAN DILLON and wife to WILLIAM C. SCOTT
29 ½ acres in Vermillion township - $900

LEVI F. LONG and wife to WILLIAM C. SCOTT
20 ½ acres in Vermillion township - $600

OSCAR B. LOWRY and wife to JOHN W. GROVES etal
66 2/3 acres in Helt township - $3,000

LYDIA A. DUNLAP to THOMAS P. PINSON
38 acres in Clinton township - $1,200

ELEAZOR HULLENWIDER and wife to ELIAS ANDREWS
Lots 1, 4, 5, & 8, block 13, Clinton - $950

CHARLES BROWN to JOHN PORTER
34 acres in Clinton township - $400

WAKEFIELD INGRAM and wife to JAMES H. DINSMORE etal
194 acres in Helt township - $5,700

GERTRUDE J. BENSON to SAMUEL E. KAUFMAN
80 acres in Helt township - $1,200

JOHN OSBORN and wife to EDGAR VANSICKLE
24 acres in Helt township - $675

HENRY OSBORN to WILLIAM A. ROEBACK and wife
113 acres in Helt township - $1,550

RICHARD MALONE and wife to GEORGE C. HUTCHINSON
Lot 20, in Finney's addition to Dana - $50

JAMES KNIGHT to MARTHA KNIGHT etal
80 acres in Helt township - $1

JACOB W. SHIRLEY to CHARLEY FREQUA
40 acres in Clinton township - $1,000

JOHN F. SMITH to HUGH S. COMINGORE
Lots 8, 9, & 10, in Riley's addition to Perrysville - $600

SAMUEL AIKMAN etal to BEN SHEPARD
Lots 17 & 18, block 11, in Dana - $100

GEORGE H. FISHER and wife to MARTIN M. WHITLOCK
Lots 27 & 28, in Fisher's addition to Dana - $60

JAMES M. REEDER to FRANK L. REEDER
50 acres in Helt township - $900

WILLIAM B. INGLE and wife to WILLIAM FONCANNON
23 acres in Helt township - $600

JOHN HAWORTH to MARTIN G. RHOADS
Lot 113, in Newport - $123.40

MARY E. INGLE and heirs to ELIZA J. JONES
19 acres in Helt township - $640

ELIZABETH HITE to SIMON S. CHAPMAN
Lot 8, in Zener's addition to Newport - $175

THOMAS J. STARK to MARTHA J. NAYLOR
240 acres in Vermillion township - $5,978

Sheriff's Sale on Decree
ROBERT J. GESSIE vs. RACHEL MACK, COURTLAND L. MACK, JOHN F. COMPTON, JOHN T. LOWE, DENNETT Harvesting Machine Co.
$1,376.25
Saturday, August 8, 1885
At courthouse between 10 and 4
NW of NE fractional ¼ Sec 18 T 18 N R 10 W – 39 acres
July 14, 1885
WARD & DAVIS attorneys for plaintiff
JOHN A. DARBY, Sheriff

Sheriff's Sale on Decree
WILLIAM B. HOOD vs. JOHN A. AYERS, MATILDA J. AYERS
$256.11
Saturday, August 8m 1885
At courthouse between 10 and 4
Lots 1 & 2, block 13, in town of Dana
July 14, 1885
M.G. RHOADS, Attorney for plaintiff
JOHN A. DARBY, Sheriff

Wednesday, July 22, 1885

Home News
WILLIAM CHILDS of Terre Haute, a young man aged 21 years, drowned in the Wabash, near that city on Saturday last while in bathing.

Jordan School House
Miss NANNIE WANN, of Fountain County, was visiting friends in this neighborhood last week.

Miss ALLIE THOMPSON, who has been spending the summer with JOHN WANN and family, will return to her home in Waterman this week.

The wife of JESSE FLEMING, living on Coal Branch, died last week.

The wife of ASA HUBBARD is lying quite low and is not expected to live many days.

Obituary
Sudden Death of JOHN P. BRILES
JOHN P. BRILES, the village blacksmith of Eugene, died very suddenly between 9 and 10 o'clock on last Thursday night. He was born in this State in 1825, and was 60 years of age. He had lived in every township of this county, and was well and favorably known by most of our citizens. He was a step-father of Sheriff DARBY. He belonged to the Odd Fellows, which order took charge of the remains and buried them on Saturday last. The deceased was a member of the last grand jury, and while here seemed to be in the enjoyment of the best of health. He was as genial and warm hearted as any man we ever met. He was lively and always full of fun. We doubt if there was a person in the county who had more friends than JOHN P. BRILES. He was esteemed and respected by everybody. He owned very little of this earth's wealth, and leaves his family in straightened circumstances.

Old Mr. BENEFIEL is lying at the point of death.

Miss CRAWLEY, of Sullivan, has for some time been here visiting her cousin, PET CRAWLEY.

Eugene Items
J.C. EDMONDS, of Vinton, Iowa, is in town visiting relatives.

Died, Thursday, July 16th, JOHN P. BRILES, aged 60 years, of congestion of the stomach. Mr. BRILES was one of the best known men in Vermillion County, having lived and worked at his trade of blacksmithing, at Perrysville, Newport, Bono, Clinton, and Eugene. His death occurred after an illness of four days, during which time he suffered greatly. He leaves a wife and 4 children, 2 sons and 2 daughters. County Sheriff JOHN A. DARBY is his stepson.

Died, Saturday, July 18th, Mrs. EVALINE HOOD, wife of WILLIAM H. HOOD, aged 40 years. Mrs. HOOD was taken sick suddenly Wednesday, from which time she sank rapidly until Saturday when death came. She leaves besides her husband, 3 children by a former marriage, for whose benefit she had her life insured for $3000.

Died, Sunday, July 19th, Miss ALICE SHEWARD, aged 25, of consumption. ALLIE had been a sufferer from the dread disease for several years, and her death had been expected for some time.

Home News
FRANK BROWN and wife, of Helt township, who went to Kansas last fall, have got all they wanted of the West, and arrived back at their old home on Wednesday last. Mrs. BROWN's son is here visiting relatives and is having a boss time.

Home News
JOHN LLOYD and WILLIAM HOUSAND left for Missouri on last Monday night.

FRANK JOHNSON, of Eugene, a young man of 17 years, leaves for Kansas this week to seek his fortune.

An infant child of FRED HIBERLY, residing 5 miles west of here, died on Monday last, aged about 3 or 4 months.

Miss ALLIE SHEWARD, an estimable young lady of Eugene, aged about 20, is lying dangerously ill with consumption.

Mrs. MARY McFADDEN and two of her little children arrived here one day last week from York, Nebraska, on a visit to her brother-in-law, GEORGE W. BRINDLEY, of Opedee. She will remain several weeks.

Mrs. CLARA H. CAMPBELL, a daughter of the late Dr. I.B. HEDGES, of Clinton, and her daughter EDITH were guests of Mrs. Judge JUMP over Sunday. Mrs. CAMPBELL is teacher of painting, drawing, and wood carving at Depauw College at New Albany, Indiana.

Obituary
The wife of WILLIAM HOOD, of Eugene, died on Saturday last after a brief illness, aged 43 years. She was a member of the M.E. Church, and was well respected by all her neighbors and acquaintances. The funeral was preached on Sunday last by her pastor, Rev. JOHN HARRISON.

CLINTON NEWMAN, residing near Indianapolis, was over here last week visiting his cousin, E.B. BROWN. He left here on Monday morning for Kansas, where he will spend two weeks in looking at the country, and then return to Newport and stop a few days before returning home.

Obituary

The town of Perrysville was cast into the deepest gloom on the night of last Tuesday, July 21st, by the dread tidings which passed from lip to ear. "Young JOE McCORMACK is drowned in the river!" The unfortunate youth went in bathing about 8 o'clock at night, and it is thought was taken with cramp, and before help could reach him sank to rise no more. Strong men and earnest comrades made every effort by diving and dragging the river to recover the body till a late hour at night. It was found that nothing could be done on account of obstructions in the river. At 8 o'clock on Wednesday morning, however, the body was recovered and taken to the sorrow stricken home. Tuesday night was a sad night. The funeral was at 5 o'clock P.M. on Wednesday, when a large concourse of sympathizing friends and neighbors met to pay the last tribute of regards to one who had been so suddenly cut off in the very bloom of youth.

JOSEPH McCORMACK, Jr., the son of SMITH J. McCORMACK and SARAH E. McCORMACK, was born September 2d, 1869, at Perrysville, where he always resided with his parents, and died July 21st, 1885. He was consequently not quite 16 years old at the time of his death. There survive him the parents, the brothers, EDWIN G., CHARLES, and an infant brother RALPH, and the sisters MARY and SUSA.

JOSEPH was a bright, good and affectionate boy, dutiful and industrious at home and respected abroad. He was promoted into the high school last fall, where he had good average standing. The Superintendent of the school, Prof. DEALAND, states that he was rarely absent and only absent and only upon sufficient excuse, and seldom, if at all tardy; and that his demeanor in school shows careful home training.

Perrysville
FRANK JONES is again employed to teach in Vermillion township. They like him down there.

Home News
M.B. HOLLINGSWORTH's 19 month old son is dangerously ill.

GRANT and JESSE GALLOWAY, of Ellettsville, are here visiting their brothers.

Miss GERTIE ANDREWS, a handsome lady of Danville, Illinois, is here visiting her sister, Mrs. JOHN ANDERSON.

SILAS HOLLINGSWORTH and wife, of Chrisman, Illinois, were in here on Sunday last to see his father. They talk of moving to Brazil in a short time.

Obituary
The infant child of WILLIAM JONES, of Eugene, a former resident of this place, died of inflammation of the stomach on Monday last, aged 6 or 7 months.

RILEY HOLLINGSWORTH has struck a streak of luck. His pension has just been increased from $12 to $16 per month, and the increase dates from 1878, giving him over $350 arrears. RILEY is feeling happy and says when he gets his money he is going to buy a home.

LEVI, LEANDER, and LUCIEN DAVIS, of New Hampshire, who have been here on a visit for several weeks, the guests of their uncle, Hon. O.P. DAVIS, left for home on Monday last. They were accompanied by Senator DAVIS and his daughter, Mrs. ALICE ODEKIRK, who will remain in the East one month or more.

A Cancer Removed
JAMES A. WHITE, Sr., one of the old pioneer settlers of Helt's Prairie, this county, and now 80 years old, has been afflicted with a cancer on his under lip for some time. It became so painful at times, that he could hardly endure his sufferings. Last week he concluded he would have it removed. His son, Dr. CHARLEY WHITE, of Clinton, accompanied him to Chicago where he secured the services of one of the finest surgeons in that city. The operation was successfully performed, and the gentleman is now reported to be without pain, and the happiest man in Helt township. We presume he will be ready to make a full hand during corn husking next fall, and to go racoon hunting every other night like he did five years ago.

Still Sick
HENRY HOLLINGSWORTH still lingers upon the sick bed, and said yesterday morning that he did not feel any better, although he is much better in appearance and looks than he was one week ago. He has to keep under the influence of morphine, and nearly everything he eats sours in his stomach. The excessive hot weather has been severe on him.

Surgery
A difficult surgical operation was performed upon Mrs. STEPHEN CRANE of Helt township, the first of last week. Several physicians of this county and Terre Haute removed from her an ovarian tumor weighing 50 pounds. She is reported to be in a very critical condition from the effects of the operation, and it is thought doubtful whether she recovers.

Death
WILLIAM BENEFIEL, Sr., of Perrysville, died on last Wednesday morning at the residence of his son, aged about 86 years. He was a member of the Odd Fellows, and was buried by that order on the day following his death. He was a good citizen and well respected by all his neighbors and acquaintances.

On last Friday night, CLAY BURSON arrived here from California, looking hale and hearty. He had not been back since 15 years ago last February, and during that time three of his sisters and one brother have died. His mother is now 80 years old and resides one mile south of town. She was overcome with joy when she met her son. He intends to remain until about the first of September, when he will leave for his western home, and probably will never see his good old mother again on earth.

J.W. PERRIN will teach school at Danville, Illinois, this year.

Sheriff's Sale on Decree
ALANSON CHURCH, admr. of JOSIAH CHURCH's estate, vs DAVID RANGER
$214.96
Sale Saturday, August 22, 1885
Sale at courthouse between 10 and 4
Lots 8 & 9, block 4, in town of Clinton
July 28, 1885
WARD & DAVIS attorneys for plaintiff
JOHN A. DARBY, Sheriff

Wednesday, August 5, 1885

Death of Miss MAMIE McMEEN
On Tuesday of last week, July 28, 1885, Miss MAMIE McMEEN, daughter of Dr. JAMES McMEEN of Eugene, died after an illness of about two weeks. Miss MAMIE was about 22 years of age, and a lady who had the respect and esteem of everybody who knew her. She had a kind and tender heart, and always had a pleasant word for everyone. In her death the people of Eugene lose as estimable citizen, and the parents a kind and dutiful daughter. Her funeral took place on last Wednesday afternoon, and was very largely attended, fully attesting the great love and esteem in which she was held. A Presbyterian minister of Danville, Illinois, performed the last sad rites, after which her remains were followed to the Groendyke Cemetery, west of town, and gently deposited in their last resting place by sympathizing friends.

Marriage
On Sunday night at the residence of the bride's mother, Mrs. MARY MATTINGLY, by Rev. H. HEAD, Miss MARY E. MATTINGLY was married to Mr. THOMAS J. CHAPMAN, in the presence of a few friends. The happy young couple began housekeeping the following day in a cottage on Oak Street in McTEGART's annex. The groom is an industrious and deserving young man, and the bride is an amiable and pretty young lady. Mr. CHAPMAN is employed at GILLICK's merchant tailoring establishment. The Democrat wishes the new couple a happy and long life.

Death of Mrs. STEPHEN CRANE
Mrs. STEPHEN CRANE, of Helt township, who was operated on by a Terre Haute physician a couple of weeks ago, and a 50 pound ovarian tumor removed from her, died on last Friday morning from the effects of the operation. She was a good Christian lady and a member of the M.E. Church. Her funeral took place on Saturday last.

Mrs. A.V. HOLMES is on the sick list from a complication of diseases. Yesterday she was considered in a critical condition. Dr. SWANK is attending her.
Williamsport Republican
Mrs. HOLMES was formerly a resident of Newport, and has a number of relatives and friends here who will regret to hear of her illness.

An infant child of Mr. and Mrs. O.P. MORGAN died on the morning of July 29th.
Clinton Argus

Death of SOPHRONIA RICHARD
Death, with its relentless hand has entered our community and taken from among us a most beloved and respected neighbor. SOPHRONIA RICHARD was born in Helt township, Vermillion County, Indiana, April 17th, 1835, and died July 27th, 1885, her age being 50 years, 3 months, and 10 days. The life of our departed friend ceased to ebb in its gentle easement and returned to God who gave it being. She was interred in the Helt's Prairie Cemetery after her funeral was preached by Rev. PALMER, a minister of the Baptist Church the day following her death. She leaves a husband and 6 step-children, 3 brothers, 3 sisters, and numerous relatives and friends to mourn her loss. Consumption preyed upon her constitution for several long years when at last her frail nature yielded to that power which will, sooner or later knock at the door of every living creature. In spite of all that could be done for her by relatives and friends, her pure spirit passed away to its eternal home. Well may her husband and children weep tears for they have lost a loving mother and a kind and dutiful wife.

Jordan School House
Mrs. NEWTON SMITH and her sister, Miss LOU LANG will go next week to Ohio to visit relatives.

Summit Grove

It is a girl and weighed 5 1/2 pounds, but J.F. LANGSTON is still in the field with bargains in groceries and dry goods. He will pay the highest market price for poultry, and show you the baby free of charge.

Home News

Miss BELL HOLLINGSWORTH, of Chicago, a former resident of this place, is here on a visit.

Judge JUMP and family attended the funeral of Miss MAMIE McMEEN, of Eugene, on Wednesday last.

A.C. LOVE is about to come in possession of his little girl ELLA according to the laws of Indiana.

S.S. COLLETT is Grandpa. His daughter, EVA LITTLEPAGE, of Charleston, West Virginia, is the mother of a fine girl baby.

License was taken out last Monday for the marriage of WILLIAM DUNTON and Miss ELLA E. WALKER, of Clinton.

Mrs. CAD HARVEY, who has been here several months visiting her mother, left yesterday for Kansas, to join her husband, who has been out there since her arrival here.

Mrs. ELLA DICKENSON has been appointed postmistress of Perrysville, VICE SMITH RABB removed on account of offensive partisanism.

Mrs. SAM MORRIS, a poor lady who had been living off the charities of the county, died on last Sunday evening, aged between 40 and 50 years. Her disease was consumption, and she had been confined to her bed for the last 6 months.

ANDY MARLATT and Miss LOU McCRARY, of Highland township, will be united in wedlock tomorrow. ANDY was down on Monday last and procured the necessary papers of the County Clerk.

Normal Institute

A List of Teachers Present the First and Second Days.

The summer Normal and county Institute now being held at Eugene starts in with a respectable attendance of teachers. The first day there were 34 present. Yesterday 4 more were added to the list, swelling the total attendance to 35 teachers. Below we give a list of their names:

A.J. WILSON, G.W. DEALAND, J.H. TOMLIN, F.D. JONES, J.L. SMITH, DENNIS ROUSE, G.H. MITCHELL, MILTON JAMES, FRED BEARD, JASPER N. FRIST, E.E. HELT, E.L. BALES, C.E. JORDAN, LOU MACK, MARY HEIDBREDER, ABBIE BUTLER, LACIE MORRIS, MATTIE McCLELLAN, JENNIE STURM, NETTIE MOORE, GRACE WHITLOCK, LAURA HARLAN, NELLIE JORDAN, LILA KERNS, ELLA DINSMORE, R.E. WHITLOCK, PORTER MILLIKIN, LEONARD CAMPBELL, CLARA SMITH, ELIZABETH MOORE, W.S. NEEL.

Second Day

JAY M. MILLS, ETTA EDWARDS, LILLIE BIRT, and C.S. FLANDERS.

Miss MOLLIE HOWARD, a former teacher in the Newport schools, and now one of the teachers of the schools in Crawfordsville, is here on a visit, and is the guest of Miss ELLA PARRETT. She will probably remain two or three weeks.

Final Settlement of Estate

Estate of NANCY FULTZ, deceased

July 15, 1885

Sheriff's Sale on Decree

GEORGE R. FINLEY vs. JESSE DONEY, ELIZABETH DONEY, MARTHA E. LEE, MERRIMAN LEE
$276.70
Sale Saturday, August 22, 1885
Sale at courthouse between 10 and 4
60 acres off W end of S ½ NE ¼ Sec 28 T 14 N R 10 W
July 28, 1885
SAWYER & GIBSON attorneys for plaintiff
JOHN A. DARBY, Sheriff

Sheriff's Sale on Decree

MAHALA JONES vs. JOHN H. FRAZIER, MARIAH FRAZIER
$135.13
Sale Saturday, August 22, 1885
Sale at courthouse between 10 and 4
SE corner Sec 20 T 17 N R 10 W – 8.51 acres
July 28, 1885
SAWYER & GIBSON attorneys for plaintiff
JOHN A. DARBY, Sheriff

Wednesday, August 12, 1885

Obituary

Death of HENRY HOLLINGSWORTH on Sunday Last

It becomes our duty this week to record the death of our old friend and comrade, HENRY HOLLINGSWORTH. He was our nearest neighbor, and we always found him to be kind and obliging to everyone. He possessed a warm and generous heart, and was ever ready to lend a helping hand to those in need or distress. His recent illness was caused by a hurt received in the army. During the last year it was very painful at times, but he bore his sufferings with great fortitude. He was only confined to his bed about five weeks, and during a part of that time no food would lie on his stomach long at a time. He grew weaker and weaker until 4:25 on last Sunday morning when the death angel claimed him for its own.

The deceased was born in this county on September 9, 1830, and died on Sunday August 9, 1885, lacking one month of being 55 years of age. On March 16, 1850, he was united in wedlock to Miss ANALIZA JAGGERS, step-daughter of Dr. JOHN GILMORE, who died February 18, 1856. On October 14, 1857, he was joined in marriage to Miss REBECCA A. WILTERMOOD, with whom he lived pleasantly and happy up to the day of his death. By his first marriage he had 3 children, all of whom are now living and grown to man and womanhood. By his last marriage he had 11children, 8 of whom are still living.

In the fall of 1863 he enlisted in Co. C, 123rd Indiana Volunteer Infantry, and served till the close of the war, when he was honorably discharged from the service. In the fall of 1857 he moved on a farm 3 miles West of town, where he resided up to 1871, with the exception of the time he served in the army, when he moved back to town, where he has resided ever since. At an early day in his life he was an active member of the M.E. Church, and the leader of a class.

His funeral took place at 9 o'clock on last Monday morning, brief services being held at his late residence by Rev. JOHN HARRISON, pastor of the M.E. Church, after which the Grand Army Post of this place took charge of the remains. The procession was headed by the Newport Cornet Band, then followed his comrades of the Grand Army Post. Next came the hearse, followed by the relatives and friends of the deceased. The procession was fully one-half mile long, and the largest witnessed in this place for many years. His remains were conveyed to the Vermillion Cemetery where the beautiful and impressive burial ceremony of the Grand Army was gone through, after which our dead comrade was lowered into the silent grave, amid the sobs of relatives and sympathizing friends. Peace to the old veteran's ashes.

Bad Accident
On last Friday, while a couple of JOE FOOS' boys were riding the horses to water, a freight came along and frightened the animal "BUCK" was riding and caused it to throw him to the ground. The horse his older brother was riding just behind him, stepped on the top of his head, inflicting a wound to the skull and nearly 3 inches long. A physician was summoned who sewed up the wound, and said he believed the skull was fractured. The boy is only 9 years old, was unconscious until Sunday morning. He is now on the mend and it is thought he is going to get well.

A Lucky Soldier
SOL JACKSON is the happiest man on Tick Ridge. After 4 years of persistent labor, DAVID A. RANGER has secured his pension. He will draw $960 back pension.

Clinton Argus

Home News
Mrs. ORPHA WIGLEY, of this place, went up to Eugene last Friday to spend a few months with her daughter, Mrs. JOHN LASHLEY.

Marriage of Miss ALMA BLANCHARD
Yesterday in Terre Haute, MARSHALL G. LEE and Miss ALMA BLANCHARD were united in bonds of holy wedlock.

Mrs. EVA FORD and her daughter, KATIE, of Lafayette, are here visiting her parents, Mr. JAMES A. FOLAND and wife.

OMER NICHOLS is in high clover. It is a boy and tips the scales at 10 pounds. It arrived here on Tuesday morning of last week.

Miss JOSIE HALL, of Champaign, Illinois, is here visiting her mother, Mrs. IRVIN LAMB, and her sisters BERTHA and EVA HALL.

Mrs. ELHANAN STEVENS, of Perrysville, who was stricken down with paralysis about 1 year ago, is lying at the point of death.

LON DRUMMOND, and Mrs. LAURA LOFFLIN, of Howard, Parke County, were in town on Thursday last visiting their sister, Miss LIZZIE DRUMMOND.

Mrs. SARAH GRIMES, who resides near Greasy Creek School house, was in town on Saturday last to visit her sister, Miss LIZZIE DRUMMOND.

Miss AMANDA KERDOLFF will leave for Cincinnati this morning to visit her parents. Her father will be 71 years of age on September 5, 1885.

Dr. McMEEN's family, of Eugene, are making arrangements to move to Danville, Illinois, sometime this month. The Dr. will not leave til sometime in the fall.

Little ETTA McCONNELL, who was hooked by an angry cow a couple of weeks since, is improving very slowly. She is not yet able to bear any weight on that limb.

FRANK HASTY in walking, takes exceedingly long steps, but his steps yesterday morning were unusually long. It is a girl, weighs ten pounds, and arrived on the 9 o'clock train the night before.

Mrs. CHARITY DAWSON, daughter of HENRY HOLLINGSWORTH, who lives at Camern, Illinois, was telegraphed last Saturday afternoon that her father was dying, but did not receive the dispatch in time to get here before the funeral. She arrived here on the early train yesterday morning.

About 25 of her lady friends gave Mrs. LIZA DILLOW a surprise by calling upon her unexpectedly and in force. It was LIZA's 35th birthday. All enjoyed a jolly good time. They made up enough money to buy her a handsome little stand table.

Obituary
An infant child of MILTON B. HOLLINGSWORTH, of this township, aged 2 years last December, died on Saturday last, after an illness of several weeks, and was buried at the Vermillion Cemetery on Sunday last.

Death of Mrs. SMITH RABB
The wife of postmaster SMITH RABB, of Perrysville, died at 1 o'clock on last Sunday afternoon, and was buried Monday afternoon. She was the mother or Judge JOE M. RABB of Williamsport. We do not know much about her history, but are informed that she was a good citizen and respected by her neighbors and acquaintances.

Perrysville
Prof. SCOTT of the Coal Branch, ran off with ELIAS SHAW's wife. SHAW went to Newport to get out papers for them and on being asked if she was his lawful wife he was unable to make it appear that she was. He came away without papers and SCOTT still has possession.

Mrs. SMITH RABB died on Sunday at 2 P.M. and was buried on Monday. A very large number of people attended the burial services. Judge RABB and wife were here during the last week.

Our Doctors
The following physicians of this county have complied with the provisions of the late law requiring practicing physicians to have license:
HENRY T. WATKINS, diploma, dated February 1st, 1872, Hanneman College, Chicago, Illinois; LEWIS SHEPARD, diploma, dated 1868, Miami Medical College, Cincinnati, Ohio; M.L. HALL, diploma, dated 1876, Bellevue Hospital, Medical College, New York; JAMES A. BARNES, diploma, dated 1875, Medical College of Ohio; HENRY NEBEKER, diploma, dated 1876, Jefferson Medical College, Pennsylvania; CHARLES W. WHITE, diploma, dated 1876, Jefferson Medical College, Pennsylvania; HIRAM SHEPARD, diploma, dated 1869, Miami Medical College, Cincinnati, Ohio; JOHN H. BOGART, diploma, dated 1868, University of Michigan; JAMES WALLACE, diploma, dated 1879, Rush Medical College, Chicago, Illinois; OTIS M. KEYES, diploma, dated 1877, Kentucky School of Medicine, Louisville, Kentucky; JAMES B. WEBB, ten year clause; GEORGE H. McNEILL, ten year clause.

Montezuma Reporter
TIM MALONE, formerly of the Dana House, has bought a hotel in Oakland, Illinois, and gone into business in that town. TIM is a good hotel man, and will no doubt make a success in the new field if his wife can strike on some plan to keep him out of the kitchen.

Death of a Pioneer
JAMES CARNEY, one of the pioneers of this township, aged 85 years, departed this life on the 2nd instant. He was an honest and kind hearted old gentleman and a large circle of friends mourn his demise. For the bereaved relatives the sympathy of the entire community goes out.
Clinton Siftings

Real Estate Transfers for July 1885

SAMUEL BOWERS and wife to WILLIAM M. LASH
Undivided ½ interest in Eugene Mills - $400

FRANCIS M. HELT and wife to Vermillion County Coal Co.
20 acres in Helt township - $800

DAVID H. BIRT and wife to JOHN H. BIRT and wife
Lot 6, block 29, Clinton - $300

JOHN H. BIRT and wife to DAVID H. BIRT and wife
Part lot 6, block 14, Clinton - $500

JOHN OSBORN etal to JOSEPH A. JACKSON etal
120 4/5 in Helt township - $274.26

AMASSA SMITH to MALINDA AIKMAN etal
67 acres in Helt township - $1

MARY A. McLAUGHLIN and heirs to LEVI H. AIKMAN
Lot 12, Burnett's addition in Dana - $300

DANIEL W. GARDNER and wife to SOCRATES K. STONER
Part lot 1, block 12, in Clinton - $1,500

MARGARET J. JAMES to JAMES M. WATSON
1/3 of 70 acres in Helt township - $700

ANDREW J. DOWDY's estate to AMANDA DOWDY
60 acres in Clinton township - $1,800

AMANDA DOWDY etal to JAMES ROBERTS
145 acres in Clinton township - $5,076

JOSEPH C. McKIBBEN and wife to ANDREW HOWARD
Lots 55 & 56, Perrysville - $350

GEORGE F. CLAYTON and wife to CHARLES FLESHMAN
Outlot 5, Perrysville - $275

GRANVILLE PUGH and wife to JANE LITTLE
45 acres in Vermillion township - $500

JOHN S. GROENDYKE to GEORGE H. FABLE
Lots 23 & 25, Eugene junction - $275

JAMES McMEEN and wife to JACOB H. ILES
Lots 57 & 58, Eugene - $1,600

DANIEL MILLER and wife to JOHN HIGHFILL
Lots 6 & 7, block 8, in Dana - $950

SAMUEL AIKMAN etal to JOHN HIGHFILL
Lots 4 & 5, block 8, in Dana - $100

FRANCIS M. DAVIS and wife to JOHN R. HOLLINGSWORTH
10 acres in Vermillion township - $120

BEN BLANCHARD to WILLIAM P. HENSON
10 acres near Newport - $300

CHARLES W. WARD and wife to EMILY L. DAVIS
Lot 41, in Newport - $12

Wednesday, August 19, 1885

Eugene Items
Marriage - Wednesday the 12th instant, SAMUEL KINDERMAN to Miss SALLIE HAWN. The happy couple left Thursday morning for Ohio on a wedding tour. They will visit Cincinnati, Columbus, and Bellaire, the latter place being the bride's former home.

Home News
J. COLE, of Hillsdale, had a picnic at his house on last Sunday. It's a boy.

WILLIAM C. MYERS is going to move out in the country on S.H. DALLAS' farm.

Uncle NEDDY JACKSON, of near Scottland, Illinois, is in here on a short visit.

Miss HATTIE HUGHES has been visiting her aunt, Mrs. COFFMAN, for some days.

CHARLEY POTTS has been appointed administrator of the estate of HENRY HOLLINGS-WORTH.

ELMER DAVIS, of Helt township, who has been attending school at Paxton, Illinois, is at home on a visit.

Miss MAGGIE SIMPSON, accompanied by Misses NANNIE and FLORA ILES of Fairmount, Illinois, and Miss EFFA ILES of Eugene, gave the Hoosier a short and pleasant call on last Monday afternoon.

The wife of THOMAS MONAGHAN, of Hillsdale, died one week ago Sunday afternoon and her remains were taken to Terre Haute for burial. She was formerly a resident of that city, and a most estimable lady.

Mrs. R.H. MYERS, of Hutchinson, Kansas, is here on a visit. She was formerly a resident of this township, and is a daughter of Mrs. BURSON, residing south of town.

ED BROWN sent back word last week that he had taken a claim of 160 Acres in Kansas. We suppose he will make arrangements to move out there about next spring.

Obituary
Mrs. EMMA PATTON, daughter of JAMES F. WELLER, a former citizen of this place, died at Ridge Farm, Illinois, yesterday.

Misses BELL and SARAH ELDER and their little brother, of Helt township, and Miss HATTIE PAIGE, of Terre Haute, a half sister, were in the city yesterday visiting their sister, Mrs. O.B. GIBSON.

Summit Grove
Mrs. CEPHUS MACK is lying very low, and is not expected to recover.

ED BROWN returned from Kansas yesterday morning. He is well pleased with the country, and says his claim lies about 75 miles southwest of Hutchinson. He did not see any of the Vermillion colony except E.Y. JACKSON and family and NORTH CRAIG and family. He says JACKSON is keeping a boss hotel and is doing pretty well. He says that NORTH has a good house, splendid barn and 26 head of cattle and is making money. He claims that he has cleared $1000 each year since he has been out there. Miss FRA JACKSON is attending Normal at Oswega.

Mr. CHARLEY JAMES lost one of his children last Monday week. That dread disease, cholera infantum, was the cause.

Obituary
Died, at Perrysville, IN, August 9, 1885, after a long and severe illness, Mrs. MARY RABB, wife of SMITH RABB. Mrs. RABB was the daughter of JAMES & JANE CARSILE who emigrated from South Carolina to Liberty, Union County, IN, about the year 1814, where the subject of this notice was born October 16, 1818, and removed with her parents to near Covington, Fountain County, IN, in the year 1826, and was married to SMITH RABB August 26, 1841. There were 9 children born to them, 7 of whom survive her. Mrs. RABB had been a citizen of Perrysville for almost 40 years, where she was favorably known for her many Christian virtues.

Postmaster
Attorney J.C. SAWYERS received a telegram from Senator VOORHEES yesterday morning announcing that JOHN A. WILTERMOOD had been appointed postmaster for this place, and Miss GERTIE BENSON postmistress at Montezuma.

Dr. A.H. DEPUY, is now permanently located in Dana. He has been practicing medicine for over 30 years, and is considered one of the best physicians in the country.

Wednesday, August 26, 1885

Elopement
W.R. PETERS, who eloped from Dana about 9 months ago with a young girl, leaving a wife and 15 year old son behind, was in town on Monday last and called at the Hoosier state office. He now claims that he did not elope with the girl and that he only took $6.00 in money with him, leaving all his property to the wife whom he had deserted. He says he had been married to her about 16 years, and that she made his home a hell on earth, and that he got tired of living that way and went out west where he had been living with a relative ever since. When informed that his wife had applied for a divorce he said he would do nothing to hinder her from getting it, but wanted it arranged so his son could come to see him occasionally. He visited his old aunt, Mrs. MARY HERBERT, near town, and left on the 2:05 o'clock afternoon train for his Illinois home. He subscribed for the Hoosier, but says he does not want his present residence known.

Birthday
Miss MYRTLE THORNTON was 8 years old on last Monday, and gave her young friends a birthday party in the afternoon. They had a jolly time, considering the inclemency of the weather. They were treated to ice cream, cake and candy to their hearts' content. The little ladies made up a purse and presented Miss MYRTLE with a handsome cream colored bunting dress pattern and enough oriental lace to trim it. The following is a list of the young guests: MABEL STEPHENS, KATIE FORD, STELLA PARRETT, MAGGIE DAVIS, LURA COFFMAN, GRACE COFFMAN, CARRIE THORNTON, MINNIE THORNTON, OLLIE BLUNK, SALLIE BROWN, NEVY DARBY, ADDIE PLACE, LUCY STOKES, SUSIE STOKES, GENEVIE HARRISON, LULA WHITNEY, ESSIE PORTER, NELLIE DAVIS, LEORA COIL, ANNA COIL, MINNIE HOLLINGSWORTH, LENA NIXON, BLANCH NIXON, GRACE DUZAN, MATTIE DAVIS, HELEN McKNIGHT, ESTA E. McCONNELL, GERTIE COOK, MAGGIE HASTY, CORA HARRISON, and GRACE HASTY.

Home News
Mrs. C.B. GALLOWAY's sister, of Ellettsville, this state, is here on a visit.

Mrs. NANCY CHAPMAN is dangerously ill, and it is thought she cannot recover.

A.B. THOMPSON of Dana, and Miss JENNIE WHITE of Helt's Prairie, are making the necessary arrangements to get married before very long.

WILLIAM C. MYERS is moving out on to S.H. DALLAS' farm this week. It is rumored that BILLY is going to marry a Knox County lady before very long.

SARAH CATHERINE DAVIS and her three youngest kids are down on Helt's Prairie visiting, and getting a few good square meals.

JOE FOOS' little son who was thrown from a horse two weeks ago last Friday and had his skull fractured, and otherwise seriously hurt, was able to set up in bed on last Sunday for the first time. He is now getting along nicely and strong hopes are entertained of his speedy recovery.

Successful at Last
At 8 o'clock on last Sunday evening at the residence of MART SEELY, A.C. BROKAW, and SALLIE PINEGAR were united in wedlock after nearly 20 years courtship. Esq. JOHN L. EGGLESTON tied the connubial knot. They went to housekeeping on last Monday afternoon in a part of the building now occupied by Marshall MILLER. Both have the best wishes of the Hoosier.

Summit Grove
Miss BELLE CAMPBELL visited SPENCER MACK last week.

Mr. MILTON JAMES, of Illinois, visited his parents, Mr. and Mrs. ED JAMES, last week.

Notice of Final Settlement of Estate
JOHN HANEY, deceased
August 22, 1885

Our Doctors
Clerk A.R. HOPKINS has issued county licenses to the following physicians for next year:
ALEXANDER KINDERMAN, Diploma 1883, Rush Medical College, Chicago, IL
A.H. DEPUY, diploma 1857, Eclectic Medical Institute, Cincinnati, OH
GRANVILLE O. NEWTON, diploma 1879, Miami Med. College, Cincinnati, OH
JAMES T. HENDERSON, diploma 1879, Butler Univ., IN
WILLIAM I. HALL, diploma 1870, Ohio Medical College, Cincinnati, OH

Obituary
Mrs. JOHN R. WISHARD, of Helt township, died at 11 o'clock a.m. on Wednesday last, aged about 68 years. Her husband died a few years ago. She was a Christian lady, a kind neighbor and an affectionate mother. In her death, Helt township loses a good citizen.

Wednesday, September 2, 1885

Obituary
Judge WILLIAM H. MALLORY, of Danville, Illinois, well known by the legal fraternity of this county, and many of our citizens, died very suddenly at Lafayette on Monday last. He had been to Logansport on business, and was on his return home when he became suddenly ill on the train and had to stop off at Lafayette where he soon expired. There was an incident connected with his life which many of our readers still remember. In 1856 he was a resident of Covington, Fountain County, and was employed as attorney in an important lawsuit. He engendered the hatred of one of the parties whom he had sued for the recovery of a debt, and this party had made threats that he would kill MALLORY on sight. They met one afternoon on the stairway leading to the court room. The party who had threatened his life started towards him when MALLORY drew a pen knife, and with one thrust severed his jugular vein. His antagonist whose name was ADLER, expired in a few moments, and MALLORY immediately gave himself up to the sheriff, and put in a plea of self defense. He was ably prosecuted by Hon. D.W. VOORHEES and others, but the jury thought it was a justifiable case and acquitted him.

A Streak of Luck

JOHN MANNING, who was granted a pension a couple of years ago of $4 per month, made an application for an increase of pension on an additional disability which was granted at the rate of $2 per month, dating back to 1865, giving 20 years arrears of pension, amounting to $472 after paying his attorney. JOHN served 10 or 12 years in the English army, and is deserving of all the pittance he gets from the government.

Death

Miss INDIANA TRUITT, daughter of GEORGE F. TRUITT, of Dana, was buried in the cemetery near Vermillion Chapel. She had been sick but a short time. February 1884, she united with the M.E. Church in Dana, and died August 27th, 1885. She was aged 19 years, 10 months, and 26 days. Her funeral services were conducted in Dana M.E. Church by her pastor, E.R. JOHNSON, according to her wishes. A large congregation was present. INDIANA was esteemed by all who knew her; dearly beloved by her sorrowing father, brothers and sisters, who received the sympathy of the entire neighborhood in which they live. May God's blessing be with them.

Teachers for This Township

The following is a list of teachers for this township and the places where they will teach this coming fall and winter. The schools will all commence next Monday, with the exception of #10, where a new building is being erected and will not be completed before the last of this month.

School #3 - MILTON W. COFFMAN
School #4 - LAURA HARLAN
School #5 - W.B. GOSNELL
School #6 - A.J. WILSON
School #7 - MINNIE LAMB
School #8 - E.L. HIBERLY
School #9 - WILLIAM BELL
School #10 - E.E. RANKIN and EMMA HAWORTH
School #11 - WILLIAM COFFIN
School #12 - EMMA BLACKMORE
School #13 - J. ROACH JOHNSON
School #14 - RICHARD WHITLOCK

Matrimony

Marriage of PERRY THOMAS to a Crawfordsville Lady

On last Sunday, at Buffalo, New York, PERRY THOMAS, of this township, who is well and favorably known by most of our citizens, was united in wedlock to ELSIE BACHELDOR, a widow lady of Crawfordsville, and for many years one of the teachers in the city schools of that place. She is the daughter of JOHN STILWELL, a merchant who formerly held forth at Waveland, in Montgomery County, but who is now dead. She is said to be an estimable lady, and we are glad to hear it, for we know she has secured a good husband. Both have the best wishes of the Hoosier State force.

Home News

JAMES HARRISON's eldest child, KATIE, is down with the fever.

O.R. JOHNSON, of Hillsdale, is making arrangements to move out to Kansas.

Miss ELLA BURNS, of Terre Haute, is visiting her uncle, MAURICE HEGARTY and family.

BEN SHEELY and his stepson, of Helt township, were in Newport on Saturday last.

SAM D. COLLETT, of this place has gone to Charleston, West Virginia, to attend college.

FRANK WELLS of Clinton is clerking for a dry goods firm in Terre Haute.

WILLIAM COMEGYS, of Ash Grove, Missouri, an old 71st boy, who moved from Perrysville out West some 20 years ago, is back here on a visit.

Married - On the 30th ultimate, at the residence of Mr. BARNES, in Highland, by the Rev. IRA MATER, Mr. JAMES MITCHELL of Vermillion County, to Miss EMMA HALL of Parke County.

The teachers for the Newport schools are Prof. COLEMAN, Danville, Illinois, principal; ED AIKMAN, Highland, grammar department; Mrs. BELLE KERDOLFF, Newport, intermediate; and Miss MATILDA HOLMES, Delphi, primary.

Fell Our of a Buggy
On last Thursday, STEPHEN JENKS and F.N. AUSTIN, of Bono, came up to this place on business. In the afternoon when they were getting ready to start for home, and before Mr. AUSTIN had got fairly seated in the rig, the horses gave a sudden start, precipitating him out of the rear end of the buggy and very seriously injuring him. He was insensible for quite awhile. Drs. HALL and WALLACE were called and soon revived him to consciousness, when he started for home. The trip did not seem to agree with him, and on last Sunday he was reported to be in a critical situation and confined to his bed. We hope to hear of his speedy recovery.

FRANK DAVIS and wife took down suddenly ill last week, and it was thought for a few days that they could not possibly recover, but at present they are convalescent. Mr. DAVIS' ailment was heart disease, and that of his wife was congestion.

Notice of Insolvency
Estate of ELLIOTT BOGGS, deceased
JOHN R. HUNTER, administrator
A.R. HOPKINS, Clerk

Killed by Falling Tree
THOMAS ROSS, residing 3 miles North of Perrysville, met with a fatal accident on Wednesday last. He was felling a tree, and in falling it struck and fell upon him, injuring him so that he died the next day. He was 66 years of age, and well respected in the neighborhood where he resided.

Notice to Non-Residents
AUSTIN W. JACKSON by LEVI S. SCOTT, guardian vs. JOHN WRIGHT, FRANK B. VANDUYN, MARIA VANDUYN, unknown heirs of THOMAS EVASTON, deceased
Complaint No. 2705
WARD & DAVIS attorneys for plaintiff
Residence of Unknown heirs of THOMAS EVASTON unknown
Must appear before second Monday of October 1885
August 29, 1885
A.R. HOPKINS, Clerk

Notice to Non-Residents
JOHN BENSINGER vs. EMERETTA BENSINGER
Complaint No, 2703
R.B. SEARS, attorney for plaintiff
EMERETTA BENSINGER is not a resident of Indiana
Must appear before second Monday of October 1885
August 22, 1885
A.R. HOPKINS, Clerk

Wednesday, September 9, 1885

Informed on the Wrong Pensioner
A certain citizen of this township who is not as warm a friend to the soldiers as he ought to be, and begrudges them the little pittance paid them by the government, concluded that ED BROWN who draws $8 per month on varicose veins, was not entitled to anything, and wrote the Commissioner of Pensions that he was an able bodied man, and just as able to earn his living by hard work as any man in the township. On the strength of this letter the Commissioner sent an agent out here to look into the case. He examined Mr. BROWN and reported to the Commissioner, who instead of dropping him from the pension rolls, increased his pension from $8 to $16 per month. ED is in hopes somebody else will inform on him before long.

Sudden Death
On last Friday, while Mrs. THOMAS HARVEY, residing a short distance southeast of Howard, Parke County, was sitting on the lounge, she dropped over and expired instantly. She was 73 years of age, and was highly respected in her neighborhood.

Eugene Items
Mr. J.H. LASHLEY and wife left Monday for Bellaire, Ohio, on a visit to relatives.

Country News
JOHN BILSLAND, of Toronto, Indiana, was a visitor in Covington during the reunion. He was a guest of his brother-in-law, W.C.B. SEWELL, during his short stay. We are glad to note that he is enjoying good health and looks remarkably well for one of his age.

Covington's People Paper

Real Estate Transfers for August 1885

WILLIAM HINES and wife to JOSEPH H. PRATHER
40 acres in Helt township - $1,000

DANIEL W. FINNEY and wife to RICHARD MALONE
Lots 21, 22, 23, & 24, in Finney's addition to Dana - $300

SAMUEL AIKMAN and wife to RICHARD MALONE
Lot 12, block 5, in Dana - $1,050

MATTHEW J. JONES and wife to BENJAMIN S. BOTHWELL
Lot 12, block 1, in Jonestown - $500

SAMUEL B. DAVIS to JOHN F. HUNT
40 acres in Helt township - $600

AMANDA J. HOLLINGSWORTH to LYDIA DUNLAP
70.40 acres in Clinton township - $400

JESSE RUNYAN and wife to CYNTHIA ANN DAVIS
40.36 acres in Clinton township - $1,500

ALBERT E. VILLARS and wife to PRESTLY MARTIN
31.92 acres in Highland township - $1,085

JAMES M. ALEXANDER etal to ELLEN ALEXANDER
Lot 14, in Eugene - $500

AMOS J. BETSON and wife to JOHN W. PARRETT
110 acres in Vermillion township - $2,000

EDMOND EDMONDS and wife to HELEN A. McKNIGHT
Part lot 49, in Newport - $300

LUCY MERRIMAN etal to JOHN W. PARRETT
Lot 109, in Newport - $200

JOHN H. BOGART and wife to HARRY B. DUDLEY
Part lots 2, 4, & 5, block 4, in Clinton - $400

DANIEL W. GARDNER and wife to HARRY B. DUDLEY
Part of lot 2, block 4 – gift

STEPHEN CRANE to LEWIS H. REED
25 acres in Helt township - $1,200

MAHLON H. LEWIN and wife to AUGUST JENKS
½ lots 9 & 10, in L. and Adams' addition to Newport - $150

WILLIAM C. JACKSON and wife to CYRUS F. DOWINS
80 acres in Helt township - $150

SAMUEL R. KAUFMAN and wife to MELVIN E. HOLLINGSWORTH
9 acres in Helt township - $150

CYNTHIA A. DAVIS to WILLIAM E. DAVIS etal
40 acres in Clinton townshiop - $1,500

ISAAC PORTER and wife to MALINDA PETTY
89 acres in Eugene township - $5,000

ELLEN CRANE etal to STEPHEN CRANE
25 acres in Helt township - $1

Home News
Mrs. JOHN W. PARRETT is out in Kansas visiting relatives.

ELMER DAVIS, son of TIP DAVIS of Dana, is teaching school at Ludlow, Illinois.

Mrs. OL. DAVIS is down seriously ill. It is thought she has the typhoid fever.

Retail liquor licenses were granted to MART ADAMS, for this place, on Tuesday last.

Our former fellow citizen, GEORGE SMITH, who is now located in Harvey County, Kansas, sent a lot of grapes back here to JOHN D. BROWN, and kindly remembered us. Many thanks, GEORGE.

Hon. O.P. DAVIS and his daughter, Mrs. ALICE ODEKIRK, returned home last week from their visit to New Hampshire and the East.

On last Wednesday a boy baby was born to WILLIAM FULTZ and wife, of Eugene. Also on the same day and in the same town a girl baby was born to JOE McCORMICK and wife.

QUILL MOREHEAD, residing one mile west of town, who has been down with the consumption for a long time, is now in a critical condition, and it looks like he could not last much longer.

Mrs. S.S. COLLETT returned home from Charleston, West Virginia, on last Friday morning where she had been on a visit to her daughter, EVA LITTLEPAGE, for several months. She had a very pleasant time, and comes back in the enjoyment of good health. She sent us a peach, larger than our fist, as a sample of the kind they raise in West Virginia.

Mrs. JOHN HASTY, who has been suffering with a tumor on her side for the last 16 years, and was scared nearly to death for fear it was a cancer, now feels much relieved. It bursted one day last week and run a large amount of corruption. She is now on the mend and her speedy recovery is predicted.

Death of NANCY CHAPMAN
Mrs. NANCY CHAPMAN, aged 70 years, and for 20 years a resident of this township, died at 6 o'clock yesterday morning at the residence of her son SIMON, with whom she was making her home. She had been in feeble health for a long time, and her death was not unexpected. She drew a pension of $8 per month from the government, which will now cease. She was kind and generous hearted, and well respected by her neighbors. She leaves 3 sons, one residing at Mattoon, Illinois, another at Washington, this State, and the other one here. Her remains will be buried in the Thomas Cemetery, the funeral taking place sometime today.

Misses ALICE and MINNIE PINEGAR, of Danville, Illinois, came down last Saturday to visit their mother and new pa.

Miss EVA DICKEN, who has been here for a number of weeks on a visit, left for her home in Mattoon, Illinois, on Monday last.

It is rumored that JOHN BLAKESLEY, of Helt township, will shortly be united in wedlock to Mrs. JANE HANNAHS of this township.

Uncle JOHN BUTLER dropped into the office on Monday last, and subscribed for the Hoosier to be sent to his daughter HAMA MILLER, at Castleton, Kansas.

Married
At 9 o'clock on last Monday night Esq. JOHN L. EGGLESTON united in wedlock CHARLES INGRAM and Miss ELIZA J. MISNER, both of Scottland, Illinois. The ceremony took place at DAVID BROWN's, one mile southwest of town. Mr. INGRAM is working at the brickyard for RILEY WHITNEY. She came here on purpose to marry him, and is only 17 years of age, while he is 22.

Mrs. HANNAH EGGLESTON, of Tuscola, Illinois, was in here last week on a visit.

KATIE, eldest daughter of JAMES HARRISON, is down with typhoid fever. She took ill 3 weeks ago today, and is pretty, sick, but thought not to be dangerous.

A letter from JOE B. CHEADLE yesterday stated that his invalid wife had been confined to her bed for the last 19 weeks, and her death is expected any minute. Sickness has been in the family for the last 6 years, and no one can tell the pangs and aches friend JOE has suffered in that time. He has our full sympathy in his sore affliction.

Sheriff's Sale on Execution
Property of ALLEN CROCKETT
Sale to be September 26, 1885
Sale at courthouse between 10 and 4
Lot 13, in Gessie and Cushman's addition to Perrysville
September 2, 1885
H.H. CONLEY, Attorney for plaintiff
JOHN A. DARBY, Sheriff

Notice of Administration
Estate of HENRY HOLLINGSWORTH, deceased
August 17, 1885
CHARLES P. POTTS, Admr.

Notice of Final Settlement of Estate
Estate of JOHN HANEY, deceased
August 22, 1885
A.R. HOPKINS, Clerk

Notice to Non-Residence
THOMAS H. EATON vs. Unknown heirs of CORNELIUS NICE, REBECCA J. BOYCE, GEORGE BOYCE, IDA M. ALLEN, JAMES M. ALLEN, METTIE V. CRABB, GEORGE A. CRABB, HARRIET A. COX, JOHN COX, ELIZABETH C. YOWELL, JOHN YOWELL, SAMUEL H. DAVIDSON, MARY A. LINDSEY, WILLIAM LINDSEY, WILLIAM S. DAVIDSON
SAWYER & GIBSON, Attorneys for plaintiff
SAMUEL H. DAVIDSON, MARY A. LINDSEY, & WILLIAM LINDSEY are not residents of Indiana
Names and residence of heirs of ALONZO LYONS and CORNELIUS NICE are unknown.
Residence of WILLIAM S. DAVIDSON is unknown
Must appear before second Monday in October 1885
September 8, 1885
A.R. HOPKINS, Clerk

Wednesday, September 16, 1885

His Wife Ran Off with Another Man
JOHN BRYANT, a farmer aged about 35 years, living on ALVA WATSON's farm near Eugene, has been in the city the past few days looking up the whereabouts of his runaway wife, who eloped with one WILLIAM FENNIMORE, of Newport, last Wednesday. Mrs. BRYANT left a one year old baby with a neighbor, just before she left. Mr. BRYANT brought the baby to this city and from here took it to his mother's, Mrs. JOHN PHILLIPS, who lives at Bismark, two miles north of the city. Mr. BRYANT states that when he went to his work Wednesday morning, he was followed by his wife with the baby in her arms, and at a distance nearly a quarter of a mile from the house she called to him to wait for her. When she got near him she asked him if he didn't want to kiss her and the baby. He did so and she walked back to the house. This act on the part of his wife seemed very strange to him, and it was in his mind all day. They had not quarreled, and he left her in the morning apparently happy as ever, and contented. He was completely dumfounded on his return to the house at night to find a note written by his wife, saying that she never expected to see him again. Mr. BRYANT is an honest, hard working man, and bears an excellent reputation. He says he don't think the elopers have gone very far as he found out they only had about $25 when they left. He has placed the matter in the hands of Deputy Sheriff HALLS to look up, with instructions to find them if possible.
Danville News

Commissioners Court for September 1885
Bridges

S.B. DAVIS	7.50
E.L. CANADY	108.50
D.E. HIGGINS	82.45
PETER AIKMAN	100.00
M. HEGARTY	12.75
L.O. BISHOP	6.00

FRED RUSH	16.00
JOSEPH HANN	1.00
Public Buildings	
R.H. NIXON	1.55
M. HEGARTY	12.55
A.R. HOPKINS	2.75
JOHN A. DARBY	67.71
THOMAS CUSHMAN	772.44
H.B. RHOADS	2.25
Poor	
JOSEPH CONRAD, poor asylum	420.00
S.B. DAVIS, Vermillion township	336.31
L.A. MORGAN, Highland township	220.68
WHITE JAMES, Helt township	192.24
JAMES MALONE, Eugene township	152.65
GEORGE W. STULTZ, Clinton township	165.50
ERASTUS MACK	25.00
JAMES WALLACE	62.00
A. KINDERMAN	37.50
C.M. WHITE	50.00
HARRY JAMES	20.00
JOSEPH HANN	1.50
Books & Stationery	
W.B. BURFORD	101.80
Gravel Roads	
W.L. PORTER, Clinton and Paris	281.40
W.L. PORTER, Hazel Bluff, bonds	1000.00
W.L. PORTER, Hazel Bluff	90.44
W.L. PORTER, Perrysville & SW	240.00
W.L. PORTER, Newport & Quaker Point	15.07
Miscellaneous	
R.H. NIXON, Criminals	16.95
R.H. NIXON, County offices	8.80
M.G. RHOADS, Attorney fees	100.00
W.L. PORTER, fees and salary	200.00
W.L. PORTER, interest on bonds	600.00
M.L. HALL, Board of Health	48.25
A.J. JOHNSON, County Superintendent	220.00
A.J. JOHNSON, Printing	2.50
DAVID AGGRAY, janitor	50.00
E. PRITCHARD, fees and salary	536.87
H.B. RHOADS, Criminals	2.75
D. DOWNING, courts	24.00
J.B. WRIGHT, courts	42.00
F.M. RILEY, courts	21.00
JOHN A. DARBY, criminals	64.50
JOHN A. DARBY, courts	10.00

Hillsdale
ORLO JOHNSON is preparing to move to his home in the great West.

WINCHESTER DOSS is prostrate with typhoid fever at LEVI BONEBRAKE's; had to be child-less when old and sick.

A 13 year old daughter of Mrs. SHORT, who has been confined by rheumatism for many weeks, is mending slowly.

Mrs. ADAM PEARMAN and CURRY LONG were called to Annapolis, Parke County, by the fatal illness of their worthy mother.

Obituary
On last Wednesday morning, September 9th, 1885, QUILL MOREHEAD, son of SAMUEL MOREHEAD, residing one mile west of town, died of consumption after a long and lingering illness. QUILL was a young man aged about 27 years, and had a host of warm friends. In fact everybody respected and esteemed him very highly. He was an honorable and upright young man, and a member of the M.E. Church. He had lain upon a bed of affliction for a long time, and at times was hopeful that he would get well. He was kindly cared for and everything did for his comfort that could be. In his death the community loses a good citizen. His funeral took place on last Thursday afternoon from his father's residence, and was very respectably attended by his neighbors and friends. Rev. JOHN HARRISON, pastor of the M.E. Church, performed the last sad rites, after which his remains were followed to the Thomas Cemetery and gently laid away to rest by kind and sympathizing friends.

Obituary
Death of JOHN W. REED at Dana
JOHN W. REED, one of the old and respected citizens of this county died at Dana on Monday last, after an illness of about 2 weeks. The deceased was born in North Carolina in 1822, and consequently was 63 years of age at the time of death. In 1832, when only 10 years of age, he emigrated to this county with his parents, and had resided in Helt township ever since. His children are all grown, and are now doing for themselves. His wife survives him. Mr. REED was a most excellent citizen, and a true Christian gentleman in every sense of the term. He was a member of church, and tried to live a consistent and upright life. His funeral took place yesterday, his remains being interred in the Sugar Grove Cemetery.

Notice to Non-Residents

ELLEN GRONDYKE vs. ANDREW J. BEAUCHAMP
Complaint No. 2706
WARD & DAVIS attorneys for plaintiff
ANDREW J. BEAUCHAMP is not a resident of Indiana
Must appear before second Monday in October 1885
August 19, 1885

A.R. HOPKINS, Clerk

Home News
CHARLEY BASSETT is the tallest man in Helt township.

HARRISON JAGGERS is down with a severe attack of the cholera morbus.

Miss ADDIE PLACE and her brother WALTER are out in Illinois visiting their grandmother.

Miss AMANDA KERDOLFF has returned from her visit to her father's at Cincinnati, Ohio.

We guess there is no question now but what BILL WIGLEY will take one of the Jonathan Creek girls into camp before long.

Attorney M.B. DAVIS has left for Lincoln, Nebraska, and located at Beatrice, a town of 6,000 inhabitants, in the same state.

Vermillion township has only two resident male teachers -- A.J. WILSON of Opedee and E.L. HIBERLY of the Eggleston School.

WILLIE BELL had to give up his school at #9 on account of poor health. Miss NAOMI EGGLESTON was employed to complete the term.

H.E. RHOADS of Waveland, father of HARRY RHOADS, came over last Saturday to spend a few days with his son and brother, MARTIN G. RHOADS.

SELDON EGGLESTON left yesterday morning for Arkansas, where he intends to remain until next spring. He is not in very good health, and is going down to see if the climate will not benefit him.

HENRY DENNIS, who has been afflicted for several weeks with a severe attack of rheumatism, is still compelled to go about on crutches.

List of Letters - September 16, 1885

CHARLES JENNINGS	HIRAM RICHARD
ANDREW REMERTER	WILLIAM PIEPLE
JOSEPH SCHRIER	JOHN M. HAZEN
Mrs. MARY PHILLIPS	Mrs. ALLA MORGAN

Rev. W.N. COFFMAN will pack his household goods the latter part of this month and move to Avalon, Livingston County, to take charge of the College Church of that place.

Our city schools bowed in on Monday last with Prof. COLEMAN as principal, ED. E. AIKMAN in charge of the grammar department, Mrs. BELLE KERDOLFF the intermediate, and Miss MATILDA HOLMES the primary.

Wednesday, September 23, 1885

Home News

F.D. JONES is attending Wabash College this year.

Mrs. LIZZIE EDMONDS, of Eugene, was in town on Monday visiting her son GEORGE.

WILBER DALLAS of St. Paul, Minnesota, is here on a visit. He is in splendid health.

JOHN L. VANDUYN has rented a large farm in Owen County and will move there next spring.

Miss GLANT CUSHMAN has gone to Attica to spend the winter with her half sister, Mrs. MAZIE SHAFER.

Mrs. NORBIN THOMAS and ROBERT J. HOLTZ, of Lodi, Parke County, were in town on Thursday last.

It is rumored that a New York gentleman will shortly lead Mrs. ALICE ODEKIRK to the hymeneal altar.

HENRY OSBORN is now at Chattanooga, Tennessee.

O.R. JOHNSON, of Hillsdale, left for Kansas last week.

BELL LINDSEY, of Sidney, Illinois, is here visiting her relatives.

Miss CLARA WHITCOMB, of Clinton, has gone to Florida to teach school.

Mrs. SIB DUNCAN, of Oskaloosa, Iowa, daughter of T.S. HOOD of Helt township, is back here on a visit.

CHARLEY CRAIG, HUNTER SHARP, WILLIAM CRAIG, and JAMES McLAUGHLIN, of Helt township, left for Missouri a few days ago, where they intend to locate.

RICHARD T. HAWKINS left for Kentucky on last Saturday to visit his mother and brothers whom he has not seen for 19 years. He expects to be gone several weeks.

Mrs. LIZZIE DALLAS, of St. Paul, Minnesota, is here on a visit, the guest of her sister, Mrs. JOHN W. PARRETT.

Our new U.B. preacher for this circuit is Rev. H. JONES, aged about 47. He has a wife and 4 children.

Death
ISAAC SHARP, of Waveland, father of WILLIAM SHARP of this place, died on last Thursday evening, aged 52 years, of typhoid fever, and was interred at the Methodist Cemetery in that city on Saturday morning. He was a responsible citizen of that town.

SAM CHANDLER of Sidney, Fremont County, Iowa, who is well known by a number of our citizens, was in town yesterday, and while here was a guest of clerk A.R. HOPKINS. Mr. CHANDLER is a Democrat, and owing to his great popularity he has twice been elected sheriff of his county, which is largely Republican, and is now serving his first term as County Auditor.

Notice of Final Settlement of Estate
Estate of ISAAC ROUSE, deceased
September 22, 1885

Teachers Institute at Vermillion County Institute
Those attending Saturday, September 19, 1885 in Newport:
A.J. WILSON, E. AIKMAN, J.R. JOHNSON, Prof. COLEMAN, MINNIE LAMB, EMMA BLACKMORE, NAOMI EGGLESTON, WILLIAM COFFIN, M.W. COFFIN, LAURA HARLAN, BELLE KERDOLFF, & E.L. HIBERLY

Death
The wife of JOE B. CHEADLE, editor of the Frankfort Banner, died on Wednesday last of consumption. The deceased had been an invalid for the last 6 years, a great portion of which time she had been confined to a bed of affliction. Her maiden name was TENBROOK, and her home before marriage was near Rockville, where her remains were brought for interment on Friday last and consigned to the silent tomb. Everyone who knew Mrs. CHEADLE was her friend. She had an amiable disposition and bore her long sufferings with much fortitude. She had a warm generous heart, and always a kind word for everybody. In her death friend JOE loses a most excellent wife, and her 4 little children a kind and affectionate mother.

Wednesday, September 30, 1885

Sudden Death
A Former Citizen of Perrysville Passes Over the River
ROBERT McCLINTOCK, for many years a citizen of Perrysville, died suddenly in Danville, Illinois, on last Friday night, to which city he moved some time ago. He and his little son, aged 8 or 9, were occupying a rented room and took their meals at a restaurant. On Friday night he went to bed in his usual health. The next morning his little son got up and then tried to wake his Pa, when he discovered he was dead and cold. A coroner's inquest was held on the body and rendered a verdict that he died from rheumatism of the heart. His wife died about 2 years ago from the same disease. She was a sister to JOSEPH B. CHEADLE, editor of the Frankfort Banner. The deceased leaves 5 children. The eldest is teaching school in Illinois, while the next oldest, a daughter aged 17, is residing in Perrysville and is reported to be in the last stages of consumption. His remains were taken to Perrysville and interred on Sunday last.

Highland Township
Miss ETTIE WITTENMYER is quite low with typhoid fever.

WARREN BAMFORD and JOSEPH BAMBRAGE started to Kansas last week where they will make their future home.

Home News
HARRY B. RHOADS has gone to Chicago to take a thorough course in chemistry.

Mrs. CAL. HUGHES, of Perrysville, sister of Mrs. Rev. W.N. COFFMAN, was down here last week on a short visit.

BYRD NEBEKER, formerly of this place, has received a position in the Custom House, at El Paso, Texas.

Clinton Argus

Rev. W.N. COFFMAN and family will leave for their new home in Missouri on Monday next. We extend to them our best wishes.

BILL SLATER, who has been out in Iowa and Colorado for the last 15 years, returned home last week looking hale and hearty. He expects to make this his future home.

Mrs. LITTLEFIELD, Mrs. LIGHT, and Mrs. SCOTT, sisters of Pastor COFFMAN who reside near Scottland, Illinois, were over here last week on a visit.

JOHN D. COLLETT left on last Wednesday with a surveying party, under the management of Capt. A.B. FITCH.

JAMES H. WHITEHEAD and wife, of Peru, Indiana, HARVEY McCLINTOCK, of Moran, and JOE B. CHEADLE, of Frankfort, came to Perrysville last Saturday to be present at the funeral of ROBERT McCLINTOCK.

The Press generally unites in expression of the deepest sympathy for Mr. J.B. CHEADLE, editor of the Frankfort Banner, in his recent loss of his loving and beloved wife.

Crawfordsville Star

The Montezuma correspondent of the Terre Haute Sunday Express says that cards are out for the marriage of OLIVER PONTON of this county, and Miss ADA AMOS of Montezuma.

JAMES CRANE and wife, of Clinton, were in town over Sunday, the guests of S.H. DALLAS and family.

When the fodder is all in shock, and the frost is on the pumpkin, BILL MYERS is going to get married to his Knox County girl.

Mrs. SERENA COATS of Veedersburg, this state, is here visiting her brother Mr. JAMES A. WHITE, Sr.

Clinton Siftings

Mr. ALONZO BRINDLEY and Miss LUCY MERRIMAN, were united in marriage at the residence of Mr. JOHN HUGHES, at 8 o'clock P.M., Wednesday, September 23rd. The ceremony was performed by Rev. JOHN HARRISON, pastor of the M.E. Church in this place. May theirs be long and happy lives is the wish of their many friends.

Toronto
Rev. THOMAS AIKMAN will move to Nebraska in a few days.

Notice of Final Settlement of Estate
Estate of SAMUEL B. PEARMAN
September 23, 1885
A.R. HOPKINS, Clerk

Jordan School House
JOHN HAINS has removed most of his family to Perrysville to attend school there.

Wednesday, October 7, 1885

Shot His Brother-In-Law
A Former Citizen of Newport Kills a Relative
The most of the people of Newport and vicinity are personally acquainted with CLAY BURSON, who was born and raised in this township. He now resides in California, where he has been making his home for a number of years. Only a few weeks ago he was back here on a visit. Shortly after his return home he had some trouble with his brother-in-law about some land, which resulted in a fight in which Mr. BURSON drew a revolver and shot his brother-in-law dead. After he had committed the terrible deed he gave himself up to the Sheriff who took him into custody. He had a preliminary trial before a justice, who set him at liberty, believing from the evidence that the murder was committed in self defense.

Dana Items
Miss CALLIE HARLAN of District #4 is attending college at Terre Haute.

Born to Mr. and Mrs. OL STAATS, last Saturday evening, a girl. Later -- Since the above was put in type we learn that this child died, last Monday morning.

Dr. GILMORE, who has been in Kansas for several weeks, looking after his real estate interests there, was called home last week on account of the illness of his son RICHARD, who has typhoid fever.

We are pleased to learn that W.H. ARMSTRONG has decided not to sell out and leave for Hot Springs, as was reported for a time here, but that he will stay with us and continue to weigh out groceries for his customers.

Home News
Mrs. GAYLORD, of Peoria, Illinois, is here visiting her daughter, Mrs. R.A. PARRETT.

JAMES BURNS and SARAH CRAIG, of Eugene, were married Sunday last.

Col. L.R. WHIPPLE and his son-in-law, WILLIAM FULTZ, of Eugene, were in the city on last Monday afternoon.

JIM JAMISON, of Ellettsville, was here over Sunday visiting his sisters, Mrs. OL. DAVIS and Mrs. ZACH GALLOWAY.

TOM MOFFATT, of Topeka, Kansas, has the thanks of the Hoosier for papers containing a full account of the soldiers' reunion held at that place last week.

Home News
WILLIAM ROACH, of Eugene township, returned from Kansas last week, where he has been for the past 5 or 6 months. We guess he got enough of that State to do him for awhile.

Got Spliced
On last Sunday afternoon WILLIAM WIGLEY was united in holy wedlock to Miss SARAH FLOYD, at the residence of her mother, on Stone Bluff, near the Jungles of Jonathan Creek. The ceremony was performed by Esq. FRED HIBERLY in his usual happy manner. Only a few special friends were present to witness the nuptials. Both have the best wishes of their numerous friends. The happy couple has our many thanks for some of the wedding cake.

Obituary
Death of B.F. MOREY of Clinton

B.F. MOREY, of Clinton, was stricken down with paralysis on Wednesday evening of last week, and died at 8:30 o'clock on last Saturday evening. On the evening of his death he was apparently in as good health as usual, and just before leaving the store in the evening, he told Mr. JOHN WHITCOMB that he had to go home to milk as he had a bad cow. He went home, took the bucket and went out into the lot to milk the cow. In the course of a half an hour his son WILLIAM came home, when the hired girl told him to go out and see what had become of his father, stating at the time that he had been gone long enough to milk half a dozen cows. His son went as requested and found his father lying prostrate in the cow lot, helpless and speechless. The alarm was given and soon help arrived and Mr. MOREY was taken to the house where able physicians were called and did everything in their power for his relief, but to no effect. He never was able to speak after the stroke.

The deceased was the third child born to WILLIAM and DEREXA MOREY, at Sommerville, Butler County, Ohio. In 1828, at the age of 16, he left home to learn the trade of blacksmithing, serving a three years apprenticeship. He came to Clinton in 1847, where he resided until his death, with the exception of two years spent in Kankakee, Illinois.

The deceased was a zealous member of the M.E. Church, and very highly respected by his neighbors and acquaintances. There were few stood higher in the estimation of the people of Clinton than Mr. MOREY. He was a member of the Odd Fellows and Masonic lodges, the last order performing the last sad rites on the day of the funeral, which occurred at 3 o'clock on last Sunday afternoon. Elder BUCKLES officiated at the residence, where short services were held. The great esteem in which he was held by everyone was fully attested to by the attendance at his funeral on Sunday which is said to be the largest ever seen in that city.

Obituary
SARAH E. BENNETT was born February 15th, 1850, united in marriage with FRANCES DAVIS April 14th, 1871, united with the United Brethren Church at Eggleston's School House, in January, 1884, under the Ministry of Rev. W.H. JONES. She retained her membership in the church with integrity, and with Christian fortitude endured her last sleep, giving assurance to her friends that all was well, that she enjoyed a well grounded hope in Christ. She died at her home in Newport on Friday, October 9th, 1885, and after appropriate services at the residence, conducted by the writer, her remains were laid to rest in the Thomas Cemetery.

Clinton Items from the Argus
WREN and JIM WHITE intend to go to Florida this fall.

Miss MAY QUICK is confined to her room with typhoid fever.

Mrs. COLLEN JAMES and daughter JENNIE, of Hastings, Nebraska, are visiting relatives and friends in this city.

Miss SARAH STAATS, the popular young dressmaker, will take her departure from our midst in the near future and intends casting her lot among the mosquitoes and alligators of Florida. Clinton society will miss her.

Rev. SAM AIKMAN, formerly of this county, paid the Argus a fraternal visit this afternoon on his way to his old home in Helt township. We used to know SAM when he was one of the 'boys' about so high. SAM is now in active charge of a flourishing Presbyterian Church in Ohio.

Obituary
Mrs. WILLIAM RANDOLPH, of Eugene township, who has lain upon a bed of affliction for several months, died of liver disease on Friday last and was interred in the Thomas Cemetery on Saturday last. She was about 60 years of age, and leaves a husband and a large family of children.

Death of a Pauper
Mrs. REBECCA SCOTT, an inmate of the poor house, died of old age at 3 o'clock on last Sunday afternoon, aged 78 years. She was a sister of Capt. WILLIAM SWAN of Clinton township, and had been cared for by the county for the last 13 years. Her remains were interred yesterday.

Got Married
On last Sunday, October 11, 1885, at the residence of the U.B. parsonage in Perrysville, Rev. J.S. BROWN united WILSON HASTY and Miss SAMANTHA WHITE in bonds of wedlock. Although we had been expecting something of the kind for quite awhile, we are willing to acknowledge they stole a march on the Hoosier. Both have been residents of this place for a long time, and are well known by all our people as honest and industrious citizens. We believe it a happy match, and hope the happy young couple may live many years to enjoy the bliss of married life. Both have the best wishes of their numerous friends.

Home News
ED and JAMES ZOOK are here on a visit to brother GEORGE.

HARRY B. RHOADS leaves for Bloomington, this state, today, to take a course in Chemistry.

Mrs. JOHN F. LEITON, of Clinton, has received $3700 insurance on the death of her husband, who died some time ago.

JAMES HASTY and wife, and his daughter NORA, and Mrs. ZACK THORNTON, spent Sunday near Georgetown, Illinois, visiting relatives and old friends.

The school at #10, with Prof. E.E. RANKIN and Miss EMMA HAWORTH as teachers, bowed in on Monday last. We understand the attendance was large.

Mrs. ELLEN JONES, who has been in Washington City for several months visiting her daughter RETA, who is employed in the pension department, returned home on Friday last.

There was born to BUCK FORTNER and wife, on E. Extension St., at an early hour on last Sunday morning, a boy baby. We did not learn its weight, but understand, BUCK says, it is not bigger than a squirrel.

The Dana public schools began operations last Monday, with the following corps of teachers: Prof. FRED RUSH, principal; Miss SALLIE KEYES, intermediate; Miss ALICE THOMPSON, primary. A large attendance is reported.

Dana News

JOHN V. LAMB's little son, aged 4 or 5 years old, and residing 2 miles northwest of town, ventured near the heels of a colt on last Saturday and was kicked in the face inflicting a very serious wound and probably ruining the sight of one eye.

Born Wednesday, September 30, 1885, to the wife of J.M. HAMMOND, a girl. Mrs. HAMMOND is said to be in precarious condition.

Hamburg, Iowa, Baby News

Mr. HAMMOND was formerly a resident of Helt township, this county.

Mrs. A.M. DICKEN, and her daughter leave for Terre Haute this morning, where they intend to reside for awhile.

Highland Township
Mrs. ELHANAN STEVENS died on Friday morning and was buried at the family burying ground on Sunday.

Miss LETTIE McCLINTOCK, daughter of ROBERT McCLINTOCK, came to visit Dr. J.D. JOHNSON's family some days before her father's death, and being in the last stages of consumption, took to her bed to rise no more. She was kindly treated by the Dr. and carefully watched and served by Mrs. JOHNSON and her schoolmates, but their care failed to restore her. She was interred on last Sunday.

Death
While at Robinson, Illinois, last week attending the fair, Mr. JOE HANN learned that W.B. HAWORTH, a former merchant of this place, and a very intimate friend while here, of E.F. DAVIS, had died about 3 months ago.

Wednesday, October 21, 1885

Obituary

On Sunday night, October 11, 1885, Rev. M.L. GREEN, died of paralysis of the heart; aged 65 years and 6 months. The funeral took place yesterday afternoon from the M.E. Church, of which he was the pastor. Presiding Elder GREEN officiating, assisted by Rev. McDANIELS and others. The burial ceremonies were in charge of the Masonic fraternity, of which order he was a worthy member.

All that was mortal of Brother GREEN now lies sleeping in the West Lebanon Cemetery. He preached at Marshfield on Sunday morning and in the West Lebanon M.E. Church the same evening, retiring to bed at his usual hour. About 11 o'clock he complained of a smothering sensation. His devoted and solicitous wife raised him to a sitting position, when he quietly passed away. His sudden death has cast a gloom over the entire town and community, and the bereaved family have the sympathy of all our people in this their darkest hour.

West Lebanon (Indiana)Gazette

Home News
JAMES HARRISON and his infant child are down with the typhoid fever.

CHARLEY COOKE, of Ridge Farm, Illinois, passed through town on last Monday evening.

Miss GLANT CUSHMAN, who is living at Attica, came down and spent Sunday with her father.

JAMES BARNHART, of Dana, died on last Sunday night from typhoid fever after an illness of 3 or 4 weeks.

Mrs. MAZIE SHAFER, of Attica, was in town over Sunday, the guest of her step-father, TOM CUSHMAN.

Hon. O.P. DAVIS went down to the French Lick Springs last week, to remain a few days. He is in quite feeble health.

Our brother CHARLEY DAVIS, and cousin Miss MAT FILLINGER, of Helt's Prairie, came up here last Saturday and stopped over Sunday with us.

D.R. GRAY and family, of Chicago, former residents of Newport, are here on a visit to relatives and their numerous friends. They are all hearty and well.

A Man Marries a MANN
On Monday last, SPICER C. HASKETT, of Helt township, took out a license to marry Miss STELLA MANN of Summit Grove.

Mrs. SARAH DENTON, daughter of GEORGE W. SHEELEY, of Helt township, is in from Kansas on a visit and will remain one month. She brought along her two little children, a boy and girl, aged 4 and 6 years.

The Frost is on the Pumpkin
Ex-Sheriff WILLIAM C. MYERS, of this place, will be united in wedlock tomorrow evening to Miss VINA ALEXANDER, of Knox County, a former teacher in the public schools of this place. Judge JUMP granted a divorce to Mrs. W.R. PETERS of Dana, on Saturday last. She is the lady whose husband deserted her and eloped with another woman nearly one year ago. She seems to be well pleased over getting released from her worthless husband.

Died
At the home of Dr. D.B. JOHNSON, in Perrysville, Indiana, Friday morning, October 9th, 1885, of spinal meningitis, LETTIE H., daughter of ROBERT M. and ANNA C. McCLINTOCK, deceased, aged 14 years and 3 days. The deceased was born in Perrysville, October 6th, 1858, where she resided with her parents until 2 years ago, when she went with her father to live in Danville, Illinois. Her mother died October 17, 1883, since which time she has had charge of her father's home. She was an affectionate daughter, a true friend and possessed a mind of rare power and beauty. She was beloved by all who enjoyed her acquaintance both at Perrysville and Danville. She was a firm believer in the doctrines of the Universalist church. She was unconscious for weeks before her death, with now and then for a moment only, a conscious interval. She died as all who are afflicted with that terrible disease die. Her funeral was preached by Rev. W.P. HARGRAVE of the M.E. Church, Perrysville, assisted by Rev. ELWELL, of the U.B. Church, on Friday evening at the home of Dr. JOHNSON, burial at the M.E. Cemetery, Saturday morning at 9 o'clock. The floral decorations were elegant and were the gifts of her former classmates and friends.

Notice of Final Settlement of Estate
Estate of ELLIOTT BOGGS, deceased
October 14, 1885

Wednesday, October 28, 1885

We have received a letter from Mrs. H.C. BURSON, of Chico, California, in relation to her husband shooting his brother-in-law a few weeks since. She thinks we did him an injustice, and sent us papers, printed in that place, giving a full account of the sad tragedy, and requesting us to read them and then see who is to blame. The papers received fully vindicate Mr. BURSON, and the Justice who examined into the facts of the case says he was justifiable in killing his brother-in-law, who first opened fire on him.

Home News
HOWARD DAVIS, of Helt township, has a new boy baby at his house. It arrived here on last Friday.

WILLIAM C. MYERS was married to Miss VINA ALEXANDER, of Knox County, on last Thursday evening as stated in the Hoosier. Both arrived here on last Friday evening and attended the bean supper at Grand Army Hall that night where they were warmly congratulated by their numerous friends. Both have our best wishes of the Hoosier for a long, prosperous and happy life.

JOE WIGLEY who has been on the sick list for the last 3 or 4 weeks, is now convalescent.

Mrs. ORPHA WIGLEY, who is residing with her daughter at Eugene, was visiting relatives here last week.

Mrs. ANNA HUGHES, residing south of town, gave birth to a girl baby on Tuesday of last week. Her husband came to town the next day and purchased 50 cents worth of the best catnip in the market.

D.R. GRAY and lady, S.H. DALLAS and lady, and Mrs. D.S. HOPKINS spent last Monday in Clinton visiting, the guests of JAMES CRANE and lady.

Dr. J.C. HARRISON came up on the early morning train last Monday morning to pay JOE FORTNER's wife a professional visit.

Notice to Non-Residents

HENRY HOLLINGSWORTH vs. REBECCA A. HOLLINGSWORTH, SILAS HOLLINGSWORTH, AURILLA NICHOLS, A. ELIZA GILBERT, CHARITY DAWSON, MARY HOLLINGSWORTH, MORTON HOLLINGSWORTH, WILLIAM HOLLINGSWORTH, ETTE HOLLINGSWORTH, MINA HOLLINGSWORTH, CARL HOLLINGSWORTH, EARL HOLLINGSWORTH, ROBERT WRIGHT, JOHN ADAMS, HARRY B. RHOADS, MARTIN G. RHOADS, ABEL SEXTON
M.G. RHOADS, attorney for plaintiff
A ELIZA GILBERT, SILAS HOLLINGSWORTH, CHARITY are not residents of Indiana
Must appear before third Monday of December 1885
CHARLES P. POTTS, administrator of estate
Petitions court to sell real estate to pay debts of estate
October 22, 1885

A.R. HOPKINS, Clerk

Application for Liquor License

JAMES M. HAIN – Perrysville
PATRICK FLYNN – Hillsdale

Wednesday, November 4, 1885

Obituary

ANNA HARPER was born March 5th, 1825, and died October 27th, 1885, at her nephew's near her old home, now owned by ANDERSON HARPER, aged 60 years, 7 months, and 22 days. She united with the M.E. Church at Salem class, Helt's Prairie, at about the age of 30 years, and remained a member of that church for near 10 or 12 years, or as long as she could conveniently attend the services at that place. Sister HARPER continued to lead a consistent Christian life in her quiet way ever since that time. During her illness, which she bore with Christian patience and fortitude she expressed herself ready to meet death, stating to her sister-in-law, Mrs. HENRIETTA HARPER, that "there is not a shadow nor a doubt between me and God." She leaves two sisters and three brothers and many kind friends to mourn her loss. Sister HARPER made friends wherever she went. She was a devoted sister in the last sickness of her sister, SOPHRONIA RICHARD, who went before her to a better land just about 3 months ago. Funeral services were conducted by Rev. L. BYRD of Tennessee Baptist church in the presence of a sympathizing and attentive audience.

Home News

LEVI BONEBRAKE, of Hillsdale, was in town on Monday.

SAM GALLAGHER, of Montezuma, has moved up to Covington.

Obituary
MARY ISABELL JONES was born May 12th, 1857; died October 1st, 1885. She was married 10 years ago this month to ISAAC H. NEWTON. She united with the U.B. Church in the year 1876 under the preaching of Brother RYE. Two years ago she was taken with the disease, which finally terminated her death. All her afflictions she bore with Christian fortitude and she gladly awaited the summons, which called her home. She leaves a husband and 3 little children, a father and a mother, 6 brothers and one sister to mourn her departure. But their loss is her eternal gain. Sister NEWTON was a kind mother, an affectionate companion and a loving sister and child. Memorial services conducted at U.B. Church at Jonestown, in the presence of a good and attentive audience by Rev. L. BYRD.

Marriage in High Life
The writer solemnized the marriage of Dr. G.C. NEWTON to Miss SUE M. GRIMES on the evening of October 27, 1885, at the residence of the bride's mother in Toronto. The occasion was one worthy of remembrance. We have known the bride from early childhood, and have been her teacher and pastor, and have always found her faithful and true. The worthy doctor has won a prize of rare value, a model woman, who will be to him a true helpmate. The young doctor is a graduate of medicine from one of our best medical colleges and has talents of a superior order. May the un-numbered years bring happiness and contentment to their minds and hearts.

SILAS HOLLINGSWORTH, of Chrisman, Illinois, was in town over Monday night.

BILLY MOREHEAD is going to start for California on Monday, to see if that climate will not help his failing health.

ROB PARRETT now has a good dishwasher in his house. His wife gave birth to an 8 pound girl baby on Tuesday night of last week.

CONLEY TAYLOR, of Clay's Prairie, Illinois, a former citizen of Helt township, this county, was stricken with paralysis on the night of October 14th, and has been lying in a helpless condition.

Mrs. S.S. COLLETT received a dispatch from West Virginia on Monday last, informing her that her daughter, Mrs. EVA LITTLEPAGE, was dangerously ill. She started at once for that place.

Dr. T.C. HOOD, son of T.S. HOOD of Dana is in New York, taking a special medical course. Next spring he will go to Edinburg, Scotland, to perfect himself in some of the special branches.
Dana News

R.W. WRIGHT of Kansas City, Missouri, a former resident of Helt's Prairie, this county, was in town overnight last Tuesday and was the guest of the editor and his family while here. He looks as young and sprightly as he did 20 years ago. Western life seems to agree with our friend.

THOMPSON ARMOUR, a former resident of this county, who now resides just across the river on JOHN COLLETT's farm, in Parke County, has been granted a pension of $30 per month from the government, with arrears dating back 4 years. His first draw will amount to $1080. He was a member of the gallant 43rd Indiana.

JESSIE P. YORK of Dana, was united in wedlock on Tuesday of last week to a Miss SUSA CLARA of Waveland. The ceremony was private, and took place in the parlors of the National Hotel, Terre Haute. Both have the best wishes of their many friends.

Mrs. GAYLORD, of Peoria, Illinois, is here visiting her daughter, Mrs. R.A. PARRETT.

JAMES BURNS and SARAH CRAIG, of Eugene, were married on Sunday last.

Col. L.R. WHIPPLE and his son-in-law, WILLIAM FULTZ, of Eugene, were in the city on last Monday afternoon.

JIM JAMISON, of Ellettsville, was here on Sunday visiting his sisters, Mrs. OL. DAVIS and Mrs. ZACH GALLOWAY.

Wednesday, November 11, 1885

Killed on the Rail
On Thursday evening of last week a horrible accident happened about half a mile south of the Eugene station, on the C. & E.I. road, by which brakeman DOUGLAS FOSSETTwas instantly killed. Just after passing the dry branch on their northern bound trip it is customary to cut the engine loose from the main train so the engine can go ahead and take water by the time the freight reaches the station, where it is usually switched to let the fast south bound passenger pass. Brakeman FOSSETT pulled out the coupling pin so the engine could pass on and by some means slipped and fell, the entire train of some 30 or 40 freight cars passing over him and grinding him to a horrible mass. The body was cut into fragments and scattered along the track for quite a distance. The most of the remains were gathered up and taken to the Eugene station and an engine and caboose dispatched for Coroner BRINDLEY, who went up that night and held an inquest, finding that the deceased came to his death by carelessness while uncoupling the engine from the train, and regrets the sad misfortune very much. DOUGLAS FOSSETT was a young man, about 25 years old, and had been working for the C. & E.I. folks for some time, but this was his first trip on this end of the road. His remains were taken to Crete, Illinois, where his relatives and friends reside.

Perrysville
On last Saturday, the 7th, there was a grand and happy surprise dinner given at the residence of Mr. and Mrs. HUGHES, it being the birthday of Mrs. HUGHES.

Home News
J.F. DUGGER, of Helt township was in Newport on Monday last.

ELMER DAVIS of Ludlow, Illinois is visiting his parents here.

Dana News

FRANK WISE, of this township, has a young farmer at his house. He put in an appearance on Saturday last.

Mrs. ALLIE BARNETT, of Newton, Kansas, is here on a visit, and is the guest of her cousin, R.E. STEPHENS, and his family.

SAMUEL HOAGLAND, Jr., a 10 year old son of SAM HOAGLAND, of Clinton township, is lying dangerously ill with typhoid fever.

LUCY MACK and WILLIAM HOAGLAND, of Helt township, are on a trade with a Kansas firm for land, and if they effect the trade they will move out to grasshopperdom.

JOHNNY GROVES is now the proud father of a real good looking girl baby. The little ootsy tootsy arrived here on Thursday last. It's dad is doing as well as could be expected.

BILLY TATE, of Butler County, Iowa, is here on a visit. He is going to help his uncle JAKE WIMSETT husk corn.

NOAH LYON, of Highland township, was taken over to Plainfield Reform School last week on order of Judge JUMP, at the request of Trustee MORGAN.

W.P. HENSON and family are again residents of Newport. Mr. HENSON and his son JOHN will open out a harness shop in the first building of the Hoosier State office.

BILLY MOREHEAD bid his relatives and friends good-bye on Monday last and left on the early train for Los Angeles, California.

JOHN McCULLOUGH, the noted actor, died at 1 o'clock on last Saturday afternoon. He had stood at the head of his profession for many years, and had a national reputation. Hid death , although not entirely unexpected, occurred quite suddenly, and was due, Dr. HUGO ENGEL, his physician says, to "an affection of the brain caused by blood-poisoning." Dr. ENGEL asserts that McCULLOUGH was not insane, and that it was a mistake to have placed him in the Bloomingdale Asylum, where he was confined for a number of weeks.

Real Estate Transfers for October 1885

HENRY WALTEN and wife to JOHN L. DEEG
Lot 2, block 30, in Clinton - $595

MARY McLAUGHLIN and husband to EPHRAIM SHUTE
10 acres in Eugene township - $300

SAMUEL GRONDYKE and wife to ELLEN GRONDYKE
1/3 of 382 acres in Eugene township - $27,636

SOLOMON CARPENTER to ROBERT CHEESEWRIGHT
10 acres in Helt township - $250

FRANCES H. MOREY and husband to HENRY L. MOREY etal
Lots 1, 3, 4, & 5, block 4, in Clinton - $100

LEVI H. AIKMAN and wife to MARY A. McLAUGHLIN
Lot 1, block 2, in Dana - $300

WILLIAM C. SHANNON and wife to JOHN SHIRLEY
2 acres in Clinton township - $200

JOHN L. EGGLESTON and wife to WILLIAM McCLELLAN
20 acres in Eugene township - $150

RICHARD MALONE and wife to W.M. TAYLOR
Lots 15, 16, & 17, Finney's addition to Dana - $150

CLARA A. STEPHENS etal to THOMAS CUSHMAN
Lots 29 & 30, in Perrysville - $500

BEN BLANCHARD to ADAM H. KILDOW
Blanchard's addition, & 7 & 8, Parrett's addition to Newport - $3,200

FRANCES H. MOREY and husband to JAMES ROBERTS
Lots 2 & 3, block 27, in Clinton - $1,200

OLIVER M. HEDGES and wife to JOHN WHITCOMB
¼ of 28 acres in Clinton township - $175

CATHERINE E. NICKELS to MALINDA J. PALMER
Part lots 22, 23, 24, & 25, block 5, in Dana - $1,235

WILLIAM HUGHES and wife to DAVID GOUTY
Outlot adjoining Gessie - $100

DANIEL W. GARDNER and wife to LON LLOYD
Part lot 5, block 2, in Clinton - $100

JOHN H. VANDUYN and wife to JOHN H. BOGART
Part lot 1, block 12, in Clinton - $750

URA SOUTHARD and wife to SAMUEL R. PORTER
18 acres in Clinton township - $500

WILLIAM L. SHUEY etal to ANDREW J. PINSON
120 acres in Clinton township - $2,600

DANIEL SHUTE and wife to SARAH R. JOHNSON
10 acres in Highland township - $2,030

JOHN L. DEEG and wife to FRANCIS M. MANN
Lot 10, block 9, in Clinton - $900

THOMAS HULL and wife to WILLIAM D. McFALL
60 acres in Helt township - $2,400

GEORGE R. HICKS and wife to ELHANAN STEVENS
Lots 7 & 9, in Steven's addition to Perrysville - $400

JAMES A. WHITE and wife to FLORENCE E. WHITE
80 acres in Helt township - $4,000

JOHN S. HOUCHIN and wife to GEORGE W. SAXTON
40 acres in Helt township - $1,200

RICHARD MALONE and wife to ALFRED C. DePUY
Lots 5 & 6, block 12, in Dana - $1,000

MARY A. STEWART to JOHN W. JARVIS and wife
Lot 23, block 3, in Jonestown - $50

JOHN R. McNEILL and wife to LYDIA HEPBURN
Outlots 24 & 25, in Perrysville - $250

JOSEPH STAATS and wife to SARAH STAATS
40 acres in Helt township – love and affection

JOSEPH STAATS and wife to JOSEPH O. STAATS
80 acres in Helt township - $1,000

JOSEPH STAATS and wife to SAMUEL STAATS
80 acres in Helt township - $1,000

PHILLIP J. ARGOTSINGER to MARY O. SMITH
Lots 1, 2, 3, & 4, in Perrysville - $140

JOHN F. SMITH etal to AMANDA SABIN
Part lots 21, 22, & 19, in Perrysville - $700

C. RICHARDSON etal to JOSEPH H. WILSON
Part lot 36, in Eugene - $160

ELLEN C. WATERMAN and husband to GEORGE A. HALD
Lot 5, in Eugene - $250

MARTHA E. HENTHORN and husband to JOHN W. ROUSE
1/3 of 80 acres in Highland township - $1,350

SAMUEL AIKMAN and wife to LEVI H. AIKMAN
27 acres in Helt township - $1,080

GEORGE F. SKIDMORE and wife to GEORGE B. TILLOTSON
60 acres in Helt township - $2,400

DAVID DEVINS and wife to HAMILTON BETSON
50 acres in Vermillion township - $1,000

Notice to Non-Residents

JOHN J. REED vs. DAVID A. REED, NANCY M. REED, ANDREW R. REED, ELIZA REED, ELIZABETH REED, HENRY REED, MARY HIDDLE, ABNER K. GREEN, MERTIE GREEN, OTHA GREEN, FRANKLIN GREEN, LOUISA COLLINS, PATSY BAUM, EMMA SKIDMORE, SARAH REED, CHARLES S. REED, SARAH R. REED, LEWIS H. REED, ALFRED M. REED, JAMES S. REED, GEORGE W. RE, JEMIMA J. REED, MARY E. MILLER, JANE P. COSLETT, and SYLVESTER MILLER
CONLEY & WILTERMOOD, attorneys for plaintiff
ELIZA REED, ELIZABETH REED, HENRY REED, MARY HIDDLE, ABNER K. GREEN, MERTIE GREEN, OTHA GREEN, FRANKLIN GREEN, LOUISA COLLINS, PATSY BAUM, SARAH REED, CHARLES S. REED, ANDREW R. REED, ALFRED M. REED, GEORGE W. REED, and JANE P. COSLETT are not residents of Indiana
Must appear before third Monday of December 1995
October 31, 1885

A.R. HOPKINS, Clerk

Wednesday, November 18, 1885

Circuit Court - October 1885

State of Indiana vs. JOHN H. WIGLEY
Selling liquor on Sunday - not guilty

THOMAS H. SMITH & Bros. vs. THOMAS H. SMITH
Administrator of ED KESPLAR, deceased - judgment - $473.44

ANDREW JACKSON vs. W.F. BALES
Administrator of C.F. KEYES, deceased - claim not allowed

J.M. HARPER vs. W.F. BALES
Administrator of C.F. KEYES, deceased - judgment - $106.85

DOWNING & HAMILTON vs. ALANSON CHURCH
Administrator of JOSIAH CHURCH, deceased - judgment - $13.40

JAMES RARIDAN vs. WINFORD M. TAYLOR
Administrator of PETER STREETMOCKER, deceased - judgment - $9.40

JERE CONLEY vs. WINFORD M. TAYLOR
Administrator of PETER STREETMOCKER, deceased - judgment $13.25

JAMES B. WEBB vs. J.F. COMPTON
Administrator of MARGARET ALDRICH, deceased - judgment $36.00

JOHN NORRIS vs. LEWIS NORRIS
Administrator of ROBERT NICHOLS, deceased - judgment $51.07

JACOB MILLER vs. LEWIS NORRIS
Administrator of ROBERT NICHOLS, deceased - judgment $12.00

DANIEL MILLER vs. LEWIS NORRIS
Administrator of ROBERT NICHOLS, deceased - judgment $25.00

State of Indiana vs. JOSEPH NORTON
Murder – State prison for 2 years

State of Indiana vs. PETER MITCHELL
Riot – continued

State of Indiana vs. JAMES T. HENDERSON
Procuring miscarriage – not guilty

State of Indiana vs. ROBERT ADAMS
Giving away intoxicating liquor on Sunday – not guilty

State of Indiana vs. JACOB T. PALMER
Selling liquor in less than one quart without license – continued

State of Indiana vs. ED KIZER
Drawing weapons – continued

State of Indiana vs. L.J. PLACE, AUGUST JENKS
Selling intoxicating liquor to minor – not guilty

State of Indiana vs. FRED CARTER
Assault and battery with intent to kill – bond forfeited

State of Indiana vs. MILFORD D. NORTON
Felony – continued

State of Indiana vs. A.C. LOVE
Assault and battery – fined

State of Indiana vs. ELIAS SHAW, EDWARD SHAW
Arson – continued

State of Indiana vs. WILLIAM FOLTZ, from J.P. Court
Continued

GEORGE A. CRABB etal vs. WINFIELD S. CRABB etal
Partition and sale – continued

HENRY C. SMITH vs. ABRAM STRAWSER, WILLIAM H. STUTLER
Continued

GEORGE R. HICKS vs. LOUIS HICKS, CAROLINE L. TINCHER
Partition – decreed

GEORGE R. FINLEY vs. JESSE DONEY
Dismissed

CHRIST GLENDMIER vs. GOTTLIEB D. HEIDBREDER
Possession – continued

GEORGE W. McCUNE vs. I.B. & W. RR Co.
Damages – dismissed

ANDERSON HARPER vs. NICHOLAS T. LEITON, from J.P. Court
Continued

GEORGE A. WOODFORD, JOHN PHALMON vs. WILLIAM T. CARMAN
Account – judgment for $278.40

PLATT Z. ANDERSON vs. JOHN WRIGHT
Complaint to forfeit title – continued

RACHEL PETERS vs. WILLIAM PETERS
Divorce – granted

Decatur County Bank vs. MARTHA E. LEE, MERRIMAN LEE
Note and foreclosure – judgment for $259.12

JOHN H. CRAIG, by next friend SPENCER H. DALLAS vs. WILLIAM H. HOOD
Quiet title – title quieted

JACOB R. RILEY vs. WILLIAM HUGHES, Admr. of ISAAC ROUSE's estate
Claim – judgment for $50

EMERY C. HODGES vs. AMOS BETSON
Damages – dismissed

HENRY T. WATKINS vs. CYNTHIA A. DAVIS
Attachment – judgment for $99.84

JOHN BENSINGER vs. EMERETTA BENSINGER
Divorce – granted

JOHN TAYLOR vs. WILLIAM B. INGLE
Damages – dismissed

AUSTIN M. JACKSON by LEVI SCOTT vs. JOHN WRIGHT etal
Partition – granted

ELLEN GRONDYKE vs. ANDREW J. BEAUCHAMP
Note – judgment for $399.79

THOMAS CUSHMAN vs. HEZEKIAH CASEBEER, JOSEPH C. JACKSON
Note – judgment for $182.40

WILLIAM L. LITTLE vs. JOHN NICHOLS, LEWIS NORRIS
Note – judgement for $76.77

RUTH E. MARLOW vs. AUSTIN MARLOW
Divorce – decreed

ELIZABETH BURSON s. JOHN DEWINE
Appeal from J.P. Court – dismissed

EDWARD G. WILSON vs. TILGHMAN UNDERWOOD
Note – judgment for $133.37

FRANCIS M. DAVIS vs. WINFIELD P. THOMAS
Account – change of venue to Parke County

THOMAS H. EATON vs. Unknown heirs of ALONZO LYONS
Quite title – title quieted

ROBERT S. McKEE, EDWARD BRANHAM vs. T.J. HUTCHINSON, SARAH HUTCHINSON
Note – judgment for $408.60

ELNORA BROWN vs. DAVID BROWN
Divorce – granted

JOHN E. JOHNSON etal vs. SAMUEL W. JORDAN, HENRY JORDAN
Note – judgment for $457.15

CHARLES W. WARD vs. JAMES HENRY, FRANCES HENRY
Foreclosure – judgment for $332.50

First National Bank of Danville, IL vs. CHARLES E. ALEXANDER
Note – judgment for $267.79

LEWIS A. MORGAN vs. WALLACE MOORE
Note – judgment for $75.45

D.M. OSBORNE & Co. vs. MORGAN HAY
Note and foreclosure – judgment for $380.15

D.M. OSBORNE & Co. vs. JOSEPH W. WILTERMOOD
Note and foreclosure – judgment for $88.81

MARY J. FULTZ vs. WILLIAM H. FULTZ
Divorce – refused

NANCY M. ELKINS vs. AMBROSE ELKINS
Divorce – continued

EDGAR VANSICKLE vs. WILLIAM C. MYERS, R.T. MITCHELL
Note – dismissed

LEWIS A. MORGAN vs. THOMAS W. STEPHENS, SARAH MOORE
Foreclosure – judgment for $598.79

COLUMBUS E. LEE vs. M. STURM etal
Change of venue from Parke County – license granted

D.M OSBORNE & Co. vs. JAMES M. MITCHELL, R.T. MITCHELL
Note – judgment for $123.35

Home News
SILAS HOLLINGSWORTH, of Chrisman, Illinois, is going to move back here in a week or two.

Attorney O.B. GIBSON and wife spent Sunday with his father-in-law, JAMES A. ELDER of Helt township.

Mrs. C.S. GAYLORD, of Peoria, Illinois, who has been visiting her daughter, Mrs. R.A. PARRETT, left for home on Saturday last.

Wooden Wedding
On Tuesday night of last week WILLIAM SHARP and wife celebrated their wooden wedding. A large number of the elite of the town was present and enjoyed the grand social event. The bride and groom received quite a lot of woodenware. We were furnished with a list of the presents and the names of the donors, but have lost it. Among them was a rocking chair for the bride, an office chair for the groom, and a handsome little rocking chair for their little boy. The groom presented the bride with a magnificent bureau. We did not learn what the bride gave the groom. At about 9:12 a splendid lap supper was furnished all present, after which the crowd had a general good time until the hour arrived for returning home. Every one seemed to enjoy him and herself. It was a pleasant gathering, and we have no doubt will be long remembered by the happy couple.

Notice of Administration
Estate of ANNA HARPER, deceased
ANDERSON HARPER, administrator
A.R. HOPKINS, Clerk

Wednesday, November 25, 1885

A Lucky Woman
The widow of IKE DICKASON, of Highland township, has been granted a pension on the death of her son who died in the army and was her main support. Her first draw will be $1900.

Uncle ROBERT DAVIS and wife, of Helt's Prairie, will celebrate their golden wedding on the 19th of January. The old gentleman will be 76 years old on the 29th of the same month, and is now in splendid health for one of his years. His good wife is 68, and nearly as spry as a 16 year old girl. May they both be spared many more years here upon earth.

Home News
JAMES H. BURNSIDE, of Helt township, was in town on Wednesday last.

JAMES KAUFMAN and JOE JACKSON, of Dana, were in town on Saturday last.

The little boys and girls of this place gave Miss EMMA WIGLEY a masquerade surprise party on last Monday night.

Uncle BILLY RUSSELL, of Helt township, is probably the oldest male citizen of Vermillion County. He is now 89 years of age, and in fair health.

A.J. WILSON, teacher at Opedee, is doing his best to retain the strength of the Democratic party in this township. It is a boy and arrived here one week ago last Sunday.

WILLIAM McLAUGHLIN and Mrs. JANE PIERCE, both of this place, were united in marriage on last Sunday evening, Rev. H. JONES, pastor of the U.B. Church, performing the ceremony.

THOMAS C. DAVIS, of Helt's Prairie, passed through here last week on his way to West Lebanon, Warren County, to take charge of his circuit at that place.

Mrs. LOU HOUGHLAND, daughter of JOE JAMES of Helt's Prairie, is lying at the point of death, caused by childbirth.

E. HAUN and son, of Glassboro, New Jersey, who have been here on a visit for several weeks, left yesterday afternoon for Beardstown, Illinois, where he intends to visit a sister until Christmas when he will return home.

Sheriff's Sale on Execution

CHARLES ALEXANDER vs. WILLIAM COLLETT
Sale Saturday, December 19, 1885
Sale at courthouse between 10 & 4
Nw ¼ sw ¼ Sec 32 T 18 N R 9 W – 6 acres
Lies W of Big Vermillion River
November 25, 1885

JOHN A. DARBY, Sheriff

Wednesday, December 2, 1885

Trustees and Teachers
Below we give the names of the several Trustees of this county, and also the name of every teacher in the county, with the number of his district and post office address. Teachers should clip this item and paste in their scrapbooks for future reference.
Clinton Township
G.W. STULTZ, Trustee

School #1 MAY WHITCOMB, Clinton
2 L.W. MASON, Clinton
3 W.H. HASKELL, Clinton
4 MAGGIE PINSON, Clinton
5. ENNIS SHIRLEY, Clinton
6. T.A. KIBBY, Clinton
7. FRED BEARD, Clinton
8. J.W. BROOKBANK, Clinton
9. ETTA EDWARDS, Clinton
10. AMON DOWDY, Clinton
11. M.C. McCULLOCH, Goshen
12. LILLIE BIRT, Clinton

Helt Township
E.W. JAMES, Trustee, Summit Grove

1. J.L. SMITH, Hillsdale
2. J.N. FRIST, Summit Grove
3. EVA MALONE, Dana
4. HATTIE AIKMAN, Dana
5. ALDA McROBERTS, Dana
6. G.W. STURM, Dana
7. NELLIE JORDAN, Dana
8. RENA RUGAN, Hillsdale
9. WRIGHT JAMES, Summit Grove
10. EUGENIA STOKESBERRY, Clinton
11. CARRIE JORDAN, Dana

12. CARRIE McDOWELL, St. Bernice
13. EFFIE F. BALES, St. Bernice
14. ALLIE RUSH, Clinton
15. E.E. HELT, Clinton
16. W.P. ANDREWS, Toronto
17. GRACE WHITLOCK, Dana
18. BELLE STAATS, Dana
19. FRED RUSH, Dana
19. S. LENORE KEYES, Dana
19. ALLIE THOMPSON, Dana
20. MILTON JAMES, Summit Grove
21. BEN BOTHWELL, St. Bernice
22. ELLA DINSMORE, Hillsdale

Vermillion Township
S.B. DAVIS, Trustee, Newport

3. M.W. COFFIN, Eugene
4. LAURA HARLAN, Newport
5. W.B. GOSNELL, Newport
6. A.J. WILSON, Newport
7. MINNIE LAMB, Newport
8. E.L. HIBERLY, Newport
9. OMA C. EGGLESTON, Newport
10. E.E. RANKIN, Quaker Hill
10. EMMA HAWORTH, Quaker Hill
11. WILLIAM COFFIN, Eugene
12. EMMA BLACKMORE, Newport
13. J. ROACH JOHNSON, Newport
14. R.E. WHITLOCK, Dana

Eugene Township
JAMES MALONE, Trustee, Eugene

1. LACIE EDMONDS, Eugene
3. J.R. STAHL, Eugene
3. JENNIE STURM, Eugene
3. LACIE MORRIS, Eugene
4. ELIZABETH MOORE, Eugene
5. NETTIE MOORE, Eugene
6. N.B. MACK, Eugene
8. MARY HEIDBREDER, Eugene
9. JAMES B. PERRIN, Eugene

Highland Township
L.A. MORGAN, Trustee, Perrysville

1. JAY M. MILLS, Perrysville
2. HATTIE SHUTE, Gessie
3. L.H. JOHNSON, Gessie
4. F.D. JONES, Perrysville
5. C.A. WHITE, Perrysville
6. G.W. DEALAND, Perrysville
6. W.A. KERNS, Perrysville
6. LILLIE KILPATRICK, Gessie
7. ETTA B. CAMPBELL, Gessie
8. D.M. CAMPBELL, Gessie

9. W.S. NEEL, Perrysville
10. J.L. WEBSTER, Perrysville
11. B.W. SCOTT, Perrysville
12. E.M. HEATON, Gessie

Clinton Corporation
J.H. TOMLIN, Clinton
JOHN A. WOOD, Clinton
MARY DeLABARR, Clinton
CLARA RUPP, Clinton

Newport Corporation
J.G. COLEMAN, Newport
EDGAR AIKMAN, Newport
BELLE KERDOLFF, Newport
M.L. HOLMES, Newport

Home News
FRED DUZAN and Miss MARY B. LAMB, both of this place, were united in wedlock on last Wednesday evening. The ceremony took place at the residence of the bride, Esq. JOHN L. EGGLESTON joining the two together in wedlock. At about 9 o'clock in the evening the Newport Cornet band, of which the groom is a member, gave them a pleasant serenade. FREDDY set up the cigars to the boys. Both have the best wishes of their many friends.

MARION HARRIER, who has been at the poor house since last March, is now in the last stages of consumption, and cannot possibly last long. He is unable to feed himself, has no appetite, and is nothing but hide and bones. He is about 35 years of age.

Mrs. LAURA NAGLE, of Oakland, Illinois, is here on a visit to her mother.

Miss M.D. STILLWELL, of Indianapolis, is here on a visit to her sister, Mrs. P.P. THOMAS.

CHARLEY COMPTON of Highland is in jail at Rockville on the charge of petit larceny.

JOHN JAMES and SUSA PATY, of Wabash, Indiana, were united in wedlock at that place, on last Tuesday evening, at the residence of Esq. JOHN L. EGGLESTON, who performed the ceremony.

H.V. NIXON and ED STEPHENS, of the DePauw University, Greencastle, came home to eat Thanksgiving turkey. They left for school on Monday morning.

Uncle JOE STAATS, of Helt township, is 84 years old, and his good wife is 80. The 5th of next January will be their 60th wedding anniversary. We doubt if there are a dozen couples in Indiana who have been trotting along in double harness that long. Both are in fair health for people of their age. Last week, JOE went out into the cornfield and helped the boys husk corn.

A Horrible Accident
A distressing accident occurred in Shawnee township, this county, last Saturday afternoon, at the residence of JOHN CARNAHAN. His little 5 year old daughter went out to the chicken coop, and with a match, set some straw on fire, which communicated to her clothing. Her screams attracted the attention to her mother, who ran to her assistance, but when she reached her, the child's clothing, with the exception of her shoes, was burned entirely from her body. The little girl lingered in excruciating pain until evening, and death relieved her.

Covington Friend

Mrs. WILLIAM SHARP is up at Danville, Illinois, visiting her cousins.

JOHN COMPTON, of Hillsdale, has moved to Illinois. Good Riddance.

Judgment
Miss CORA RUSSELL, a handsome young lady of Perrysville, who got mashed on Dr. NORMAN L. JONES of Lodi, Parke County, and was cheated out of her prize by another lady, brought suit against the frisky doctor for $5,000 for lacerated affection. The suit was brought in this county, and afterwards to Fountain County for change of venue, where it came to trial last week. After the suit was instituted, Dr. JONES who was township Trustee, became involved in the school supply swindle, and had to light out for Canada, where he still remains. H.H. CONLEY, her attorney, obtained judgment for $3,000, but would probably be willing to compromise now at $1,000. The doctor's present wife is residing at Lodi.

Notice to Non-Residents
MAURICE HEGARTY vs. BEN BLANCHARD, ADAM H. KILDOW
Complaint No. 2745
SAWYER & GIBSON, attorneys for plaintiff
BEN BLANCHARD is not a resident of Indiana
Must appear before third Monday in December 1885
November 10, 1885
A.R. HOPKINS, Clerk

Sheriff's Sale on Execution
JOHN J. BRAKE vs. SIDNEY VANOSTRAND & ELIZA VANOSTRAND
Sale Saturday, December 26, 1885
Sale at courthouse between 10 and 4
Undivided ¼ of 2/3 and undivided 1/3 of 32 acres
W ½ NW ¼ Sec 13
Along road leading from Clinton, IN to Paris, IL
JOHN J. BRAKE, attorney for plaintiff
December 1, 1885
JOHN A. DARBY, Sheriff

Wednesday, December 9, 1885

A Drunken Man Frozen to Death at Rockville
On last Saturday an old farmer of Parke County, 58 years of age, went to Rockville and got on a big spree. He filled his tank too full for navigation, and after night, took lodging on the sunny side of the court house, where he was found about 8 o'clock the next (Sunday) morning, frozen stiff and nearly dead. Sheriff MUSSER took him to the jail, undressed him and put him in a comfortable bed, wrapping him up well in quilts. The Sheriff then retired, but returned in a short time to see how his patient was getting along. He peeped through the grates and could not notice him move. He opened the door and stepped in, and found the old genleman dead as a mackerel. His name was JOSEPH RICHEY. He lived about 4 miles southwest of Rockville, and leaves a family in uncomfortable circumstances.

Burned
On last Sunday morning an old lady by the name Mrs. ELIZA HOGAN, of Terre Haute, met with an accident that will probably cause her death. She had just arisen from bed, and stepping too near an open stove to dress, her clothing caught fire, and as there was no one near to render help she is thought to be fatally burned. When assistance arrived she was lying on the floor prostrated, and her skin burned to a crisp.

Real Estate Transfers for November 1885
C.A. GARLINGHOUSE and wife to S.R. GARLINGHOUSE
Lot 27 in Alta - $50

WILLIAM SOUTHARD and wife to HENRY BROCK
5 acres in Helt township - $100

GEORGE H. McNEILL, assignee, to MARTIN B. RUDY
60 acres in Eugene township - $3,000

NANCY TAYLOR etal to RICHARD F. CHURCH
1 acre in Helt township - $50

JOHN R. SPURGEON and wife to EDGAR VANSICKLE and wife
South half, block 6, Hillsdale - $100

DAVID SANDERS and wife to MARGARET J. RUHL
Lot 86 in Perrysville - $175

LEANDER M. CRAFERAFT and wife to ALBERT HENDERSON
20 acres in Vermillion township - $425

JOSEPHINE HARVEY to LEOTA MOREHEAD
Lots 23, & 24, in Newport - $500

McKENDREE RANDALL and wife to DAVID W. CARITHERS
55 acres in Highland township - $900

SAMUEL MOREHEAD to ROBERT H. NIXON
195 acres in Vermillion township - $5,000

NANCY J. FENNIMORE and husband to MARTIN PETTY
30 acres in Vermillion township - $800

WILLIAM E. FULWIDER and wife to WILLIAM McCAULIFF
2 acres in Helt township - $225

MARTIN PETTY and wife to NANCY J. FENNIMORE
14 acres in Clinton township - $400

LEOTA MOREHEAD to JOSEPH A. MOREHEAD Jr.
Undivided ½ lots 23 & 24, in Newport - $250

E.T.H. & C. RR Co. to EDGAR RANKIN
Lot 2, block 5, Summit Grove - $30

FRANK RICHARDS etal to SILAS JONES
116 acres in Vermillion township - $1,540

FRED P. GROVES etal to JOSEPHUS COLLETT
16 acres in Vermillion township - $900

SAMUEL B. PEARMAN to MARGARET E. BARNHART
70 acres in Helt township - $975

MATILDA NICCUM and wife to HENRY VOLKEL
2 acres in Highland township - $50

CRAWFORD FAIRBANKS and wife to MARGARET H. OLIVER
Lots 13 & 14, in Gessie - $40

WILLIAM J. ANDREWS and wife to WILLIAM D. McFALL
6 2/3 acres in Helt township - $200

ABRAHAM CARTER and wife to JOHN S. HOUCHIN
20 acres in Helt township - $225

CLARA EHTES to JOHN H. BOGART
South ½ lot 4, block 10, in Clinton - $250

LEWIS NORRIS and wife to JOSEPH JACKSON
.27 acres in Helt township - $10

Home News
Liquor Licenses Granted
PAT FLYNN, of Hillsdale
JAMES M. HAIN, of Perrysville

Our Friend Esq. JOHNSON intends making application through Attorney CHARLES WARD at the December term of Circuit Court to practice law in this state. Mr. JOHNSON has proven a fair and competent justice and we predict he will make a success in his new step.

Roll of Honor
List of pupils who were neither absent nor tardy during the month ending November 27th.
BERTHA FOOS, NORA MILLER, BERT FOOS, JOHN THOMAS, SARAH MILLER, MELLIE HOLLINGSWORTH, FRED WILTERMOOD, JAMES THOMAS, ALLIE HUGHES, ETTIE HATON, BUCK FOOS, SARAH THOMAS, PERRY HOLLINGSWORTH, LISSIE HUGHES, and ELMER BUSH.
A.J. WILSON, teacher

Agents for the Hoosier State
J.J. RABB – Perrysville
W.H. SALTSGAVER – Gessie
HOSFORD & BELL – Eugene
J.E. BISLAND – Dana
F.N. AUSTIN – Toronto
J.R. FINNELL – St. Bernice
THOMAS C. DAVIS – Summit Grove
JOHN F. LEITON – Clinton
Mrs. H.M. WOOSTER – Montezuma

Sheriff's Sale on Decree
CHARLES WARD vs. JAMES HENRY, FRANCES HENRY
$339.79
Sale Saturday, December 19, 1885
Sale at courthouse between 10 & 4
NW part of SE ¼ of NE ¼ Sec 20 T 18 R 10 W – 31 acres
WARD & DAVIS attorneys for plaintiff
November 25, 1885

E.C. HODGES
Monuments
Terre Haute

L.H. REED
Notary Public
St. Bernice

J.C. JACKSON
Dry Goods
Hillsdale

RILEY WHITNEY
Dry Good, Boots
Newport

O.B. LOWRY
G.H. FISHER
Walking plows, farm implements
Dana

BEN BLANCHARD
Money to loan on Real Estate
Vermillion County abstracts
Newport

JOHN GALLOWAY
JAMES GALLAGHER
Blacksmiths
Newport & Montezuma

H.H. CONLEY
J.A. WILTERMOOD
Attorneys at Law
Newport

S.B. DAVIS
Editor of Hoosier State
Newport

FRED RUSH
County Surveyor
Dana

W.H. ARMSTRONG
Groceries, cutlery
Dana

Wednesday, December 16, 1885

Gravel Road Items
Miss MARY KINGSBERRY, of Homer, Illinois, is visiting her sister, Mrs. JOHN McCRARY.

Messrs. JAMES and WILLIE THOMAS, from Nebraska, are visiting relatives in this vicinity.

Home News
L.H. BELLUS and wife, of Bloomington, Monroe County, this state, former residents of Clinton, are back on a short visit.

H.S. CADY and his son WILLIE, who have been working on the railroad across the Wabash, in Sullivan County, are at home for the winter.

BOB WHITE, who moved out to Kansas a couple of years ago, has got all he wants of the West, and is now on his way back to Old Vermillion. They will all be back here in the course of time.

W.H. NEWPORT, residing 2 miles west of town, has a young dutchman at his house. The little fellow arrived here on Tuesday night of last week, and will vote the Democratic ticket when he gets old enough.

Mrs. V.A. KOONSE, and her good looking daughter, Miss ALLIE, of Lafayette, are now on a visit to relatives in this county. They went from here to Dana on Saturday and will return on Friday to spend a few more days before leaving for home. Miss KOONSE may possibly stay until after Christmas.

Miss NANCY HELT, of Helt township, aged about 60, fell on the ice Tuesday, sustaining a fracture of the arm near the wrist. At this writing she is doing well.

Clinton Argus

The Democratic population of this township was increased by one new arrival on last Sunday night. The little fellow is stopping with JOHN BLUNK for the present.

Wednesday, December 23, 1885

Killed on the Rail

An Intoxicated Man Meets a Sad Fate While Stealing a Ride

On last Saturday afternoon a man by the name of BENJAMIN FRANKLIN WILLIAMS, who claimed to reside at Grape Creek, in Vermilion County, Illinois, met a horrible death just north of the Eugene station. He had come to Eugene to rent a house where he intended to move in a short time. He was out of money, but expected a man on the afternoon southbound passenger who owed him. When the train arrived a little before 2 o'clock he mounted the train and passed through the coaches, but failed to find his man. He made the remark that he was going to steal his ride to Danville on the freight that was nearly ready to pull out. He got on the freight when it came along, and did not ride more than a half or three quarters of a mile until he fell off and was horribly mangled. The side of his head was all mashed in, his right arm near the shoulder cut nearly off, and also one foot cut off, the thigh of one leg nearly severed, the thigh bone protruding out fully six inches. He was sitting on the bumpers, about midway of the train, and as he was considerably intoxicated, and in attempting to climb up to get on a car, he slipped and fell under the train. Notwithstanding he was seriously cut, mangled and nearly every bone in him broken, he lived until they conveyed him down to the depot, where he soon breathed his last. Coroner BRINDLEY was telegraphed for and went up immediately to hold an inquest. The Coroner says he was a man addicted to strong drink, about 35 or 36 years of age, dark complexioned. He leaves a wife and 3 or 4 little children. He has a brother-in-law residing near Perrysville who is said to be in fair circumstances.

Obituary

Death of TEMP JACKSON

On Thursday morning, December 10th, 1885, at 5 o'clock A.M. at the Hay Springs House of pneumonia, D.T. JACKSON, aged 45 years. Mr. JACKSON, with his 4 sons, came from Hillsboro, Alabama, only 2 weeks ago, to take land in this vicinity. They had made improvements, but the filing had not been made. His sudden death causes the sympathy of the community to go out to his unfortunate boys. The funeral was held from the Hay Springs House, today at 10 A.M.

Hay Springs, News, December 11, 1885

Mr. JACKSON moved to Hillsboro, Alabama, about 2 years ago from this township, where he resided up to the latter part of November, when he and his 3 sons moved to near Hay Springs, Nebraska, arriving there about the first of this month. The sudden change from a warm to a cold climate gave him pneumonia. He only lingered 2 weeks, when death put an end to his life here on earth. The deceased had many relatives in this county, and a large acquaintance among our people. Everybody respected Mr. JACKSON. He was an industrious and kind hearted man, and was ever ready to render a favor to anyone needing assistance. There were few better or more generous hearted citizens lived in Vermillion County than TEMP JACKSON.

Obituary

At about 3 o'clock on last Friday morning the wife of RICHARD F. GILLMORE, of Dana, who has been ailing with a combination of diseases for 2 or 3 months, passed beyond the river of death. During the greater part of her illness, her husband was confined to his bed with disease, but notwithstanding this she was kindly cared for by friends, and everything possible that could be done to alleviate her sufferings was done. In her death her husband loses a good wife, and the town an exemplary and Christian lady. Her funeral took place on Saturday last, her remains being interred in the cemetery at Vermillion Chapel, this township.

Marriage

Rev. F. NEWHOUSE and Miss RENA POMEROY were married at Williamsport on last Monday. They at once left for New York from which city they will sail for Bombay, India, where Mr. NEWHOUSE has been assigned mission work.

Attica Ledger

Mr. NEWHOUSE was formerly a resident of Clinton, this county.

R.H. WHITE and family, who moved to Jackson County, Kansas, more than a year ago, arrived back here on Friday last, and will stay in old Vermillion the rest of their days. Mr. WHITE says it takes 3 bushels of corn in that county where he lived to buy one bushel of coal. Here a person can buy 3 bushels of coal for one bushel of corn.

Home News
DICK WIMSETT has returned home from Missouri.

CHARLES GRAY, of Chicago, is down here on a visit.

FIRMAN ALLEN, formerly of Rockville, has located at Attica.

Mrs. LEN WHEELER is down at Marshall, Indiana, visiting relatives.

FRANK JONES, of Wabash College, has come home to spend the holidays.

DAVE CADE, of Perrysville, is back from his western trip, and is ready for trial.

Mrs. CLENDENNING, of Perrysville, this state, daughter of ELIAS LAMB, is here on a visit.

HENRY STURM, CALE BALES, WILLIAM F. BALES, and JOE JACKSON, of Helt township, were in town yesterday on legal business.

JOHN P. DUNLAP will leave this morning for Howard, Elk County, Kansas, where he intends to make his future home. His wife has been out there sometime. We are sorry to lose them from our society. Both are good citizens.

Miss MATILDA HOLMES, teacher of the Primary department, has gone to Delphi, her home, to spend the holidays.

The two sons of JOHN RYAN, residing 7 miles west of town, who have been dangerously ill with the typhoid fever, for a long time, are now convalescent.

R.A. FENDLY, of this township, will leave for Hutchinson, Kansas, this week, where he expects to make his future home.

Prosecutor CONLEY and family went down to Helt township, on Saturday last to visit his mother, who is in very feeble health.

THEODORE SHANNON, of Clinton township, has just received notice that his pension has been allowed. His first draw will be $973.07. He was a member of the 123rd Indiana.

Mrs. S.S. COLLETT, who has been in Virginia for several weeks visiting, returned home last week, accompanied by her daughter, Mrs. ADAM LITTLEPAGE.

A.J. SANDERS, of Scottland, Illlinois, and ELIZABETH SMITH, of St. Bernice, Indiana, were united in wedlock on the 15th instant by Esq. JOHN L. EGGLESTON.

REUBEN FORTNER and Miss ADALINE NICHOLS, both of this township, were united in marriage on the 15th instant by Esq. JOHN L. EGGLESTON.

Married Money
ROLAND JACKSON and Miss ELIZABETH MONEY, of this township, were united in wedlock by Esq. JOHN EGGLESTON on last Sunday evening. Mr. JACKSON will have one advantage over most persons. He will always have money.

WILLIAM RUSSELL and Miss ALMA HELT, both of Helt township, will be united in wedlock on Christmas eve, Thursday night of this week. The ceremony will take place at Salem Church, Helt's Prairie, and will be performed by Rev. J.T. WOOD.

Wednesday, December 30, 1885

Perrysville Paragraphs
Miss LURA DUNLAP, of Des Moines, Iowa, is visiting in the city.

Miss JENNIE McNEILL who has been attending school at St. Mary's, and BRUCE FERGUSON, a student at the Rose Polytechnic at Terre Haute, are spending vacation at home.

On last Thursday evening, at the residence of the bride's father, Miss MAGGIE HAINS and SILAS KERNS were united in bonds of sacred wedlock, Rev. HARGRAVE officiating.

Home News
JASPER HASTY, of Lafayette, is here visiting relatives.

EBENEZER CROSS, of New York, was here visiting his brother, JOHN W. CROSS.

D.C. JOHNSON, of Clinton, was admitted to the Newport Bar yesterday, on motion of C.W. WARD.

Miss LAURA CARTY, of Annapolis, who is teaching at Lodi, spent Christmas with her uncle, E.D. WHEELER of this place.

WILLIAM HAMMAN, of Harveysburg, Fountain County, was in town on Monday last. He is talking about moving back to Old Vermillion.

GERTIE and GRACE HARRISON, daughters of Pastor HARRISON, went up to Danville, Illinois, yesterday, to visit Mr. AL HARPER and family of the Commercial.

DONALD DEWAR and lady, of Sanford, Edgar County, Illinois, came over here on a visit last week, and were the guests of Mr. JOHN H. KERDOLFF and wife while here. Mrs. DEWAR is a cousin of Mrs. KERDOLFF, and will remain here until the latter part of the week.

ENOS HANN of Glassboro, New Jersey, was united in wedlock on Tuesday afternoon to Miss SALLIE BROWN, of this township. The ceremony took place at the residence of the bride, and was performed by Rev. JOHN HARRISON, Pastor of the M.E. Church. Both have the best wishes of the Hoosier for a long and prosperous life. They will leave for their eastern home in a few days. Mr. HANN is a brother of JOSEPH HANN, of this place, and is said to be in fair circumstances.

Sheriff's Sale on Decree
RACHAEL MILLER, EMMA J. MITCHELL, by LEWIS A. MORGAN, Agent vs.
JOHN LUSADDER and LAURA LUSADDER
$1,780.24
Sale Saturday, January 23, 1886
Sale at courthouse between 10 and 4
S part of NE fractional ¼ Sec 22, T 19 N R 9 W – 113 acres
WARD & DAVIS attorneys for plaintiff
December 30, 1885
JOHN A. DARBY, Sheriff

NAME INDEX

www.ingramcontent.com/pod-product-compliance
Lightning Source LLC
LaVergne TN
LVHW061239100826
845148LV00008B/989

* 9 7 8 0 7 8 8 4 4 2 0 5 6 *